UK
POLITICS TODAY

(Second Edition)

Frank Cooney
(Head of Social Studies, Northern College)

Peter Fotheringham
(Lecturer, Department of Politics, University of Glasgow)

Pulse Publications

CONTENTS

ACKNOWLEDGEMENTS
The authors and publishers would like to thank
the following for permission to reproduce copy-
right material:
The Press Association for photographs on pages
12, 18, 20, 35, 36, 39, 41, 42, 43, 45, 46, 49, 52, 53,
57, 59, 60, 62, 67, 68, 71, 73, 75, 77, 79, 80, 83,
84, 85, 87, 90, 91, 92, 93, 94, 97, 99, 101, 102, 104,
105, 107, 112, 114, 115, 118, 119, 120, 125, 127,
129, 132, 133, 135, 136, 140, 151.

Published and typeset by
Pulse Publications
45 Raith Road, Fenwick,
Ayrshire, KA3 6DB

Printed and bound by
Thomson Colour Printers

British Library Cataloguing-in-Publication Data
A Catalogue record for this book is available
from the British Library

ISBN 0 948 766 80 8

© Cooney & Fotheringham 2002

ELECTIONS

ELECTIONS AND DEMOCRACY

Elections are central to democracy. Elections permit the people collectively to decide who should govern them. British democracy is representative and indirect meaning that the people do not rule or govern directly. Rather the people are governed by the individuals they have elected to represent them in the legislature, the House of Commons, some of whom also become members of the executive.

Democratisation, the process whereby countries become democratic, is character-ised above all by two achievements—universal suffrage and free elections devoid of corruption. The process of democ-ratisation in Britain took a long time. In the nineteenth century the right to vote was extended to most males. Women did not get the right to vote until the 1920s.

The electorate used to decide only who should represent them in the Commons and on local government coun-cils. Today, voters also take part in elections to the Euro-pean Parliament and, if they live in Scotland or Wales, to the Scottish Parliament or the Welsh Assembly.

THE BRITISH GENERAL ELECTION

The principal election in Britain remains the general election which must be held once every five years. The Prime Minister may call a general election before the five year period is up if that is likely to increase the govern-ment's chances of re-election. Formally the Prime Minister must ask the Monarch to dissolve Parliament before the election can be held. However, circumstances may leave the Prime Minister with little choice about the election date. Such was the case in May 1979 when James Callaghan went to the country after losing control of the House of Commons as a result of being defeated in a Motion of Confidence. The Prime Min-ister may also be forced to wait until almost the last possible moment of the five years allowed if opinion polls suggest that his or her party will not be re-elected (for instance, John Major in 1997). In 2001 Prime Minister Blair was forced to delay the date of the election by one month because of the foot and mouth crisis.

Constituencies

When a general election is held, all 659 Members of Parliament are elected. Every one of the 659 constituencies in Britain is represented by a single MP. Constituencies do not all have the same number of voters. The Western Isles has the smallest number (21,807 in 2001) while the Isle of Wight has the most voters (106,305 in 2001). (See *Redrawing the Electoral Map* on page 5.) In 2001 the average constituency had 69,892 voters in England, 66,170 in Northern Ireland 55,718 in Wales and 55,291 voters in Scotland. The voters in each constituency choose one individual from a number of candidates for the job of MP in that constituency. Although voters are officially voting for an MP, they tend to think more about which party they support and who will form the government. The name of the party which the candidate represents is now noted beside his/her name on the ballot paper. In addition to selecting their own candidates, the major political parties effectively organise the election campaign.

Candidates & deposits

Under the procedures established over many decades, candidates are required to submit their nomination papers together with a deposit of £500 to the Returning Officer, who has responsibility for managing the smooth running of the election. The regulations require that any candidate who fails to gain at least 5% of the votes cast in the election will lose his or her deposit. This is a considerable sum of money for any individual to lose. In 1997, a total of 3,245 candidates contested the Election, of whom about 2,000 lost their deposits. In 1997 only one Labour candidate, three Conservatives and eleven Liberal Democrats lost their deposits, so the great majority of deposits lost were by the candidates of minor parties with no hope of winning seats.

Polling Stations

On general election day, polling stations up and down the country will be open from 7.00 a.m. until 10.00 p.m. Voting is fairly straightforward with the electors marking an 'X' beside the name of their preferred candidate. At the close of the polls the ballot boxes are carefully sealed and sent on to the numerous counting centres which have been set up. It is here that the votes are counted and the results announced. Any voting slips which have been agreed as being 'spoiled' are set aside and not counted. Results are announced from midnight onwards, with the outcome of the election usually being fairly clear by about 3.00 a.m.

THE PURPOSE OF ELECTIONS

What is it, then, that voters hope to gain out of a general election?

? A change of Prime Minister and Cabinet?

? A new MP to represent their views at Westminster?

? Manifesto promises carried out?

In many ways the voting public will get all of these things. They certainly get a constituency MP who will represent them whether they voted for him/her or not. These constituency representatives select the government. That government will, during its lifetime, find time to carry out some of its manifesto promises.

Selecting a government

Governments are chosen by the electoral process, even though in the British parliamentary system only members of the legislature (the MPs) are elected directly by the people. Which political party makes up the government is effectively decided by the collective voice of individual voters who usually return to the Commons a majority party from whose ranks the Prime Minister, Cabinet and junior Ministers are drawn. The government receives legitimacy from being elected. The rule of law is much easier to achieve when those who make the law have been elected by the people who must obey the law.

Power to the people?

The voice of the people is turned into political reality by the electoral system, i.e. by the rules governing general elections. The representation of parties in the legislature and the party composition of the government to emerge from the legislature after an election are influenced by:

✗   the way that a country is divided into constituencies,

✗   the number of representatives per constituency,

✗   the way votes are counted,

✗   the number of votes required to elect an MP.

Electoral systems are not neutral. Different rules lead to different results in terms of the number of parties with significant representation in the legislature and the number of parties represented in the government. There is a conflict between two of the principal purposes of an election—representation of the people and the establishment of a government. How representative is the House of Commons and the government following a general election? What is the best type of government—one based on a single majority party or one based on a coalition of two or more parties none of which individually enjoys a majority in the legislature?

THE HOUSE OF COMMONS ELECTORAL SYSTEM

Britain has a long history of having two major parties along with single majority party government. The rules of the electoral system contribute in no small measure to these central features of British politics. The British electoral system has developed into a controversial political issue in recent decades for a number of reasons.

●   The apparent electoral invincibility of the Conservative Party from 1979 until 1992 led some to believe that the only way to overcome Conservative strength was to change the electoral system.

●   The decision to use different forms of proportional representation in 1999 for elections to the European Parliament, Scottish Parliament and Welsh Assembly.

●   The two-party dominance of the British party system at the electoral level is weakening. (See Table 1.2.)

REDRAWING THE ELECTORAL MAP

A basic principle of representative democracy is 'one person, one vote; one vote, one value'. The movement of population, especially from the cities to the suburbs, can, over time, distort the respective size of constituencies in Britain. Historical political decisions can also create unequal treatment of voters. For example Scotland and Wales are over-represented in Westminster.

The *House of Commons (Redistribution of Seats) Act* 1944 introduced regular reviews by an independent Boundary Commission and the *Boundary Commission Act* 1992 requires that reviews take place every eight to twelve years.

Separate Boundary Commissions exist for England, Scotland, Wales and Northern Ireland. The English Boundary Commission began its latest review of constituencies in February 2000. The four Commissions are not required to report until 2007.

What is certain is that Scotland will eventually see a reduction in the number of MPs sent to Westminster. The *Scotland Act* 1998, which established the Scottish Parliament, removed the legislation which guaranteed Scotland at least seventy seats. The Scottish Boundary Commission must use the quota system used in England which would entitle Scotland to about sixty seats at Westminster. Such a dramatic reduction in the number of seats (possibly twelve) would lead to a substantial redrawing of Scotland's electoral map and significant in-fighting between the political parties. In the long term, such a change will reduce the Scottish influence and could affect the outcome of future general elections. This will especially impact on the Labour Party as it is the dominant party in Scotland. Future Labour leaders may see the wisdom of concentating on 'middle England' as the influence of the Scottish electorate will decline.

The reduction in the number of MPs will not apply to Wales as its Assembly does not have the decision making powers bestowed on the Scottish Parliament. Wales currently has forty MPs (it is guaranteed thirty six) and it is likely that the Boundary Review will retain the present allocation.

Scotland Act 1998

CHAPTER 46

£11·95

Inverness East, Nairn and Lochaber

	% SHARE OF VOTE	
	1992	**1997**
Liberal Democrats	**26.0**	17.5
Labour	25.1	**33.9**
Conservative	22.6	17.5
SNP	24.7	29.0

Table 1.1 Figures in bold indicate the winning party

Source: *Times Guide to the House of Commons 1992 and 1997*

Table 1.1 illustrates what can happen when four candidates are evenly matched. In 1992 Sir Russell Johnstone won the seat with only 26% of the votes cast. This highlights one of the criticisms of FPTP, namely that it creates a situation whereby many individual MPs and the victorious party overall, which goes on to form Her Majesty's Government, do not receive the support of a majority of the electorate. The people who vote for those parties which form the Opposition may still have their views represented by the opposition MPs. They will not, however, see these representatives in government. Since there are no prizes for coming second they get nothing in terms of power or influence. As we will see, those who get nothing comprise a substantial proportion of the electorate.

Plurality system

The British electoral system depends on majorities rather than on proportion. It is popularly known as a first-past-the-post system (FPTP) or plurality system because the winning candidate is the one with the most votes in each single-member constituency. In other words the one winner in each constituency is the candidate with more votes than any other rival candidate. The required number need not be an absolute majority.

Election results based on the first-past-the-post principle, such as those reported in Tables 1.1–1.3, give rise to claims that the electoral system used to elect members of the House of Commons is essentially unfair and that it leads to many individual votes being 'wasted'.

The three most striking features of the general election results reported in Tables 1.1–1. 3 are:

➡ The clear discrepancy between the proportion of total votes gained by a particular political party and the proportion of seats it has in the House of Commons. The difference varies from one election to another.

➡ The clear parliamentary majority achieved by one single party in twelve of the sixteen elections since 1945. The exceptions are 1950, 1964, February 1974 and October 1974. (See column 9, Table 1.2.)

➡ The persistence of a two-party system at the parliamentary level in spite of the decline in the combined Conservative and Labour share of the popular vote. (Compare columns 3 and 6, Table 1.2.)

FEATURES OF FPTP

Table 1.2 illustrates trends in the percentage shares of votes and seats won by British political parties in general elections since 1945. The discrepancies between party shares of individual votes and shares of seats in the legislature define the 'representative' character of the electoral process in Britain. There are three main conclusions to be drawn from Table 1.2.

All rewards to the victor

Firstly, the winning party always wins a bigger share of seats than of votes. In 2001, Labour won 42% of the popular vote and 62.6% of the seats in the House of Commons. The party coming second overall in the share of the popular vote usually benefits from the first-past-the-post system by winning proportionately more seats than votes. The impact of the electoral system is evident when the two-party or major-party share of the vote (i.e. the combined Conservative and Labour share) is compared with the major-party share of seats in the Commons. The decline in the popularity of the two major parties is shown in column 3. Conservative and Labour together won close to 90% or more of the popular vote from 1945 until 1970. However, in the 1974 Elections their share fell well below 80%. Their lowest share was recorded in 1983 when they won less than three-quarters of the popular vote. Column 6, which gives the major-party share of seats in the Commons, shows that, despite this decline in their share of the vote, the share of seats won by the two major parties has not declined to the same extent.

Since 1974, the two major parties have been winning slightly fewer seats than before. In 1997 the much stronger Liberal Democrat performance in winning forty six seats reduced the Conservative–Labour share of seats (88.6%) to less than 90% for the first time in the post-war era. In 2001 that share was reduced further to

THE BRITISH TWO-PARTY SYSTEM

AND THE ELECTORAL SYSTEM: 1945–2001

	% Share of the Vote			% Share of Seats			Liberals		Overall Majority
	Con.	Lab.	C+L	Con.	Lab.	C+L	%Votes	%Seats	
	1	2	3	4	5	6	7	8	9
1945	39.8	**47.8**	87.6	33.3	61.4	94.7	9.2	1.9	146
1950	43.5	**46.1**	89.6	47.7	50.4	98.1	9.1	1.4	5
1951	**48.0**	48.8	96.8	51.4	47.2	98.6	2.5	1.0	17
1955	**49.7**	46.4	96.1	54.7	43.9	98.6	2.7	1.0	58
1959	**49.4**	43.8	93.2	57.9	40.9	98.8	6.0	1.0	100
1964	43.4	**44.1**	87.5	48.1	50.3	98.4	11.2	1.4	4
1966	41.9	**47.9**	89.8	40.2	57.6	97.8	8.5	1.9	96
1970	**46.4**	43.0	89.4	52.4	45.6	98.0	7.5	1.0	30
1974	37.9	37.1	75.0	46.6	47.4	94.0	19.3	2.2	–
1974	35.8	**39.2**	75.0	43.5	50.2	93.7	18.3	2.0	3
1979	**43.9**	36.9	80.8	53.4	42.2	95.6	13.8	1.7	43
1983	**42.4**	27.6	70.0	61.0	32.2	93.2	25.4	3.6	144
1987	**43.4**	31.7	75.1	57.7	35.2	92.9	23.2	3.4	101
1992	**41.9**	34.4	76.3	51.6	41.6	93.2	17.9	3.1	21
1997	30.7	**43.2**	73.9	25.0	63.6	88.6	16.8	7.0	179
2001	32.7	**42.0**	74.7	25.1	62.6	87.7	18.8	7.9	167

- The figures in bold denote the share of the vote of the party which won a majority of seats in the House of Commons. In 1974 (Feb.) no party won a parliamentary majority.
- Shares of votes and seats are based on results in the United Kingdom as a whole. Until 1970 Northern Ireland votes are included under the appropriate British parties. From 1974 this is not done because the Northern Ireland parties broke away from their British counterparts which did not, by and large, campaign in the province.

Table 1.2   Source: Butler and Butler, *British Political Facts 1900–1994* and *Times Guide to the House of Commons 1997, 2001*

87.7%. Such trends suggest that the electoral system protects the parliamentary representation of the two major parties from limited and temporary declines in their popular support.

The 'winning' party, i.e. the party with the most seats, nearly always wins more votes than any other party. However, in 1951 the Conservatives won more seats than Labour in spite of winning a slightly smaller share of the popular vote. This can happen because of single-member constituencies. A party winning some of its seats by large margins may win fewer seats but more votes than a party which wins its seats by narrower margins. In February 1974 these positions were reversed. The Conservatives, who had called the election after three years and eight months in office, won almost 230,000 more votes than Labour. This difference in number of votes represented less than 1% of the total vote in the United Kingdom.

Nevertheless, the Conservatives won four seats fewer than Labour.

Third parties smothered

Secondly, the first-past-the-post system makes it difficult, though not impossible, for 'third' parties to gain significant representation in the House of Commons. In Table 1.2, columns 7 and 8 illustrate the mixed electoral fortunes of the most significant 'third force' in post-war British politics, the Liberals from 1945 to 1979, the Liberal/SDP Alliance in 1983 and 1987 and the Liberal Democrats since 1992.

The two major parties always won a larger share of seats than votes. In sharp contrast, the third party has been winning a lot more votes than seats for many years. In 1951 the Liberals won six seats with 2.5% of the vote. In 1992 the Liberal Democrats won twenty three seats with 17.9% of the vote. In other words the third party vote

share went up seven times but its share of seats went up only four times. The 'third party' fared particularly badly in 1983 when it took the form of the Liberal/SDP Alliance (an alliance of the old Liberal Party and the newly formed Social Democratic Party which had broken away from Labour in 1981). The Alliance won 25.4% of the vote in Britain compared to Labour's 27.6%. Yet the Alliance won only twenty three seats (3.6%) compared to Labour's 209 (32.2%).

The Liberal Democrats' share of seats has increased from 3.1% in 1992 to 7.9% in 2001. This increase reflects a change in Liberal Democrat strategy which involves 'targeting' seats with relatively small majorities.

After the 1997 Election, which produced the largest overall majority of the post-war era, 'New' Labour and the Liberal Democrats appeared to be discussing a common approach to issues of

7

The Electoral System: *A Scottish Dimension*

	Percentage of votes			Percentage of seats			Number of seats		
	1992	1997	2001	1992	1997	2001	1992	1997	2001
Labour	39.0	45.6	43.9	68.0	77.8	77.8	49	56	56
Conservative	25.7	17.5	15.6	15.2	0	1.4	11	0	1
Liberal Democrats	13.1	13.0	16.4	12.5	13.9	13.9	9	10	10
SNP	21.5	22.1	20.0	4.2	8.3	6.9	3	6	5

Table 1.3

constitutional reform, including reform of the electoral system.

The electoral system encourages long-term two-party domination at the parliamentary level, but a particular two-party system may not be indestructible. It took the Labour Party, established by the trade union movement in 1900, forty five years to win a general election. During that period Labour replaced the old Liberal Party as the second major party as it gained the support of an increasing proportion of the working class. To overcome the biases of the first-past-the-post electoral system, third parties have to attract the support of significant sections of the electorate. Labour accomplished this task very gradually during the first thirty years of the twentieth century.

The influence of third parties depends as much on the gap between the two major parties as on their own strength in the Commons. The narrower the margin between the major parties in the legislature and the smaller the winning party's overall majority, the greater is the influence of the small parties which have some representation in the Commons. The contemporary Conservative–Labour two-party system has tottered sometimes, particularly in the 1970s when on two occasions no party enjoyed a Commons majority. In the February 1974 Election, no party won a parliamentary majority. Labour formed the government because the Liberals made it clear that they would not support the continuation of

Edward Heath's Conservative government. In October 1974 Labour 'won' with a majority of only three. Labour lost its majority in by-elections and had to rely on a 'Lib-Lab Pact' to survive in Parliament until the summer of 1979.

Comfortable Government

Thirdly, the electoral system and the electorate usually combine to produce a government with a comfortable working overall majority in the House of Commons. (Column 9 in Table 1.2.) 'Comfortable' is a variable which depends upon such factors as how the governing party fares in by-elections and whether a suitable opportunity arises for the government to call a general election which will increase its parliamentary majority. Labour's majority of five in 1950 was not sufficient to withstand a determined Conservative Opposition which forced all-night sittings and brought the government to its knees. The Labour government which won narrowly in 1964 after thirteen years of Conservative rule was able to call an election after eighteen months and win a large Commons majority. In contrast, the Labour government elected in October 1974 with an overall majority of three never found an opportunity to go to the country to strengthen its mandate.

The three Conservative victories in 1979, 1983 and 1987 were all 'comfortable'. The somewhat unexpected victory for the Conservatives under John Major in April 1992 provided a majority of twenty one which was whittled

away by by-election defeats and the defection of three Conservative MPs until, at the beginning of 1997, the government lost its overall majority. However, the government survived some votes of confidence because the Ulster Unionists did not vote against it. A government without an overall majority can survive if some third party MPs vote for it or do not vote against it. Prime Minister Major was unable to call an election until the last possible moment because the polls had suggested for several years that Labour would win.

Concentrated support

The present system suits parties with significant traditional support nationally (Labour and Conservative) or strong, if limited, regional support (the nationalist parties in parts of Scotland and Wales in 1974). Such support leads to the parties coming first in certain types of constituency. For example, Labour dominates in the central cities such as Glasgow where all the seats were won by Labour in 1992, 1997 and 2001. It does not suit parties whose vote is spread evenly, but thinly, throughout most of the country (the Liberal Democrats in England and the SNP since 1979).

Table 1.3 illustrates further variations in the results possible in the first-past-the-post electoral system. Labour has been the dominant party in Scotland since 1959. Its dominance in terms of seats has grown in spite of the increase in support for the two smaller parties, SNP and Liberal Democrats, which now contest all Scottish constituencies. In 1966 Labour won almost 50% of the Scottish vote and forty six seats. In 1992 Labour won less than 40% of the vote but won forty nine seats. Labour's social base has remained sufficiently loyal to ensure that the number of Scottish Labour MPs contributes to Labour's overall strength in the Commons. In contrast, the Conservative Party, which won 50.1% of the Scottish vote in 1955, has experienced a massive loss of votes which reduced its share of seats to 15% in 1992 and no seats in 1997. In the 2001 General Election the Conservatives won back Galloway and Upper Nithsdale. This gain was attributed to the fallout from the foot and mouth crisis which badly affected this rural constituency.

The Conservative decline is due, in part, to the increase in support for the SNP and the Liberal Democrats whose strength has been most evident in the rural areas of Scotland outside the industrial and urbanised belt in central Scotland. The Conservatives have, since 1959, progressively lost out to Labour in urban and industrial Scotland.

The advantages of having your votes concentrated in certain areas can be seen in the changing electoral fortunes of the third and fourth party challenges to Labour and Conservative. Since 1983 the Liberal Democrats have been winning more seats than the SNP in spite of a much smaller share of the Scottish vote. This is because Liberal Democrat voters have been effectively concentrated in certain areas such as the Borders, Grampian and the Highlands and Islands. The SNP has much more support than the Liberal Democrats in most parts of Scotland outside the seats won by the Liberal Democrats. In 1997 the SNP came second in every one of Glasgow's ten constituencies and won 19% of the vote compared to the 7% won by the Liberal Democrats. However, such strength only goes to increase the SNP's share of the popular vote without winning the Party any seats in urban Scotland. In contrast, the Liberal Democrats' parliamentary representation (13.9% of Scottish seats) was directly proportional to its share (13%) of the popular vote.

PROPORTIONAL REPRESENTATION IN ACTION

case study IRELAND

(Single Transferable Vote)

1992 & 1997 GENERAL ELECTIONS IN IRELAND

	1992			1997		
	% share of votes	N°. of seats	% share seats	% share of votes	N°. of seats	% share seats
Fianna Fail	39.2	68	40.9	39.3	77	46.4
Fine Gael	24.5	45	27.1	27.9	54	32.5
Labour	19.3	33	19.9	10.4	17	10.2
Progressive Democrats	4.7	10	6.0	4.7	4	2.4
Democratic Left	2.8	4	2.4	2.5	4	2.4
Others	9.6	6	3.6	9.9	7	4.2
Green Alliance	—	—	—	2.8	2	1.2
Sinn Fein	—	—	—	2.5	1	0.6

Table 1.4   Note: The Irish Parliament has 166 seats, so 84 seats are needed for an overall majority.

Looking at Table 1.4, you can see that shares of seats are clearly much closer to shares of votes. The result is that no party wins a majority of seats which means that coalition government is necessary. Smaller parties receive much greater and fairer representation in the legislature. The government which was formed after the 1992 Election included members of Fine Gael, Labour and the Democratic Left. The largest party in terms of both votes and seats, Fianna Fail, was not represented in government. The Irish coalition government, based on three parties, enjoyed majority support in the legislature from 1992 to 1997.

The 1997 Irish Elections led to a change of government which was in fact a minority coalition government. The major change in voting behaviour was a severe decline (almost 50%) in support for Dick Spring's Labour Party. Although Irish Prime Minister Bruton's Fine Gael Party increased its share of both votes and seats, the coalition formed after the 1992 Election could not hold on to its legislative majority in the face of Labour's loss of sixteen seats. Fianna Fail once again emerged as the biggest single party and its leader, Bertie Aherne, formed a minority government along with the Progressive Democrats who won only four seats. One Cabinet seat went to Mary Harney of the Progressive Democrats. The new government, which was three seats short of an overall majority, depended on the votes of the five Independents.

PROPORTIONAL REPRESENTATION (PR)

PR is based on the principle that every party winning an agreed minimum number of votes should be awarded a number of seats in the legislature. This number should be approximately proportional to the number of votes the party receives in the country as a whole. Some small parties, who gain very few votes, would not be awarded any seats at all even under PR.

In Scotland the FPTP electoral system works massively in favour of Labour compared to the shares of seats which would emerge from any type of proportional representation. Exactly how important the principle of proportionality is in determining the number of seats won by each party can be clearly seen by comparing the results in Scotland in Table 1.3 with the results of the 1992 and 1997 Elections in Ireland (Table 1.4) where a form of PR is used. If the shares of the vote won by the parties in Scotland in 1992 (Table 1.3) were to be translated into shares of seats on the basis of proportionality, there would have been no majority of seats for the Labour Party, the SNP would have won more seats than the Liberal Democrats and the Conservatives would have won eighteen seats rather than eleven.

The Alternative Vote (AV)

The alternative vote is, in effect, only a modified form of the first-past-the-post system. It would not require any boundary changes and the constituencies would still return one MP. Where the alternative vote system differs is that voters would have two votes instead of one. The voter would indicate his or her preference among the candidates. In this situation the winner would be that candidate who secured an absolute majority of the votes cast (more than 50%). Should this not happen after the first count, then the candidate with the fewest votes would be eliminated with

Euro Elections in Great Britain, 1994 and 1999

	% share of votes		% share of seats	
	1994	1999	1994	1999
Labour	44.2	28.0	73.8	34.5
Conservative	27.9	35.8	21.4	42.8
Liberal Democrats	16.7	12.7	2.4	11.9
UK Independence	0.8	7.0	0	3.6
Greens	3.2	6.3	0	2.4
Nationalists	4.3	4.6	2.4	4.7

Table 1.5

his/her second preferences being distributed among the other candidates. If this did not produce a candidate with more than 50% of the votes, the procedure would be repeated until it did. The main criticism of the alternative vote system is that it fails to give a fairer share of the votes to the smaller political parties.

The Additional Member System (AMS)

The additional member system is of great interest in Britain because it was chosen as the system to be used for elections to the Scottish Parliament. The voter in the additional member system casts two votes. First the voter selects the candidate whom he/she wishes to represent him/her in the local constituency. The rationale here is to maintain a link between constituencies and their elected representatives. Therefore, the first seventy three members of the Scottish Parliament are elected from seventy three single-member constituencies. These are the seventy two British parliamentary constituencies in Scotland with the Orkney and Shetland constituency allocated two seats in the Scottish Parliament.

Under AMS the voter also has a second vote in a multi-member constituency, choosing from a regional party list which contains the names of candidates in order of preference decided by the parties. This second ballot determines the composition of the legislature. The additional members are chosen in such a way as to ensure a high degree of propor-

tionality in the overall allocation of seats to parties. In elections to the Scottish Parliament, the then eight existing Euro constituencies, which themselves were each made up of nine British parliamentary constituencies, were used to select fifty six additional MSPs. The operation of the additional member electoral system in Scotland is explained in detail in Chapter 8.

National/Regional List

This form of PR has been used in many European countries and was employed for the first time in Great Britain (but not in Northern Ireland) in the 1999 Elections for the European Parliament. Under this system, the electorate does not vote for individual party candidates but for party lists. The candidates are selected and ranked in order by the parties so that it is known in advance which candidates will be elected depending on how successful each party's list is. The counting system which was used in 1999 is called the d'Hondt system. The degree of proportionality achieved and the consequences for party representation are illustrated in Table 1.5 by comparing the results of the 1994 and 1999 Elections to the European Parliament. In 1994 the traditional first-past-the-post system was used. In both systems the voters have one vote only.

In 1994 the first-past-the-post system based on the simple plurality rule in single-member constituencies was massively favourable to Labour at a time when it led the Conservatives comfortably in the opinion polls.

The Operation of the *Party List Electoral System*: 1999 European Parliament Elections in Scotland

	Votes	Share of Votes	Percentage of Seats	No. of Seats
Labour	283,490	28.7	37.5	3
SNP	268,528	27.2	25.0	2
Conservative	195,296	19.8	25.0	2
Liberal Democrat	96,971	9.8	12.5	1
Green	57,142	5.8	0	0
SSP	39,720	4.0	0	0

Table 1.6

The Liberal Democrats suffered their usual fate: the plurality counting system did not turn their votes into seats.

In 1999 Great Britain was divided into eleven multi-member constituencies. Nine English 'Euro' constituencies elected a total of seventy one MEPs while Scotland (eight MEPs) and Wales (four MEPs) each constituted one 'Euro' constituency. In each constituency votes were counted and seats allocated among the parties according to the following formula:

$$\frac{\text{Number (or \%) of Votes}}{\text{Number of Seats Gained} + 1}$$

The operation of this system may be illustrated by working out the allocation of the eight Scottish MEPs. (See Table 1.6.)

To allocate the first of the eight Scottish 'Euro' seats the votes of each party were divided by one. Labour was thus allocated the first seat because it had won the most votes in Scotland. In the second count Labour's votes total was now divided by two according to the d'Hondt formula. This left the SNP with the largest number of votes, so it was allocated the second seat. Then the SNP total was divided by two, leaving the Conservatives as the strongest party in the third count. By this stage the three strongest parties had now had their vote totals halved. In the fourth count Labour's total divided by two still

exceeded the Liberal Democrats' total, so Labour got the fourth seat. By the same process the SNP and the Conservatives won the fifth and sixth seats. Now the three strongest parties, each with two MEPs elected, had had their vote totals divided by three. This left the Liberal Democrats marginally ahead of Labour in the seventh count, so they got the seventh seat. Labour then got the eighth and final seat.

In 1994 Labour won six of the eight single member 'Euro' constituencies and the SNP won two. In 1999, the combined effect of the new electoral system and a big fall in the Labour vote in a low turn-out election produced a much more 'proportional' allocation of seats among the parties and Labour's loss of three MEPs. In Britain as a whole the 1999 results were characterised by a much closer relationship between shares of votes

and shares of seats. The new electoral system also helped the Greens and the UK Independence Party (opposed to membership of the European Union) to win seats which they were unlikely to do under first-past-the-post. The larger the number of seats per constituency the more proportional the results will be. A national party list system would be still more proportional than the results achieved in 1999 in multi-member constituencies.

The Single Transferable Vote

This system is used in the Republic of Ireland (see page 9), and in Northern Ireland for elections to both the European Parliament and the Northern Ireland Assembly. Using a quota system for counting votes and allocating seats in multi-member constituencies, STV usually introduces a high degree of proportionality into election results. Voters have as many votes as there are representatives to be elected from each constituency. In a five-member constituency voters indicate their preferences using the figures 1–5 from the total number of candidates standing. Often the number of candidates will be in double figures. Finding the winning candidates using STV is complicated. It is achieved by using a formula to calculate the minimum number of votes, known as the quota, required to win one of the several seats in each constituency.

STV and the 1999 Elections to the European Parliament in Northern Ireland

	CANDIDATE	NUMBER OF VOTES
Democratic Unionist (DUP)	Paisley	192,762
Social Democratic Labour (SDLP)	Hume	190,731
Ulster Unionist (UUP)	Nicolson	119,507
Sinn Fein (SF)	McLaughlin	117,643
Others		58,166
Total		678,809

Table 1.7

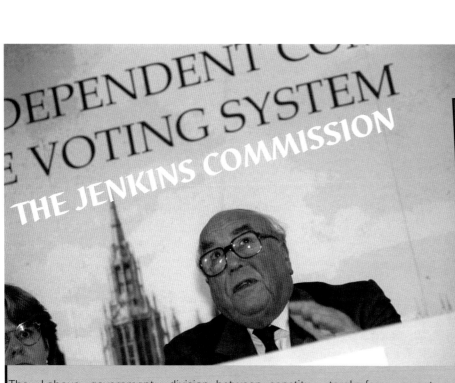

INDEPENDENT C[U]
[TH]E VOTING SYSTEM
THE JENKINS COMMISSION

> "We are committed to a referendum on the voting system for the House of Commons. An independent commission on voting systems will be appointed early to recommend a proportional alternative to the first-past-the-post system."
> (Labour Party Manifesto, 1997)

The Labour government elected in May 1997 followed up on its Manifesto commitment by establishing an independent commission on voting systems to be chaired by Lord Jenkins of Hillhead. Lord Jenkins, a one-time Labour MP and Cabinet Minister, left the Labour Party in 1981 to set up the Social Democratic Party to represent right-wing Labour supporters dismayed at the Party's move to the left after the 1979 Election defeat. Lord Jenkins subsequently joined the Liberal Democrat Party which, in its previous identity as the Liberal Party, had long campaigned for electoral reform.

The Jenkins Commission at first recommended an AMS electoral system with a 2/1 division between constituency representatives and top-up party list members. This was not acceptable to the Labour government. The Jenkins Commission subsequently reported in October 1998, recommending that 543 MPs be elected by the alternative vote system used in Australia with another 116 members to be elected from multi-member constituencies similar in operation to the second ballot in Scottish Parliament elections. The alternative vote system requires that winning candidates in single-member constituencies achieve majority support by the method explained on page 10.

In spite of the Manifesto commitment to a referendum on PR, the idea of electoral reform was not popular among Labour MPs elected in 1997 because the party had won such a massive majority that victory in the next election seemed guaranteed. Labour's flirtation with PR had been encouraged by the run of four Conservative election victories from 1979 to 1992. In addition, the use of different forms of PR in Scotland, Wales and Northern Ireland, and in elections to the European Parliament, established pressures to extend electoral reform to the House of Commons. Some Labour leaders, including the Prime Minister, were also motivated by a desire to maintain a cooperative relationship with the Liberal Democrats, partly in order to ensure that the

two parties would be allied against the Conservatives. The strong opposition within the Labour Party to electoral reform for the House of Commons was widely perceived to have killed off the chances of implementing Labour's 1997 Manifesto commitment. In March 2001, Tony Blair and Charles Kennedy, the new leader of the Liberal Democrats, reached agreement on a face-saving compromise to review the operation of the PR electoral systems after the next elections to the Scottish Parliament and the Welsh Assembly due in 2003. This watering down of the 1997 Manifesto commitment annoyed both Labour MPs who thought that the PR issue was dead and buried and Liberal Democrats who thought that the promised referendum on PR would be held soon after the 2001 Election.

STV FORMULA

$$\text{Quota of Votes} = \frac{\text{Number of Votes Cast}}{\text{Number of Seats} + 1} + 1$$

In a five-member constituency where 180,000 votes were cast a candidate would require 30,001 votes in order to be elected. (Work it out!) Candidates exceeding that total when votes are counted are immediately declared elected. It is unlikely, though not impossible, for all five seats to be allocated in the first count. Certainly more than five candidates cannot win. If votes were evenly divided among six candidates with 30,000 each, none would be elected in the first count. In practice, votes are unevenly distributed with perhaps two or three candidates from the major parties securing immediate election. The second and subsequent preferences of voters are then taken into account to decide the allocation of the remaining seats. The 'surplus' votes of the first candidate or candidates elected are redistributed among the candidates not yet elected in proportion to the second preferences of all the voters who supported the winning candidate. This process continues until the five seats are all filled.

(continued on page 14)

PROPORTIONAL REPRESENTATION

The sustained increase in the Liberal share of the vote from 1974 onwards (see Table 1.2) stimulated a debate about which type of electoral system Britain should have. Successive Conservative election victories, beginning in 1979, convinced some Labour supporters that reform of the electoral system was one way of preventing a recurrence of long-running Conservative government (as happened from 1951–1964 and 1979–1997). The 1997 Labour Party Manifesto included the electoral system in its list of British institutions in need of reform. It moved quickly to propose one of several types of proportional representation, the additional member system, for elections to the Scottish Parliament. Labour also decided to fall into line with the rest of the European Union by introducing proportional representation for elections to the European Parliament in 1999.

Different electoral rules tend to produce different outcomes. In particular, the number of major parties, the influence of minor parties and whether there is a single majority party in the legislature are largely determined by the electoral system. The first-past-the-post system used in Britain has tended to produce two-party politics and an executive branch (Prime Minister and Cabinet) drawn from one party only. In sharp contrast, electoral systems based on proportional representation, such as the German additional member system or the Irish single transferable vote system, tend to produce multi-party systems, which give minor parties more representation in the legislature and more participation in government. They tend to produce more coalition or minority governments. (See Table 1.4.)

The United Kingdom now employs four different electoral systems.

1 General Elections
Traditional first-past-the-post syste which has been the subject of an independent inquiry.

2 Scottish Parliament and Welsh Assembly
Additional member system.

3 European Elections
Regional party list system.

4 Northern Ireland
Single transferable vote in a three-member constituency for elections to the European Parliament and also for elections to the Northern Ireland Assembly.

The 1997 Labour Manifesto promised that the British people would be asked to state their views on the 'voting system'. It is likely that the following arguments will be presented to them by the supporters of the rival systems available. Voters in any future referendum on the voting system will have to decide whether proportionality, which certainly seems fairer in terms of representation, is also capable of producing governments as 'good' or as 'strong' as the government Britain has enjoyed, or endured, under first-past-the-post.

ARGUMENTS FOR
FIRST-PAST-THE-POST
(Strong Government)

1 Usually produces a strong government drawn from one party enjoying a majority in the House of Commons.

2 Single party government allows the Prime Minister and Cabinet to pursue policies clearly stated in the Manifesto without having to compromise with smaller parties in the coalitions associated with PR.

3 There is no tradition of coalition government in Britain. PR encourages coalitions or minority government which may allow minor parties to hold larger parties to ransom.

4 PR may lead to a coalition between a minor party or parties and the second largest party in Parliament. This leaves the largest section of public opinion unrepresented. (See Table 1.4.)

5 Coalitions encourage compromise so that fewer voters—Conservative or Labour voters—get what they really want.

ARGUMENTS FOR
PROPORTIONAL REPRESENTATION
(Fair Representation)

1 PR is 'fair' because it produces a close correlation between shares of votes and shares of seats and avoids such results as Labour winning 74% of European Parliament seats with 44% of the popular vote as it did in 1992.

2 PR gives minor parties more parliamentary representation and encourages voters to vote for them without feeling that their votes will be wasted.

3 Coalition government increases the percentage of the electorate supporting the government parties.

4 Coalition government gave Germany better government than Britain for many years.

5 Coalitions encourage consensus which is the result of compromise. In other words more voters get some of what they want and less of what they do not want.

STV in practice

The operation of STV can be illustrated by examining the results of the 1999 Euro elections in Northern Ireland which, as one multimember constituency, elects three MEPs. (See Table 1.7.)

Northern Ireland is a three-member constituency, so the quota required to win any of the three seats is:

$$\frac{678,809}{3+1} + 1 = 169,703$$

The Protestant community, the Unionists, are divided between the Democratic Unionists and the Ulster Unionists. The nationalist community is divided between the SDLP and Sinn Fein. Paisley and Hume achieved the required quota in the first count and were immediately elected, so that the two sides of the community each gained representation in the European Parliament. The second preferences of all the 'others', the candidates with no hope of winning the third seat, were then redistributed with 43,120 going to Nicolson and 1,709 going to McLaughlin. That was not enough to elect Nicolson. Paisley's 23,059 'surplus' votes, i.e. the second preferences of his supporters,

were redistributed with 22,162 going to the second unionist candidate, Nicolson, and only thirty two going to Sinn Fein. That redistribution took Nicolson above the required quota and he won the third seat.

The impact of STV on party representation in elections with many more seats at stake is illustrated above with the results of the 1998 elections to the Northern Ireland Assembly. The Assembly has 108 seats elected in eighteen constituencies, six representatives per constituency.

The share of votes column demonstrates that Northern Ireland

is a divided community in party terms with five major groups defined mainly in religious terms and two smaller parties which try to bridge the religious and political divide. The choice of STV was motivated by the expectation that elections under this system would give significant and 'fair' representation to all the principal political forces in the province. This was certainly achieved in 1998 with the result that no one party or religious group could dominate the Assembly or the Executive. The outstanding feature of the results in 1998 is the close correspondence between shares of votes and shares of seats.

Party	Share of Votes (%)	Number of Seats	Share of Seats(%)
UUP	21	28	26.0
DUP	18	20	18.5
Other Protestant	10	10	9.3
Alliance	6	6	5.5
SDLP	22	24	22.0
Sinn Fein	18	18	16.6
Women's Group	3	2	1.9

1998 Northern Ireland Assembly Election Results under STV

Table 1.8

A SUMMARY OF THE RIVAL VOTING SYSTEMS & THEIR IMPACT ON ELECTION RESULTS

System	First-Past-the-Post (FPTP)	Alternative Vote (AV)	Supplementary Vote (SV)	Additional Member System (AMS)	Single Transferable Vote (STV)
How it works	Very simple, the Westminster way. It retains traditional single-member constituencies in which the candidate who gets the most votes wins the election.	Single-member constituencies, but voters list preferences among the candidates (1,2,3,4, etc.). Unless one gets more than 50% of the first preference votes—and wins outright—the subsequent preferences of candidates with fewest votes are distributed until someone does pass the 50% mark.	Simple variation of AV, used to elect London's Mayor. Voters only get two votes. If no one wins in the first ballot, the second preference votes of candidates with fewest votes are distributed between top two candidates. ('AV-Plus' or 'SV-Plus' is a mixed system in which up to half the seats are not directly elected. Instead they are distributed to candidates on a party list.)	Voters have two votes. One would be used to elect up to two-thirds of MPs in traditional way under FPTP. The other would be cast for the party and remaining MPs would be elected from party lists.	Large multi-member constituencies would each have four or five MPs. Voters list candidates in order of preference and can pick between contenders in the same party as well as rival ones.
1997 election result using each system	Labour 419 Con. 165 Lib. Dem. 46 Others 29 **Lab. majority 179**	Labour 436 Con. 110 Lib. Dem. 84 Others 29 **Lab. majority 213**	Labour 436 Con. 110 Lib. Dem. 84 Others 29 **Lab. majority 213**	Labour 303 Con. 203 Lib. Dem. 115 Others 38 **Lab. majority 27 short**	Labour 342 Con. 144 Lib. Dem. 131 Others 42 **Lab. majority 25**
Pros	Clear result: tends towards stable one-party government; good link between local MP and local voter.	Retains direct link between MP and constituents; ensures winner has majority support at local level; fairer to small parties.	SV is straightforward, SV- and AV- Plus variations produce highly proportional results.	Produces effective proportional results while retaining constituency link and increasing voter choice.	Gives the voters what they want, no wasted votes and due weight to minority views. Encourages turnout in areas previously 'safe' for one party.
Cons	Can deliver near-absolute power via huge majorities on less than half the popular vote: unkind to small parties; limits voter choice.	Can produce wildly unproportional results, thanks to tactical voting. Was recommended for Westminster in 1910 and 1916.	Under landslide conditions the leading party gets too much dominance at constituency level.	Makes it hard for one party to win outright majority and thus gives small parties power out of proportion to their votes or seats.	Complex, hard to understand or count votes. Too parochial. Huge 200,000-plus constituencies.

15

VOTING BEHAVIOUR

Voting behaviour—the way in which people decide which political party to vote for—is a complex issue. Voters' choice is influenced by factors such as social class, age, sex, family background, neighbourhood, ethnic background and region. Elections and voting behaviour determine who governs us and, to a large extent, what they do in office.

CONTINUITY AND CHANGE

British electoral patterns are characterised by a great deal of stability. The Conservative and Labour Parties have been the only two major parties in Britain for more than sixty years. The Conservatives won four elections in a row between 1979 and 1992, giving them control of the powers of government for eighteen years. Labour has won a majority of Scottish seats in all twelve elections since 1959. Such continuities in election results are the product of a great deal of stability in individual voting behaviour over time. When a political party acquires or loses major party status, or loses an election in a landslide as the Conservatives did in 1997, it does not win or lose all its supporters overnight. That is why minor parties such as the Liberal Democrats in Britain and the SNP in Scotland find it difficult to achieve major party status.

Voters tend to acquire a loyalty to the party of their choice, a loyalty which is not easily or quickly overturned. However, one of the interesting questions about voting behaviour today is whether individual voters are less loyal to parties than they used to be, and if this is the case, why.

In every general election result we see a mixture of continuity and change. The study of voting behaviour is concerned with identifying and explaining both the continuities and the changes which determine ultimately what political parties attempt to do in office when they win elections. The principal continuities and changes in the decisions of the British electorate in the sixteen elections since 1945 are illustrated on page 17.

Table 2.1 illustrates the elements of continuity and change by comparing the 1992 and 2001 Election results in two areas—Scotland with seventy two constituencies and the south-east of England (excluding Greater London) with 117 constituencies. Continuity is represented by the fact that Labour was the strongest party in Scotland and the Conservatives were the strongest party in the south-east of England in both elections. There was very little change in the 'third' party shares of the votes between the two elections. Clearly, Scotland is a Labour stronghold and a Conservative political desert, while the South-east is a Conservative stronghold (11% ahead of Labour in the 2001 popular vote) even in a disastrous election for the Party.

CONTINUITY and CHANGE
IN BRITISH POLITICS

EVIDENCE OF AN *UNCHANGING* POLITICAL LANDSCAPE

1   The British electorate has sustained a Conservative–Labour two-party system since 1945. Only once, in 1983, has the 'third' party come within 5% of the weaker of the two major parties.

2   The winning party usually wins over 40% of the popular vote, the only exceptions being the two closely fought elections of 1974.

3   The Conservatives have twice won more than two elections in a row (1951, 1955 and 1959, and 1979, 1983, 1987 and 1992), holding governmental office for thirteen years and eighteen years respectively. Labour has yet to win more than two successive elections.

4   The performance of the principal 'third party' challenge to the two-party system in Britain divides neatly into two periods. From 1945 until 1970 the Liberals only once exceeded 10% of the vote. However, since February 1974 the 'Liberal' challenge has attracted close to 20% support.

5   For most of the post-war period the degree of major party 'swing', i.e. the relative changes in the Conservative and Labour shares of the popular vote, was within a range of 1–4%, suggesting that many individuals tended to remain loyal to one party. In other words, Britain possessed a stable electorate. This was much lower than the degree of swing in American presidential elections during the same period.

EVIDENCE OF A *CHANGING* POLITICAL LANDSCAPE

1   Six of the sixteen elections since 1945 have resulted in a change of government (1951, 1964, 1970, February 1974, 1979 and 1997).

2   The Conservative–Labour two-party system within the electorate has been considerably weaker since 1974. From 1945 to 1970 the two major parties averaged 91.2% of the popular vote. Their combined share has averaged only 75.6% since February 1974. This trend has been described as partisan dealignment.

3   The 'third party' challenge has strengthened considerably since 1974. Since 1974 the 'third force' in British politics has averaged 19.4% of the vote. In the 1950s the Liberals stopped contesting every constituency because their share was falling drastically. However, by 1974 the Liberals and their successors were back to contesting the great majority of seats. In 1997 the Liberal Democrats' share of seats more than doubled in spite of a slight decline in vote share because they successfully 'targeted' seats they thought they had a chance of winning. They were also helped by tactical voting by Labour supporters seeking to deny seats to the Conservatives

4   The electorate has become much more volatile since 1979. Prior to the first Thatcher victory, the average gap between the votes of the two major parties was only 3.4%. Since 1979 that gap has averaged 10.7%. The Labour landslide in 1997 was based on a large swing of 10%. Labour won a few seats which had been considered 'rock solid' for the Conservatives with a swing of 15%. A swing of just over 1% to the Conservatives in 2001 made virtually no difference to the result.

5   From 1950 to 1966, turnout never fell below 75%. (1945 was exceptional because wartime conditions made it impossible for many individuals on the electoral register to vote.) However, since 1970 turnout has fallen below 75% on four occasions. In 1997 turnout fell to 71.3% but in 2001 it fell even more dramatically to a post-war low of 59.1%; two voters out of five did not go to the polls.

CONTINUITY & CHANGE	1992		2001	
	% Votes	Seats	% Votes	Seats
Scotland				
Labour	40.0	49	43.9	*56
Conservative	26.0	11	15.6	1
SNP	22.0	3	20.0	5
Liberal Democrats	13.0	9	16.4	10
Total		72		72
South-east England				
Labour	21.0	3	32.0	35
Conservative	54.0	106	43.0	73
Liberal Democrats	23.0	0	22.0	9
Total		109		117

Table 2.1 *Includes the Speaker

17

1997 A 'RECORD-BREAKING' ELECTION?

The Conservatives

The Conservative share of the vote, 30.7%, was the lowest since 1832. Only twice before in the post-war period, in the two indecisive elections of 1974, had the Conservative share fallen beneath 40%. The Conservative presence in the House of Commons, 165 MPs out of a new total of 659, was the lowest since 1906. Labour had won 209 seats in 1983 when its share of the popular vote was only 28.3%. Seven Cabinet Ministers lost their seats, the second highest total ever. (In 1906 eight lost their seats including the Prime Minister.) For the first time ever no Conservatives MPs were returned from Scotland or Wales. In the words of one journalist the Conservatives were reduced to being "a party based almost entirely in the countryside and some suburbs". Conservative MPs were banished from Britain's cities, though a small rump of Conservative voters remained faithful. On Merseyside, with its sixteen seats in Liverpool and its urban hinterland, the Conservatives won no seats and a mere 19.7% of the vote.

Labour

Labour's overall majority of 179 was its biggest ever, beating 146 in 1945 and 96 in 1966. Labour's margin of victory over the Conservatives in the popular vote was, at 13%, its biggest ever though its vote share in 1997 (44.4%) was smaller than in 1945 (47.8%) and 1966 (47.9%).

Liberal Democrats

1997 was the best 'Liberal' performance in the post-war period. Their Commons delegation of forty six MPs was the highest total since the fifty nine seats won in 1929. The Liberal Democrat vote share was lower than the Liberal/SDP Alliance achieved in 1983 and 1987. However, the Liberal Democrats' campaign strategy was much more successful in 1997 when they 'targeted' (put more resources into) seats where they had a realistic chance of winning.

Swing

The degree of relative change in the major parties' shares of the vote in 1997 was 10%. This is the highest swing in the post-war period apart from 1945 when the 12% swing relative to 1935 was partly due to the ten-year interval between elections caused by the Second World War. The 10% swing in 1997 was almost double the Labour–Conservative swing of 5.2% in 1979, which was the highest recorded between 1950 and 1992. The large swing suggests that many more voters than usual changed their party allegiance and thus provoked the 'record' features of the 1997 Election. Why they changed will be examined below.

Turnout

The 71.3% of the registered electorate voting in 1997 was the lowest since 1945. The average turnout in the four Conservative victories between 1979 and 1992 was 75.4%. The relatively sharp fall in 1997 has provoked a debate about its significance. Conservatives argue that the fall was due to many Conservatives not voting rather than moving to support other parties. Another explanation offered for the low turnout was that the result was widely anticipated (the opinion poll predictions were accurate) because of the long-running problems experienced by the Major government.

The 1997 Election also produced the lowest majority in an individual constituency since 1910. The Conservative Gerry Malone was defeated in Winchester by two votes—a result he was to contest in court.

'Tory-Free Zones'

In 1997, Scotland and Wales were proclaimed 'Tory-Free Zones' because no Conservative MPs were returned to Westminster.

VOTING BEHAVIOUR

There are two very general types of explanation of individual voting behaviour and collective voting trends.

☞ The first emphasises the specific *social characteristics* of individual voters. These social explanations tend to explain long-term continuities and gradual changes in electoral trends.

☞ The second explanation focuses on the political background to particular elections such as the *significant issues* of the day which may influence individual voters. Issues tend to explain short-term changes such as Labour's defeat in 1979 which led to the Thatcherite era in British politics and the 'record' characteristics of the 1997 result. Issues may also be related to long-term continuity in so far as they provide a motive for individual allegiances to a particular party which are then sustained over a long period of time.

Class and Voting

Social class dominated explanations of voting behaviour until the 1970s and is still considered to be influential today. The dominance of social class among the various influences on the decisions of the British electorate was dramatically expressed in 1967 in a celebrated claim by the Oxford political scientist P J Pulzer:

> "Class is the basis of British party politics; all else is embellishment and detail."

(PJ Pulzer *Political Representation and Elections in Britain*, Allen & Unwin, 1967).

Pulzer's statement was widely accepted as an accurate description of the key characteristic of such elements of British party politics as voting behaviour, party membership and party policies. Studies of voting behaviour were discovering that many people voted for the same party throughout their lives and that choice of

(continued on page 22)

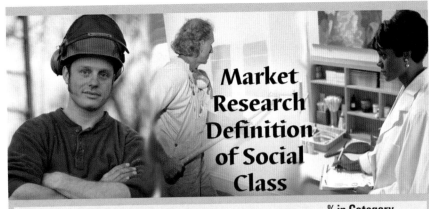

Class	Categories		% in Category		
---	---	---	1966	1992	2001
A	Higher Managerial	A+B	12	19	}50
B	Lower Managerial				
C1	Skilled Supervisors		22	24	
C2	Skilled Manual		37	27	}50
D	Unskilled Manual/Manual				
E	Residual/Unemployed/Poor	D+E	29	30	

Table 2.2   Categories A, B, and C1 constitute the non-manual 'middle class' categories, while C2, D and E make up the manual 'working class'.

WHAT IS SOCIAL CLASS?

A social class is generally taken to be a set of individuals who share certain social characteristics which collectively give them a similar attitude to life in general and to politics in particular. Individuals who are brought up in the same neighbourhood and who then live and work in similar conditions might be expected to develop similar views on politics (which party to support), sport (which team to support), religion (which church to attend), leisure activities (bingo or bridge) and so on. There are many social conditions which are included in lists of variables defining social classes: occupation, housing, education, income and wealth. Some individuals are born into poor families, others into wealthy families. The children of richer families tend to go to private fee-paying schools and on to higher education; the children of less wealthy families are more likely to go to comprehensive schools and are less likely to go on to higher education.

Such a simple division of the population is not accurate enough for the purposes of political scientists. They have tended to make use of the social class categories employed by market research organisations in their efforts to find out why consumers buy certain products and not others. The market research definition of the British class structure uses six categories, namely A, B, C1, C2, D and E, which are based on a classification of occupations. These categories and their relative sizes are described in Table 2.2.

Table 2.2 illustrates a significant change in British social structure in the three decades between the late 1960s and the early 1990s. Britain is slowly becoming more middle class. The percentage of the workforce classified as middle class increased from 34% in 1966 to 43% in 1992. By 2001 the middle and working classes were almost equal in size. The two classes experiencing most change have been the upper middle class (A+B) which has increased in size, and the skilled manual class which has reduced in size. Before the 1997 Election this change in the relative sizes of the two principal social classes was considered to be a disadvantage for the Labour Party. This was partly responsible for Labour leaders after Michael Foot redesigning the policies, the image and the electoral strategies of the 'working-class party'.

The market research categories are employed by most polling organisations to produce data on voting behaviour linking social class to party support. Even though occupation is the sole criterion assigning individuals to particular class categories, the assumption is made that individuals in every social class category share similar social features with others in the same class category. They share a common 'lifestyle' which differs from that of the other categories.

A T FIRST SIGHT the General Election contested in June 2001 produced remarkably few changes relative to the pattern of party support registered in 1997. The shares of both votes and seats won by the two major parties hardly altered. The Conservatives enjoyed a net swing of 1.6% from Labour but could win only one more seat than in 1997. The small Conservative net gain from Labour, five seats, was offset by a net loss of four seats to the Liberal Democrats. Apart from Northern Ireland, where there were significant changes, only twenty one seats changed hands, the lowest number since 1910.

	Share of Vote %	Changes in Seats Won
Labour	-1.2	-6
Conservative	+2	+1
Liberal Democrats	+2	+6

2001 ANOTHER RECORD

POLLING PLACE

LANDSLIDE & APATHY

Labour was granted another massive overall majority of 167, a mere twelve down on the record of 1997. On the surface, the 2001 Election looks like a rerun of 1997 with almost exactly the same outcome. Nevertheless, that is not how the 2001 result was interpreted by most political analysts. This is because relative party performance does not indicate the most dramatic feature of voting behaviour in 2001. For that we have to look at the turnout which was at its lowest since 1918.

Turnout

Only 59.1% of the registered electorate voted on 7 June 2001, only 2% more than the record low turnout of 57% in 1918, a wartime election. Fewer than three out of every five voters made it to the polling booths. Only 25% of the registered electorate voted for the winning party. The drop of 12.2% relative to the 1997 figure, itself the lowest since 1945, was the largest recorded between two peacetime elections. Labour attracted 2.8 million fewer supporters than in 1997 and almost 800,000 fewer than when it lost in 1992. John Major's Conservative Party won almost 6 million more voters in

1992 than did William Hague's Party in 2001. The lowest constituency turnout was 34% in Liverpool Riverside. The lowest turnout in Scotland was 39% in Glasgow Shettleston. Even in the Prime Minister's constituency, Sedgefield, turnout at 62% was 10% lower than in 1997. The largest turnout of all was 81.3% in Ulster Mid; the largest turnout in mainland Britain was 78.7% in Winchester. Turnout failed to reach 50% in sixty eight constituencies. Low turnout was particularly marked among new and young voters. Only one-third of voters under 25 went to the polls but 70% of pensioners did so.

There are several theories to account for the long-term decline in turnout since the early 1970s and the dramatic falls in 1997 and 2001.

"The result was a foregone conclusion"
Public opinion polls throughout the four years following New Labour's 1997 victory provided little or no hint of a Conservative revival in time for the next election. Polls close to the 2001 Election gave Labour a very comfortable lead. Thus it is argued that many voters did not feel that they could make a difference or else felt

that their particular votes were not needed by their preferred parties.

"The result is an instruction to do better"
The Prime Minister's own interpretation of voting behaviour in 2001 was based on an analysis of the low turnout which claimed that many voters had not been greatly impressed by the government's attempts to improve such public services as education, health and transport. Abstention was a way of warning the government that improvements were necessary before the next election if a third Labour victory was to be achieved.

"The end of ideology"
There have been several changes in the image of British politics as a contest between two class-based, ideologically divergent parties. Labour has more or less lost its socialist and trade union dominated image. The private finance initiative (PFI) to provide some public services is a far cry from the nationalised industries of the 1945–1979 era. Conservatives have accused Labour of "stealing the Emperor's clothes". The middle class has become the biggest class in our allegedly 'classless society'. In the post-industrial society the

ideological dimension in policy is much less important to consumers of health, education and other services than efficiency. However, deciding how to vote by judging the relative efficiency of political parties in government is much more difficult than doing so out of an emotional commitment to a political ideology. Thus fewer observable policy differences between the parties and less ideological commitment on the part of voters combine to explain the long-term decline in turnout in general elections in many western capitalist democracies.

Turnout was higher where local or regional issues were stronger than national issues. Turnout was higher in Northern Ireland where the Good Friday Agreement divided both nationalists and loyalists. Turnout was 75% in Wyre Forest where an independent, Dr Richard Taylor, won a seemingly 'safe' Labour seat. Dr Taylor ran as a protest against developments in the NHS in his constituency.

Compulsory Voting?

The 2001 turnout immediately prompted calls for the introduction of compulsory voting by those who are worried that lower turnout cheapens or weakens British democracy.

	SEATS		VOTES	
	1997	2001	1997	2001
Ulster Unionists (UUP)	10	6	32.7	26.8
Democratic Unionists (DUP)	2	5	13.6	22.5
SDLP	3	3	24.1	21
Sinn Fein	2	4	16.1	21.7
Others	1	0		

Table 2.3

Northern Ireland

The political gulf between mainland Britain and Northern Ireland was highlighted by the major changes in voting behaviour in Ulster where there was neither a landslide nor apathy. Ian Paisley's DUP, opposed to the Good Friday Agreement and less likely to make concessions to the nationalists, ran David Trimble's Ulster Unionists close in the race to be first in the loyalist camp. For the first time Sinn Fein won more nationalist votes than the more moderate Social Democratic and Labour Party led by John Hume. David Trimble resigned as First Minister in July 2001 to be reelected in November 2001.

The Liberal Democrats

The Liberal Democrats gained six seats overall, proportionately the biggest change in party fortunes, leading to claims that Charles Kennedy had performed best out of all the party leaders. No fewer than nine of the twenty seats to change hands switched between the Liberal Democrats and the Conservatives with seven going to the Liberal Democrats and two to the Conservatives. The Liberal Democrat gains emphasised that the Party has at last learned to live with the first-past-the-post electoral system by concentrating its vote where it has a chance of winning. Kennedy's party won almost three million votes fewer than the Liberal/SDP Alliance in 1983 but won more than twice as many seats.

Every election creates new titles to describe the key voters in marginal constituencies who can influence the outcome of a general election. Below is an example of the terms used in the 2001 Election.

"The Conservatives last night set their election sights on winning the votes of 2.5 million 'pebbledash people' in marginal seats as William Hague pledged a future Tory government to a public service revolution akin to Margaret Thatcher's reform of the trade unions. Like Mondeo man and Worcester woman of the last general election, Tory strategists have identified a key group which they feel, if won over, would put Mr Hague in 10 Downing Street.
As the name implies, they are middle-income families who live in pebbledashed 1930s semi-detached houses. They are found in around 180 marginals, mainly in the Midlands. A Tory Party spokesman said the target seats operation would form an important part of the party's election campaign but added that the label "pebbledash people" was "not part of official language".
'They've been given other names like Mondeo man, but they're always the same people: voters in three-bed semi-detached houses.' "

PEBBLEDASH PEOPLE: Some 2.5 million voters living in 180 marginal seats, mainly in the Midlands and the north-west of England. Many live in 1930s-style pebbledashed semi-detached houses.

MONDEO MAN: Created after Tony Blair, during the 1997 campaign, came across a man washing his Mondeo car. A 30-something middle-income home owner who was the bedrock of Labour's election victory.

SIERRA MAN: The lifelong Tory voter whom Labour targeted as a switcher.

WORCESTER WOMAN: Targeted by the Tories and replaced Essex man (sometimes dubbed Basildon man), who had become a lost cause for John Major in 1997.

FLORIDA WOMAN: Replaced Worcester woman. More affluent and regularly holidayed in the sunshine state.

Adapted from *The Herald*, 31/1/01

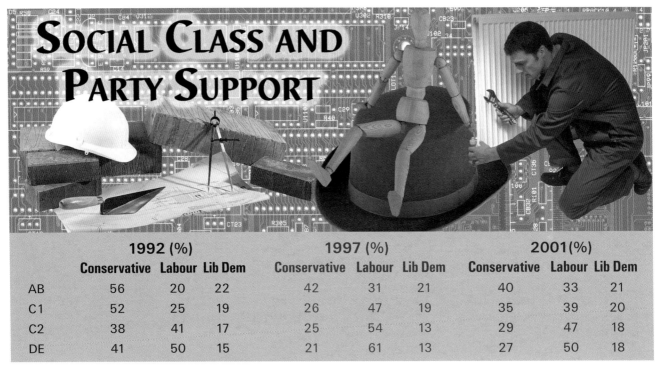

SOCIAL CLASS AND PARTY SUPPORT

	1992 (%)			1997 (%)			2001 (%)		
	Conservative	Labour	Lib Dem	Conservative	Labour	Lib Dem	Conservative	Labour	Lib Dem
AB	56	20	22	42	31	21	40	33	21
C1	52	25	19	26	47	19	35	39	20
C2	38	41	17	25	54	13	29	47	18
DE	41	50	15	21	61	13	27	50	18

Table 2.4   Source: Butler & Kavanagh *The British General Elections of 1992 and 1997; The Observer* 2001

party was strongly linked to 'social class'. Given its central position in explanations of British political behaviour, it is essential to define 'social class'. (See page 19.)

The changing relationships between social class, as defined by the market research categories, and party support/voting behaviour are illustrated in Table 2.4.

In 1992 the Conservatives enjoyed their fourth consecutive victory, though this time their overall Commons majority was reduced to twenty one and the gap in the popular vote between Conservative and Labour was reduced from 11.7% to 7.1%. An intriguing feature of the 1992 result was that the still large Conservative vote won fewer seats than was the case in 1983 and 1987. This was because Labour did much better in marginal constituencies and held on to or won seats which would have been lost if the swing had been uniform.

As in the 1983 and 1987 Elections, there was still a relationship between social class and party support in 1992 but it was much reduced. Although Labour regained its position as the strongest party in C2, the skilled working class, its lead was very small at 3%.

There was still more working-class Conservative support than middle-class Labour support. The proportion of the electorate voting for the natural class party rose to 49% in 1992. The Liberal Democrats had more of a class look to their support, the middle classes being several points more supportive than the working classes although the class connection remained much less pronounced than in the case of the two major parties.

Studies of voting behaviour in the twenty years prior to 1997 concentrated on Labour's electoral weakness. The changing class structure and the four successive Conservative victories suggested that Labour faced long-term difficulties which were not due to the particular circumstances of each election. Then in 1997 Labour was elected following the largest swing in support between the two major parties since 1945.

The 1997 Election has been described previously as a record-breaking election. The record-breaking theme may also be applied to the survey findings linking class to party support. For the first time ever the larger middle-class category, C1, gave more votes to Labour than to the Conservatives and by a wide

margin (21%). The highest social class, AB, remained faithful to the Conservatives, but for the first time fewer than 50% of ABs voted Conservative. There were now many more middle-class radicals (Labour voters among ABs and C1s) than working-class Conservatives (Conservative voters in C2/DE). In 2001 Labour increased its vote in the AB category but its lead over the Conservatives in the working class decreased.

The 1997 relationships between social class and party support were largely repeated in 2001. Labour retained the lead in the lower middle class (C1). One intriguing feature was that a small overall swing of 1.8% to the Conservatives hid a small swing to Labour in the two middle-class categories (AB and C1) and a larger swing from Labour to the Conservatives in the two working-class categories (C2 and DE). These swings are probably based on differential turnout. The Labour vote declined most in safe Labour seats but held up well in more marginal seats. Labour's considerable working-class vote declined most in safe seats which Labour held onto comfortably. But this decline contributed to a small swing to the right.

RIVAL EXPLANATIONS OF SOCIAL CLASS AND VOTING TRENDS
Dealignment or Trendless Fluctuations?

British society and British voting patterns have changed since it was claimed in the 1960s that "class is the basis of British party politics". That claim has to be re–examined in the light of the changes in the links between social class and party support illustrated in Table 2.4.

Two rival explanations have been offered to explain the links between social class and party support illustrated in Table 2.4. One explanation is the dealignment thesis put forward by Professor Ivor Crewe and others. The second explanation put forward by Heath, Jowell and Curtice in *How Britain Votes*, published in 1985, focuses attention on problems inherent in efforts to define social class meaningfully.

Dealignment

Dealignment means a weakening relationship between social class and party support—a decline in the class basis of British politics. The evidence supporting the dealignment thesis may be seen in the fall in the proportion of the electorate voting for their natural class party from 64% in 1966 to 44% in 1987.

Crewe explained dealignment by distinguishing between an 'old' and a 'new' working class. Members of the 'old' working class still shared such definitive characteristics as

- an unskilled manual occupation in a traditional 'heavy' industry
- trade union membership
- living in council housing
- they were to be found in greater numbers in North Britain (North of England, Scotland and Wales) than in South Britain

Members of the 'new' working class were

- more likely to be skilled
- owner occupiers
- working in newer 'high tech' industries
- located in the Southern half of England

Two sets of evidence supported Crewe's division of the working class into two parts.

- Several social and political indicators suggested a growing 'North-South' divide.
- In the 1980s the skilled working class had moved from the Labour camp to the Conservative camp.

New definitions of Class

Heath et al challenged the dealignment thesis. First they focused attention on the widely accepted market research class categories in such a way as to strengthen the links between class and voting behaviour. Their new class categories are described below.

* *Salariat* (27%): managerial, supervisory and professional 'workers' with secure employment, relatively high income and some authority and autonomy.

* *Routine non-manual* (24%): clerks, salespersons and secretaries; subordinate position in the workplace but still 'white collar'.

* *Petty bourgeoisie* (8%): farmers, small proprietors and self-employed manual workers; essentially individuals who work for themselves and who are not subordinate within the workplace.

* *Foremen and technicians* (7%): 'blue-collar' elite, supervisory positions in the workplace.

* *Working class* (34%): rank-and-file skilled and semi-skilled manual occupations in industry and agriculture.

Heath et al argued that the voting behaviour of these redrawn class categories supported their view of social class in Britain. The most Conservative class between 1983 and 1992 was the 'petty bourgeoisie'. 'Foremen and technicians' were more evenly divided between the parties, moving from favouring the Conservatives in 1983 to favouring Labour in 1992. Both were more Conservative than the working class because their possession of some authority and independence allowed them to see themselves as closer to the 'salariat' in the workplace.

If individuals leaning to the Conservatives and assigned to the working class by the market research classification are removed from the working class, two consequences follow. Firstly, the residual working class is smaller and therefore Labour's natural pool of class support is smaller. Secondly, those remaining in the working class will be more loyal to Labour.

Heath et al concluded that there had not been a significant reduction in the links between social class and party support—that dealignment was not a satisfactory explanation. Rather the variations in the links between class and party support evident in voting behaviour since the 1970s, including 1997 when Labour took over from the Conservatives as the dominant party, suggest that the circumstances of each election might explain the result. Hence they talked of 'trendless fluctuations' beyond the control of the parties and the government. It had so happened that circumstances had favoured the Conservatives from the 'winter of discontent' in 1978–79, through Labour's profound internal divisions before the 1983 Election to the economic recovery in the years immediately before and after the 1987 Election.

Ethnicity and voting

One in twenty potential voters comes from an ethnic minority but this ignores the potential concentration of their votes in a limited number of inner city constituencies. Some commentators suggest that in as many as forty nine seats, the majority of the sitting MPs was less than the total number of local ethnic minority votes.

Asian and Black voting intentions 1997 (%)		
	Asian	Black
Conservative	25	8
Labour	70	86
Liberal Democrat	4	4

Table 2.5
Source: based on Saggar (1997)

Previous tough Conservative legislation on asylum seekers and William Hague's hard line on immigration, alienated some support among ethnic minorities. The high profile of ethnic minority MPs, such as government Minister, Paul Boateng, and the complete absence of any Conservative ethnic minority MPs, reinforces the popularity of Labour among ethnic minority voters.

In the 1997 Election, the Conservatives made a significant effort to woo the Asian vote which included a high profile tour of India by the then Conservative Prime Minister, John Major. While Table 2.5 clearly highlights the overwhelming ethnic support for Labour, it indicates a difference between Asian and Black voting intentions. Conservatives had the support of a quarter of Asian voters compared with only 8% support from Black ethnic minorities.

Age & party support

Age does appear to be a factor in voting preference (see Table 2.6) but the reasons for this are not easy to identify. Different age groups may vote differently because they have had different experiences of life and of political history. In 1997 and 2001 the Conservatives 'won' among the over-65s, in spite of pensions becoming a prominent issue during the campaign, but 'lost' elsewhere. These older voters hardly changed allegiance overall compared to 1992. Younger voters, including new voters, were particularly strong supporters of Labour.

Age hardly influenced the Liberal Democrat vote at all. The Party's ability to poll evenly across both class and age divisions suggests that its appeal is not dependent on social factors. This may limit its ability to develop its electoral base. Parties which achieve major party status usually depend on securing the allegiance of particular sections of society.

Age Group	Conservative	Labour	Lib. Dem.
18-24	29	47	19
25-34	29	47	18
35-44	28	44	20
45-54	34	39	20
55-64	34	40	19
65+	42	37	18

Table 2.6
Source: The Observer 10 June 2001

In the 1950s and 1960s a higher percentage of men than women voted Labour, while a higher percentage of women voted Conservative. This was explained by Labour's strong 'male' identity with the trade union movement. Certainly, as the links between the Labour Party and the unions have weakened, so the gender gap has narrowed. In the 1997 and 2001 Elections there was no significant difference between the way the genders voted. (See Table 2.7.) Labour's selection of a significant number of women candidates and the more moderate policies of New Labour have played their part in this change.

For two decades now, British women have been more likely than men to cast their votes; in the General Election of 1997, 3% more women voted than men—a turn-out gap of almost two million votes.

Gender and Party Support

| | Conservative | | | Labour | | | Liberal Democrats | | |
	1992	1997	2001	1992	1997	2001	1992	1997	2001
Men	39	31	33	36	44	42	18	17	18
Women	43	32	33	34	44	42	18	17	20

Table 2.7   Source: 1992 data ITN/Harris exit poll; 1997 BBC/NOP exit poll; 2001 ICM/Observer poll

| | Conservative | | Labour | | Liberal Democrats | |
	1992	1997	1992	1997	1992	1997
Home owners	47	35	30	41	14	17
Council tenants	19	13	64	65	10	15

Table 2.8   Source 1992 data ITN/Harris exit poll; 1997 data BBC/NOP exit poll.

Table 2.8 illustrates the fact that there is a strong correlation between form of housing tenure and vote. It is clear that council house tenants identify strongly with Labour and that one-third of council tenants who voted Conservative in 1992 switched to the Liberal Democrats in 1997. The 1997 Election witnessed, for the first time, greater support among home owners for Labour than for the Conservative Party.

Residence and Party Support

ISSUE VOTING

How can we explain the scale of the change in party support in 1997? Explanations based on sociological terms—class, gender, age etc.—are inadequate. Other influences were clearly at work. The impact of specific 'issues' on the voters was perhaps of increasing importance.

Election campaigns revolve round two themes:

➡ who will form the government?

➡ what will they do in office?

The 'what' is usually defined in policy terms—what the parties

stand for and what they say they will do. The 'who' is often determined by the voters' impresssion of how well each party has performed in office.

An election result might depend on the performance of the sitting Prime Minister and Cabinet or on memories of the performance of the major party rival the last time it held office. Some voters may be swayed by what the parties say they will do if elected.

The 1992 and 1997 Elections with their very different outcomes offer

an opportunity to look at the impact of several types of issue.

Table 2.9 indicates that in 1992 the Conservatives were preferred on inflation, taxation, defence and relations with Europe. Labour was preferred on education, the NHS and unemployment. The Conservative lead on the issues on which they came out ahead as 'best able to handle a particular problem' was considerably greater than Labour's lead on issues where it came out ahead.

In 1997 Labour overtook the Conservatives on both taxation and relations with Europe andf increased its lead considerably on unemployment, the NHS and education. Labour's lead was greatest in relation to the NHS. The Conservatives were still ahead on defence and inflation but by greatly reduced margins.

Why did public perceptions of how the rival parties would handle decisive issues change after 1992? After all, Labour had been ahead on issues before, though not nearly so decisively, and had lost the Elections of 1987 and 1992.

According to John Curtice there was a drastic change in the public's perception of the strengths and weaknesses of the Conservative Party sometime following the 1992 Election. (See Table 2.10.) The surveys were held in the spring and early summer of the years in question. In 1992, shortly after the closely contested General Election, the Conservative image was much more positive than Labour's on party unity and on whether the parties were likely to offer strong and capable government. The parties were equally rated on 'moderation' which suggested that Labour had by then lost its radical left-wing image. By 1994 the Conservative image had been severely tarnished on both party unity and the ability to provide strong government. In contrast, Labour's image had improved so much that from 1994 onwards Labour was widely perceived as more moderate, more united and more likely to provide strong, capable government.

Curtice explains this dramatic switch in the public's perception of the attributes of the two major parties to 'Black Wednesday' in September 1992 when the Conservative government had to withdraw Britain from the European Exchange Rate Mechanism and accept devaluation of the pound. Conservative disunity on Euro-

ISSUES & PREFERRED PARTY: 1987 & 1992

Which party would handle a particular policy best?

ISSUE	PREFERRED PARTY LEAD	
	1992	1997
NHS	Labour 17	Labour 49
Unemployment	Labour 19	Labour 38
Education	Labour 6	Labour 39
Defence	Conservative 41	Con +86
Prices/Inflation	Conservative 29	Con +59
Taxation	Conservative 20	Labour 12
Relations with Europe	Conservative 34	Labour 12

Table 2.9   Source: Dunleavy et al. *Developments in British Politics*

Although the Conservatives campaigned to 'Keep the Pound' at the election in 2001, the issue of Britain's place in Europe split the Party from the early 1990s. This disunity helped to create a lack of confidence among the voters about the Party's ability to govern.

pean issues was highlighted by Eurosceptics rebelling in Parliament against the passage of the Maastricht Treaty and later on the issue of the single currency. The 1997 result has been interpreted as a negative judgement on the performance of the Conservative Government elected in 1992.

IMAGES OF THE PARTIES, 1992–1996

IMAGE		1992	1994	1995	1996
Moderation	Conservative	61	48	48	51
	Labour	61	72	76	74
Capable, strong government	Conservative	84	32	27	27
	Labour	35	60	67	62
Party unity	Conservative	67	10	8	9
	Labour	30	64	67	54

Table 2.10 Source: Based on data derived from John Curtice, *Anatomy of a Non-Landslide'* in the Politics Review, September 1997.

TACTICAL VOTING

Tactical voting was encouraged by the electoral strategy of the Liberal Democrats who targeted seats where they had a chance of winning—often seats where they had come second in 1992.

Tactical voting had two consequences. Firstly, the Liberal Democrats won forty six seats with a lower share of the vote than the Liberal/SDP Alliance had achieved in 1983 and 1987. Secondly, in spite of considerable agreement on constitutional issues between the Labour and Liberal Democrat leadership elites, there was often bitter fighting in the campaign between the two parties challenging the Tories in seats where both felt they had a chance of victory. The Liberal Democrats had some victories which upset the Conservatives. For instance, they defeated Norman Lamont in Harrogate. However, the Liberal Democrats also campaigned less vigorously in many marginals where they felt they would not win. This left such seats open to the possibility of a Labour gain which duly transpired. Labour won about forty seats more than the most optimistic projections.

GEOGRAPHICAL INFLUENCE

Regional and national variations in voting behaviour and election results have become a major focus of interest in recent years. The Labour governments elected in 1950, 1964 and 1974 were dependent on winning a comfortable majority of Scottish and Welsh seats to overcome Conservative majorities in England. Nationalist electoral successes in Scotland and Wales in 1974 appeared to pose a potential threat to Labour's favourable position outside England and so prompted Labour's conversion to favouring devolution.

A North-South divide?

After 1979 the combination of Labour dominance in Scotland and long-term Conservative government at Westminster raised the spectre of the 'Doomsday Scenario'. Liberal Democrat seats were concentrated in Scotland from 1983 until the 1997 breakthrough in England. Finally, there was increasing talk of a deepening North-South economic and political divide under Thatcherism. The Conservatives were much stronger electorally in the southern half of England, including the English Midlands, than in northern Britain including Scotland and Wales. The electoral division seemed to be accompanied by economic trends which saw lower unemployment and higher incomes in the South than in the North.

What, then, are the territorial dimensions to British elections and what explains them? *The British General Elections Studies* reports election results using nine standard English regions, Scotland and Wales as shown in Figure 2.1.

Table 2.12 illustrates regional variations in voting behaviour in 1987 when the Conservatives won decisively and in 1997 and 2001 when Labour won even more decisively. In 1987 the Conservatives were

NUMBER OF SEATS IN ENGLISH REGIONS

		1987	2001
South of England	South-east (excluding Greater London)	108	117
	Greater London (Outer & Inner London)	84	74
	South-west	48	51
English Midlands	West Midlands	58	59
	East Midlands	42	44
	East Anglia	20	22
North of England	Yorkshire and Humberside	54	56
	North-west	73	70
	Northern England	34	36
	(England)	(521)	(529)

Table 2.11

Figure 2.1

Conservative & Liberal Strength by Region and Nation

Region	CONSERVATIVE MPs			CONSERVATIVE share of vote(%)			LIBERAL MPs			LIBERAL share of vote(%)		
	1987	1997	2001	1987	1997	2001	1987	1997	2001	1987	1997	2001
South-east England	107/108	73/117	73/117	55.6	41.4	43	0	8	9	27.2	21.4	22
Greater London	57/84	11/74	13/74	45.4	31.2	31	3	6	6	21.3	14.6	18
South-west England	44/48	22/51	20/51	50.6	36.7	31	3	14	15	33.0	31.3	39
West Midlands	36/58	14/59	13/59	48.6	33.6	35	0	1	2	20.8	13.8	15
East Midlands	31/42	14/44	15/44	45.5	34.9	37	0	0	1	20.9	13.6	15
East Anglia	19/20	14/22	14/22	52.1	38.7	42	0	0	1	25.7	17.9	19
North-west England	34/73	7/70	7/70	38	26.4	28	3	2	3	20.2	14.3	17
Yorkshire & Humberside	21/54	7/56	7/56	37.4	28	30	0	2	2	21.6	16.0	17
North of England	8/34	3/36	3/36	32.3	22.4	25	1	1	1	21.0	13.3	17
England	357/521	165/529	165/529	46.2	33.7	35.2	10	34	40	23.8	17.9	19.4
Wales	8/38	0/40	0/40	29.5	19.6	21	3	2	2	17.9	12.4	14
Scotland	10/72	0/72	1/72	24	17.5	15.6	9	10	10	19.2	13.0	16
Great Britain	403/631	165/641	166/641	43.3	31.5	32.7	22	46	52	23.1	17.2	18.8

Table 2.12

the dominant party in terms of both seats and votes in the south of England where Labour was desperately weak outside Inner London. The Conservatives almost monopolised seats in the south-east and south-west of England, winning all but five out of 156 seats on the basis of over 50% of the popular vote. Rural East Anglia was just as strongly Conservative. Inner London, where Labour won twenty out of twenty nine seats, was an exception to Conservative dominance in the south of England. The Conservatives were also the strongest party in Greater London and the Midlands where they won well over 40% of the vote and well over 60% of the seats.

Only in the northern regions of England did Labour win more seats than the Conservatives in 1987 though Labour's margin, 94 seats out of 161 in the North-west (mainly Lancashire), Yorkshire and Humberside and northern England (essentially the border region) was much smaller than the Conservative margin in its Southern stronghold. Scotland and Wales were even less sympathetic to the Conservatives than the north of England with their vote

down below 30%. The north of England was electorally closer to Scotland and Wales.

The distribution of votes and seats in 1987 supported the concept of a 'North-South divide' in British politics and society. (See Table 2.13.) The Conservatives won over 80% of the 360 seats (55.6% of the Commons) in the south of England and the English Midlands combined. Labour won over 60% of the 271 seats in the north of England, Scotland and Wales. The 'South' side of the 'divide' could be sub-divided into two sections:

☞ the South-east, not including Greater London, the South-west and East Anglia where the Conservatives were supreme;

☞ Greater London and the English Midlands where the Conservatives held two-thirds of the seats.

The 'North' side of the 'divide' comprised Scotland and Wales where the Conservatives were extremely weak winning fewer than 20% of seats, and the three northern regions of England where Labour won more seats

than their major party rivals but by much less convincing margins than in Scotland and Wales.

The 1997 and 2001 Elections produced similar geographical patterns though the fortunes of the parties had changed radically. There were massive Labour majorities in the Commons and comfortable Labour majorities in the popular vote. A North-South divide was still visible. The much weaker Conservative performance was relatively in line with the regional patterns of support evident in 1987. The Conservative vote and share of seats fell as we moved north. The political centre of gravity of Britain shifted decisively to Labour and moved northwards. Indeed the dividing line between North and South shifted because Greater London and the English Midlands became Labour territory.

The Conservatives remained, even in their worst electoral performance of the twentieth century, the strongest party in the south of England outside London. Nonetheless, there were considerable territorial divisions in the South. Conservative strength was con-

The North-South Divide:
Conservative and Labour Seats (%), 1987 – 2001

	1987		1997		2001	
	CONSERVATIVE	LABOUR	CONSERVATIVE	LABOUR	CONSERVATIVE	LABOUR
The Conservative South (SE /SW) & East Anglia	96.6	1.7	57.4	31.1	56.3	30.5
Greater London and the English Midlands	66.7	30.4	22.0	74.0	23.2	71.2
North-west & Yorkshire/Humberside	43.3	54.3	11.0	84.9	11.1	84.9
North of England, Scotland and Wales	17.8	70.6	2.0	81.2	2.7	82.4

Table 2.13

fined to the suburban and rural constituencies of the South-east where they won seventy three out of 117 seats in 1997 and 2001. The only other region to favour the Conservatives was rural East Anglia where they won fourteen out of twenty two seats in both elections.

The Conservatives lost their status as the dominant party in the south-west of England, losing both seats and votes heavily to Labour and particularly the Liberal Democrats. The South-west now supports a clear three-party system in terms of both votes and seats. The Liberal Democrats won more votes in 2001, 39%, than both major parties but won five fewer seats (fifteen) than the Conservatives (twenty) and one fewer than Labour (sixteen).

In 1987 more than half of the twenty two seats won by the Liberal Democrats were Scottish (ten) and Welsh (two) seats. In 2001 they won forty of their fifty two seats in England. Although they have won seats in all English regions their strength is concentrated in 'southern' Britain— south-east and south-west England and Greater London. (See Table 2.12.) The Liberal Democrats

have not made any significant advances in Scotland since 1983. (See Table 8.1.)

Outside southern England and rural East Anglia Labour was dominant in 1997. Greater London became a Labour stronghold. The Conservatives lost three-quarters of their seats in the suburbs of Outer London. Labour became the majority party in the English Midlands where Conservative losses were particularly heavy. Labour's superiority in north of England constituencies was dramatically extended and rivalled the Labour lead in Scotland and Wales.

The geographical divisions in British voting may be explained in part by the class factor. The clue here is the presence of the Labour stronghold of Inner London at the height of Conservative electoral dominance in the 1980s. Inner London remained true to Labour because there were enough working-class voters in its inner city constituencies. Similarly Scotland, Wales and the north of England have more working-class constituencies than their southern counterparts. However, the territorial divisions are not simply a mirror image of social divisions because the differences are greater than

social factors alone would lead us to expect. Even here the explanation relies on class. It was established in the 1960s that the minority class in constituencies which were strongly working class or middle class crossed the party line to a greater extent than in constituencies where the classes were more evenly matched. Economic trends were also significant. The 'South' generally experienced less unemployment and attracted a higher proportion of the supervisory and skilled jobs in new industries based on technology. The 'North', where unemployment rates were higher, had more than its share of unskilled jobs in heavy industries which were dying out. Another clue lies in Crewe's 'old'-'new' working class distinction. Members of the new working class who were more inclined to vote Conservative than their older working-class brethren were more likely to be found in the 'South' than in the 'North'. Scottish and Welsh support for Labour and hostility to the Conservatives is also explained by political issues such as devolution. Conservative intransigence on this issue in the face of support for devolution from the other parties added to the forces turning voters away from the Tories.

POLITICAL PARTIES

The electoral system, described in Chapter 1, ensures that Britain enjoys 'representative democracy'. The voters, whose behaviour was analysed in Chapter 2, have to be organised. The political institutions which have developed throughout the world in order to organise elections and voters are called political parties.

THE BRITISH PARTY SYSTEM

Political parties contest elections, organise voters by giving them meaningful choices, represent them in the legislature, and organise the business of government once the electorate has had its say. The members and supporters of a political party share distinctive ideas and philosophies. It is this which provides the bond that in turn allows for the pursuit of agreed policies and objectives. This is not to say that political differences will not emerge within a party. Intraparty differences— conflicts over policy positions within individual parties—are often as significant as interparty differences between rival parties. It could be argued that internal Conservative Party differences over the EU and a single European currency were the crucial factors in the heavy Conservative defeats in 1997 and 2001.

Political parties represent the views of their members and supporters in Parliament. Parties compete in elections in the hope that they will win governmental office in order to implement agreed policies. In performing the functions of 'electioneering' and representation, political parties effectively organise the democratic process.

The range of parties in any country reflects its social composition, taking in class, religious, national and regional, linguistic, ideological and other divisions. Countries with several major social divisions tend to generate several significant or major political parties. Countries with a limited number of social divisions generate fewer major parties. Parties may be broadly or narrowly based. Comprehensive or 'catch all' parties, common to two-party systems, try to cover as wide a range of political beliefs and interests as possible to ensure a broad-based support capable of winning elections. Smaller parties, especially in multi-party systems which are encouraged by proportional representation, receive the support of such a limited social group that they cannot hope to form a government by themselves.

There are many commentators who argue that the political parties have become much too influential—particularly in the way in which the majority party dominates Parliamentary procedures and Parliamentary business. Nevertheless, although parties have become much more centralised and disciplined, they still offer many ordinary people the opportunity to become involved in the political process.

Parties have remained the principal organisers of the political process in Britain even on the few occasions when referenda have been used as the mechanism for achieving some popular control over major decisions. The decision to hold referenda in 1975, 1979 and 1997 led to parties temporarily abandoning strict party discipline as cross-party alliances emerged to campaign for or against the questions being put to the electorate. However, this did not occur quite as much during the 1997 Scottish devolution referendum campaign.

A TWO-PARTY SYSTEM?

The number of parties in any country with a parliamentary system has significant implications for the nature of government and also for the range of opinions represented in both the government and the legislature. It should be noted that

➥ the fewer the number of major parties, the less likely it is that a country will have a coalition or minority government;

➥ the greater the number of parties winning parliamentary seats, the stronger is the ability of every party to represent faithfully the views of its supporters in the electorate.

Historically, the British electorate has preferred a two-party system. The Labour and Conservative Parties have dominated political life since the 1930s. The last Liberal to hold Prime Ministerial office was David Lloyd George, 1916–22. Governmental office has been confined to Conservative and Labour since 1945. In only one of the sixteen general elections since 1945 has one of the two major parties failed to win a parliamentary majority, though the governing party has lost its majority on occasion in between general elections. Nevertheless, many other parties do exist, some of which win seats in general elections. The situation in which a third party determines which major party should hold office after a general election has arisen only once in fifty years. In Feb-

(continued on page 34)

2001 *General Election* in Scotland

	Share of Votes (%)	Number of Seats
Labour	43.9	56
SNP	20.0	5
Conservative	15.6	1
Liberal Democrat	16.4	10

Table 3.1

GENERAL ELECTION RESULTS 1974-2001

Election Results		Cons.	Labour	Libs.[2]	Others
February 1974	Votes (millions)	11.9	11.7	6.1	1.7
	Seats	296	301	14	24
	% Vote	38.0	37.0	19.0	6.0
October 1974	Votes (millions)	10.4	11.5	5.3	1.9
	Seats	276	319	13	27
	% Vote	36.0	39.0	18.0	7.0
1979	Votes (millions)	13.7	11.5	4.3	1.7
	Seats	339	268	11	17
	% Vote	43.9	36.9	13.8	4.0
1983[1]	Votes (millions)	13.0	8.4	7.8	1.0
	Seats	397	209	23	21
	% Vote	42.0	27.6	25.4	3.0
1987	Votes (millions)	13.7	10.0	7.3	1.4
	Seats	375	229	22	23
	% vote	42.3	30.8	22.6	4.4
1992[1]	Votes (millions)	14	11.5	5.99	2.1
	Seats	336	271	20	24
	% Vote	41.9	34.4	17.8	5.9
1997[1]	Votes (millions)	9.6	13.5	5.2	
	Seats	165	419	46	29
	% Vote	30.7	43.2	16.8	5.8
2001	Votes (millions)	8.35	10.74	4.82	
	Seats	166	413	52	29
	% Vote	32.4	41.7	18.7	6.5

000 Denotes government
1   Number of seats increased to 650 in 1983, 651 in 1992 and 659 in 1997
2   Liberal/SDP Alliance in 1983 and 1987; Liberal Democrats from 1992

Table 3.2

THE POLITICAL SPECTRUM

Left · Centre · Right

Left
- Public ownership of large industries especially utilities like water and gas.
- Big government—providing for needs of all in community through free health care, free education and social security.
- Workers' rights are defended.
- Community needs are given priority over individual needs.
- Promotion of greater equality by means of a redistribution of resources from the wealthy to the poorer sections of society.

Centre
- A mixed economy with public and private ownership.
- Toleration of opposing viewpoints with each individual guaranteed freedom to live as he or she wishes.
- Accept the marketplace as a means of organising the economy but believe that the government has a duty to intervene to ensure that individuals are not exploited.
- Support the existence of a Bill of Rights.

Right
- All industries should be run by private companies without government interference. The marketplace is supreme in making economic decisions.
- The individual should be free from government restrictions to decide how to live his/her life.
- Small government—each person is responsible for her/his own life and the government should not be involved in providing services.
- Government should only support the destitute.
- Government role should be limited to defence, providing a strong money supply, controlling relations with other nations.
- Stresses patriotism and authority with strong support of social discipline and law and order.

Post-war consensus based on the Welfare State

Left	Centre	Right	Left	Centre	Right
	LABOUR			CONSERVATIVE	
		LIBERAL			

Polarisation in the 1980s

Left	Centre	Right	Left	Centre	**Right**
LABOUR					CONSERVATIVE
		LIBERAL/SDP			

The early 1990s—return to a new consensus based on the market

Left	**Centre**	Right	Left	**Centre**	Right
	LABOUR—		—CONSERVATIVE		
	LIBERAL DEMOCRATS				

Late 1990s— New Labour, New Consensus

Left	Centre	**Right**	Left	Centre	**Right**
	LABOUR—		—CONSERVATIVE		
	LIBERAL DEMOCRATS				

Both major parties are themselves made up of competing groups or factions which disagree about policy and ideology. In spite of often bitter internal conflicts over policy, British MPs rarely change their party allegiance. When any do so this is an indication of ideological conflict within the party. In 1995 two Conservative MPs left to join rival parties. On 7 October Alan Howarth (Stratford upon Avon) made the long jump from Conservative to Labour. Howarth was found a safe Labour seat (Newport East) and rewarded after the 1997 Election with a ministerial post (Parliamentary Under-Secretary in the Department of Education and Employment) in the new Labour government. On 29 December Emma Nicholson (Devon West and Torridge) left the Conservatives to join the Liberal Democrats. She did not contest the seat at the 1997 General Election and received a Life Peerage after the Election.

WHY DO WE NEED POLITICAL PARTIES?

Political parties fulfil a great many functions which can be summarised as follows.

Candidate Selection

Political parties select election candidates. Candidates at an election need the back-up of a political party if they are to have any chance of being elected to Parliament. Voters tend to vote for a particular party rather than for a particular candidate. Only one Independent was elected in 1997, the first since 1950. Martin Bell, who was a widely recognised BBC reporter, was elected as an anti-sleaze candidate in Tatton. This unusual Independent success was made possible by the tacit support of the Labour and Liberal Democrat Parties. Their candidates stood down in what had been considered to be a safe Conservative seat in order to secure the defeat of Neil Hamilton who had been accused of committing 'sleaze'. In 2001 the voters of Wyre Forest elected an Independent MP, Richard Taylor, who stood on a local health issue—'Save Kidderminster Hospital'.

Electioneering

Parties provide the money required for an election campaign. They publicise their policies and their candidates nationally and also locally where their members and supporters may canvass, deliver leaflets and so on.

Policy Making

Parties make elections meaningful by publicising their rival positions on the most important issues of the day. Most voters have a rough idea of what the different parties intend to do if elected. The parties encourage this awareness by publishing Election Manifestos which state their policy programmes. This allows voters to choose a party whose policies are closest to their own point of view. American parties pay much less attention to policy making than to electioneering, whereas British parties focus strongly on the policy making function.

Governing

Government is organised by the winning party whose most senior MPs take control of government Departments. This is why British government is frequently described as 'party government'.

Organising the Parliamentary Process

With the aid of the Whip System (see page 57) parties organise the business of the House of Commons. This allows both government and opposition to be effective. As we shall see in Chapters 5 and 6, the British Constitution, in the shape of the conventions of ministerial responsibility to Parliament, encourages centralised and disciplined parliamentary parties.

The party functions listed so far describe what political parties do on their own behalf. Parties, however, also perform functions for the benefit of the political system and of society as a whole.

Representation

Parties represent the views and expectations of those who participate in politics. Through elections, parties ensure that Britain maintains a representative form of indirect democracy, although it should be noted that parties in office have been tempted occasionally in recent decades to resort to the more direct form of democracy provided by referenda. The people have been asked to state their collective view on issues such as membership of the European Community and devolution for Scotland and Wales. By the procedures of elections and referenda, parties help to ensure that government is legitimate because through these methods it receives the consent of the people who are being governed.

ruary 1974, a minority Labour government was formed after the Liberals decided to support Labour in the Commons rather than the Conservative administration led by Edward Heath.

The 1997 and 2001 Election results provide contradictory evidence in relation to the issue of whether Britain still has a two-party system. In 2001the Labour and Conservative Parties, the two 'major parties', won their lowest combined share of parliamentary seats in the post-war period —87.7%. The Liberal Democrats won the largest number of seats, fifty two, to go to a third party since 1945. No fewer than five parties won seats in Great Britain (England, Scotland and Wales). Another four parties won seats in Northern Ireland. Nevertheless, the two major parties still won almost three-quarters of the popular vote. Furthermore, the winning major party, Labour, achieved the two largest parliamentary majorities of the post-war period.

Divergence in Scotland and Wales

There are national and regional variations in the strength of 'two-partyism'. Indeed one could argue that the 'British' two-party system is an English phenomenon only. It cannot be applied at all to Northern Ireland which has its own party system. In Scotland the Conservatives, a major British party, could win only one seat in the two elections, (Galloway

and Upper Nithsdale in 2001) and came fourth in the popular vote in 2001. In Wales they have not won any seats since 1992.

Scotland and Wales no longer support a Labour-Conservative two-party system. Rather Scotland and Wales may be said to have one-party dominant, four-party systems under the first-past-the-post electoral system still used in British parliamentary elections. In Scotland in 1997 and 2001 this system favoured Labour and the Liberal Democrats and penalised the Conservatives and the SNP. (See Table 3.1.) From 1997 to 2001 the Conservatives suffered the embarrassment of not having a Scottish or Welsh MP to act as 'Shadow' Secretary of State for the two nations in Parliament. During this period the Liberal Democrats argued in vain that one of their MPs should act as the 'Shadow' Scottish Secretary.

In spite of these strong national variations in party systems the 2001 Election continued the 'norm' of the electoral system producing 'majority party government', one of the key strengths of the two-party system. The long-term resilience of two-partyism in the UK as a whole, which is dependent on the English electorate, is indicated by Labour's recovery from winning only 27.6% of the vote and 32.2% of parliamentary seats in 1983 to win 43.2% of the vote and 63.6% of seats in 1997, a position which was maintained in essence in 2001.

IDEOLOGY AND POLICY

Ideological and policy differences between British political parties have long been expressed in terms of a spectrum running from left to right. Thirty years ago Labour was thought of as left of centre, the Conservatives as right of centre and the Liberals as the centre party. For most of the fifty-year period following the Second World War these ideological party images were defined in relation to economic issues and the role of the state in society.

Ideologically Labour was a socialist party. It stood for a redistribution of wealth in society in order to reduce major differences between the rich and the poor. Labour believed that the state should provide health and welfare for its citizens and should control the economy to achieve its aims. Labour promised radical reforms of both society and the economy.

The Conservative Party was opposed to socialism. It believed in leaving most economic decision making in the hands of the market economy while accepting the welfare state, the NHS and certain aspects of a mixed economy. Ideologically the Conservatives preferred gradual evolutionary change to radical reform.

Consensus

In spite of ideological differences and intense electoral competition from 1945 until the late 1970s, British politics were characterised as 'Consensus Politics'. There was a broad range of agreement over a number of key economic and social policies such as a mixed economy, the welfare state and the nationalisation of some, if not all, public utilities.

The 1970s proved to be a decisive turning point in British politics. After the long period of Conservative government from 1951 to 1964, the electorate rejected Labour in 1970, the Conservatives in 1974 and Labour again in 1979. British governments during that period experienced major economic problems which troubled most Western capitalist countries. They were confronted by rising rates of inflation and found themselves having to choose between low inflation and low unemployment instead of being able to achieve both simultaneously. The humiliation of electoral defeat stimulated both parties to think out new policies in opposition. The 'Post-war Consensus' came to an end. It gave way to ideological polarisation, a divergence rather than a convergence in the ideological beliefs of the major parties.

Polarisation

Conservative defeat in the two 1974 Elections was followed by the right-wing Margaret Thatcher replacing the moderate Edward Heath as leader in 1975 and by a radical policy rethink. Mrs Thatcher's name and her policies gave rise to the theme which was to dominate British politics for more than a decade after the Conservatives regained power in 1979. Her policy programme was summed up as 'Thatcherism'; her supporters were the 'Thatcherites'. 'Thatcherism' was considered to be radical and neo-liberal rather than conservative and evolutionary. It echoed Ronald Reagan's famous dictum that "Government is the problem, not the solution".

Electoral defeat in 1979 led to the Labour Party moving to the left because of discontent with the record of the Wilson and Callaghan governments. The left wing demanded, and temporarily achieved, a more socialist programme including a unilateralist defence policy and a commitment to withdraw from the EEC. However, successive electoral defeats in 1983, 1987 and 1992 forced Labour leaders Neil Kinnock, John Smith and Tony Blair to bring Labour policies into the ideological centre ground. By 1997 the change was so dramatic and the left so marginalised that Labour was commonly referred to as 'New Labour'.

The ideological and policy changes of both major parties are outlined below. Page 32 shows the broad picture of the changing ideological spectrum of British politics. The left–right ideological spectrum retains some validity, especially because that is how the major parties prefer to see one another. Nevertheless, the left–right ideological dimension has to be qualified by three recent developments.

● Firstly, both major parties have been shifting their ideological position. The Conservative Party has moved to the right and the Labour Party has redefined its socialism during its move to the centre.

● Secondly, a significant feature of recent British politics has been the dramatic impact of constitutional issues, such as devolution and Britain's membership of the European Union. Such issues have cut across normal party rivalries.

● Thirdly, neither party is without internal disputes about where the party should stand on the main issues of the day.

THE CONSERVATIVE PARTY

Thatcherism:
Ending the consensus

From May 1979 until May 1997 British politics and government were dominated by the Conservative Party which won four elec-

tions in a row (1979, 1983, 1987 and 1992). For much of that period, until she was forced out of office in November 1990, the dominant figure was Britain's first female Prime Minister. 'Thatcherism', the decisive radical policies associated with Mrs Thatcher and her supporters on the 'dry' wing of the Conservative Party, constituted a policy agenda which ended the 'post-war consensus' and changed the face of British politics. If 'conservatism' is associated primarily with preserving the status quo, then Mrs Thatcher was clearly less 'conservative' than her predecessors Harold Macmillan and Edward Heath were.

The main elements in the Thatcherite Agenda included:
❑ Monetarism
❑ Trade Union Reform
❑ Community Charge (Poll Tax)
❑ Control of Inflation
❑ Reducing Income Tax
❑ Sale of Council Houses
❑ Consumer Choice
❑ Privatisation
❑ Greater Reliance on the Market
❑ Internal Markets applied to Education and the NHS

Underlying these policies, which were implemented in stages as the 1980s unfolded, was a basic determination to reduce the role of government and to replace much of the public sector of the mixed economy, for example utilities and railways, with a privatisation pro-

Mrs Thatcher was Conservative leader and Prime Minister from May 1979 until November 1990. Under her leadership the Conservatives won three elections and enjoyed comfortable parliamentary majorities. Her policies were radical and not always popular, provoking internal opposition from more traditionally minded Tories who were dismissively known as the 'wets'.

Guard Pat Kennedy flagged off the last British Rail passenger train at Glasgow's Queen Street Station on 1 April 1997. By the time it arrived in Edinburgh, the train was privatised and run by National Express.

gramme. In two much publicised interviews Mrs Thatcher claimed that she intended to destroy socialism in Britain and to resist the interventionism of Conservatives such as Michael Heseltine whose policies "were more akin to Labour Party policies".

Efforts to capture the essence of Thatcherism have used terms such as 'individualism', 'laissez- faire' and 'anti-statism'. Mrs Thatcher demanded that individuals be allowed to make their own choices whenever possible. Conservative educational reforms such as allowing schools to opt out of local authority control in favour of grant maintained status applied the principle of individual choice to education. The preference for market decision making over the bureaucratic alternative was behind the attempt to create a market within the NHS known as an 'internal market'. GPs became 'fundholders' who could 'shop around' for the best hospital treatment for their patients. Catering and cleaning services were put out to tender. Hospitals could become Hospital Trusts, independent of regional hospital boards. Thatcher's ideological belief in the primacy of the market was clearly evident in the 'privatisation' of publicly owned utilities such as communications, electricity and water.

The pro-market and laissez-faire emphasis in policies such as privatisation and the internal market

prompted the claim that Thatcherism was closer to nineteenth century liberalism than to twentieth century conservatism of the type associated with Harold Macmillan and Edward Heath. Thatcherism sought to achieve limited government interference and a strong state. The state was to be strong, especially in its representation of British interests abroad, but at the same time it was to be severely restricted in both its functions and its revenue-raising capacity. Tory 'wets', who lost influence progressively as the Thatcherite agenda unfolded, called for a return to 'One Nation Conservatism'. The Conservative Party had long claimed that it represented the interests of the whole nation, hence 'one nation', while accusing Labour of representing narrow class interests, basically trade union interests. A frequent criticism of Thatcherism

was that its free market and 'anti-state' principles were enlarging the gap between rich and poor and so contributing to 'two nations'.

Thatcherism frequently combined ideological and political objectives. Council house sales were justified ideologically by references to the desirability of a property-owning democracy. However, they also reduced the role of local government, which was often Labour controlled in urban areas, and they increased the number of owner-occupiers who were more likely than council house tenants to vote Conservative. Industrial relations reform could be justified for its own sake, but it could also be seen as weakening the powers of unions and their leaders who were strong supporters of the Labour Party. Legislation was introduced to force the unions towards greater internal democracy and to require ballots of union members before a strike could be called.

Running out of Steam

The Major government elected in April 1992 ran into serious political trouble almost from the start. The issue which was to cause Major severe difficulties which he never quite overcame was the same issue which had stimulated the revolt against Thatcher (though not against all aspects of 'Thatcherism')—Europe. John Major and others had persuaded Mrs Thatcher, against her

Black Wednesday—16 September 1992—when the Conservative Chancellor was forced to let the value of the pound fall from $1.90 to $1.60. The public lost faith in the Conservative's ability to manage the economy.

instincts, to take Britain into the Exchange Rate Mechanism, which allowed limited exchange rate movements. It was argued at the time that the exchange rate was much too high, especially against the German mark. The drastic fall in stock market share prices which happened on 16 September 1992 (Black Wednesday) proved too much for the pound which was allowed to fall from 1.9 to 1.6 against the dollar. This was, in effect, a devaluation and Britain came out of the Exchange Rate Mechanism.

Unfortunately for Mr Major the next step on the horizon of European integration was to be the establishment of a common currency and a common monetary policy. The Conservatives were hopelessly divided internally between Eurosceptics on the right who argued that a common currency meant the end of the British state and more pragmatic Europhiles who believed that, given the right conditions, a common currency could be beneficial to the British economy. Major adopted a 'wait and see' policy as the 1997 Election approached.

The Conservatives lost by a massive margin. John Major resigned as Conservative Party Leader to be succeeded by the youthful William Hague (36) who proclaimed himself a Thatcherite and received her support in the third ballot against Kenneth Clarke. The 1997 Election relegated the Conservatives to the opposition benches and gave the new leadership the opportunity to consider the organisational and policy reforms which many deemed essential if the Party was to regain office.

REFORM OF THE CONSERVATIVE PARTY

William Hague immediately set out to reorganise the Party through his 'Fresh Future' proposals. It was clear that the Party faithful favoured greater Party democracy and unity. At the October 1997 Conference, during the debate on Party structure, speaker after speaker denounced the Tory MPs whose division, they argued, had been the main cause of John Major's defeat. The massive Labour victory had transformed the Conservatives' traditional deference to their leaders to feelings of anger and concern. Some delegates even argued that the power of MPs to choose their leaders should be removed in favour of a 'one member, one vote' election by Party members. The 'Fresh Future' proposals were debated and approved at a Special Reform Convention held in March 1998. (See page 38.)

The reforms introduced by William Hague were based on the principle of democratisation. Every Party member now has the opportunity "to be involved in the decision making process of the Party". Party members can influence policy through the Conservative Party Forum and direct ballots of Party members. Party leaders after William Hague are now chosen by all members of the Party. This enabled Scottish and Welsh Party members to participate in the election of the leader in 2001. (William Hague was elected Party leader by the Conservative MPs from England as there were no Scottish or Welsh Conservative MPs at that time.)

THE DECLINE IN PARTY MEMBERSHIP

It is perhaps no coincidence that the decline in electoral turnout and the rise in voter apathy are matched by the sharp decline in membership of political parties. While Labour witnessed an increase in individual membership in the mid-90s , the Conservatives witnessed a dramatic drop. The 1997 General Election was the first in which the Labour Party's individual membership (410,000) exceeded that of the Conservative Party (400,000). The Liberal Democrats' membership was around 100,000. In 1994, by way of contrast, Conservative membership was twice that of Labour and, going further back, in 1979 it was five times that of Labour.

Especially worrying for the Conservatives is their inability to attract young members. (See Figure 3.1.) In 1949 there were 160,000 young Conservative members. Today the figure is about 2,000. Two-thirds of Conservative members are either retired or near retirement and as such are unrepresentative of voters as a whole. Patrick Seyd, Professor of Politics at the University of Sheffield, estimates that membership could have fallen as low as 240,000.

Age Breakdown of Conservative Party Members %

Figure 3.1

REFORM OF THE CONSERVATIVE PARTY

	STRUCTURE	MEMBERSHIP	POLICY	ORGANISATION IN PARLIAMENT	LEADERSHIP ELECTION
OLD	There were separate Party structures for MPs, Central Office and the National Union (the Party's volunteers). The main central body of the Party was the National Union of Conservative and Unionist Associations.	Members belonged to a Constituency Party only. There were no national figures for membership. It is estimated that total membership had fallen from over a million in 1979 to under 400,000 by 1997.	This was decided by the Shadow Cabinet and the Conservative Party leader. No other body had the power to make policy.	Conservative MPs met as the 1922 Committee and discipline was enforced by the Party Whips. Disunity in Parliament under John Major made it difficult for the Whips to impose their authority. Withdrawal of the Whip was not used and, consequently, dissent and improper conduct by a minority of Conservative MPs went officially unpunished.	Only MPs voted for the Party leader.
NEW	There is now a unified party structure under a single governing body entitled The Board of Management. This body is responsible for all matters relating to Party organisation and management, with direct powers over Central Office. It has the power to: • refuse membership to anyone; • replace constituency officers; • disband local associations. It also oversees campaigning and organises the Party Conference. It is chaired by the Party Chairperson who is appointed by the leader. The remaining thirteen members are either directly elected by the National Convention or have automatic membership, e.g. chairperson of the 1922 Committee.	Such was the disarray of the Party that in 1997 there were no precise figures for membership. A national membership database has been set up. This is intended to aid recruitment and identify areas and local Parties which are failing to enlist young members. (The target of a million members by the year 2000, set by Mr Hague, was far too ambitious and membership remained at the 1997 level.)	Two new bodies—The National Conservative Convention and The Conservative Political Forum—were set up. Both allow members to influence policy, but they remain advisory. Hague attempted to make the Party more democratic by the use of direct ballots of Party members on specific policy issues. Since 1997 there have been four ballots and in every case Party members have overwhelmingly endorsed the proposals of their leader. The leadership has control over this mechanism and grass roots members cannot initiate their own proposals and ballots.	An Ethics Committee can impose penalties for misconduct, including expulsion from the Party. Tighter discipline has been imposed on MPs. Peter Temple Morris, a pro-European Conservative MP, publicly disagreed with Hague's declaration that Britain would remain outside a single European currency for the lifetime of two Parliaments. The Party Whip was withdrawn from him in 1997 and in 1998 he 'crossed the floor' and joined Labour.	A new two stage process to elect the Conservative leader was introduced: Stage 1 involves only Conservative MPs; Stage 2 involves grass roots members of the Party. (See Figure 3.4.)

Tory Leader William Hague, and Shadow Chancellor Michael Portillo in St Albans on the first leg of a nationwide 'Save The Pound' tour. Mr Hague attempted to highlight his determination to turn UK membership of the Euro into a major issue at the 2001 election

HAGUE'S LEADERSHIP

Under William Hague the 'Thatcherite' influence within the Party gained the ascendancy. In his first Shadow Cabinet several Eurosceptic right-wingers received key posts, with Peter Lilley as Shadow Chancellor, Michael Howard as Shadow Foreign Secretary and John Redwood as Shadow Trade and Industry Secretary. Hague imposed a new, harder line on the single currency of "not for the next ten years" in place of the earlier "not for the foreseeable future". This dismayed the pro-European Conservatives such as Ian Taylor and Kenneth Clarke.

The return of Michael Portillo as a Conservative MP did not impact on William Hague's leadership. Portillo displayed his loyalty and, while the press spoke of secret talks to dispose of Hague if the general election went badly, this was denied by the leaders of the Party.

Common Sense Revolution

Hague used the 1999 Conservative Party Conference to inspire his Party when he launched the 'Common Sense Revolution'. In a forty three page document, which was to form the basis of the Conservative Manifesto for the 2001 General Election, Hague included sixty populist policies, such as a promise to reduce the nation's tax burden, a pledge to limit the voting rights of Scottish MPs at Westminster, and a partnership with private health care to give every NHS patient a guaranteed waiting time based on the need for treatment.

By late 2000 it seemed that William Hague had restored the unity of the Party and had gained the trust of the electorate. Labour's poor handling of the fuel crisis, the Dome fiasco and the award of a 75p increase to pensioners by the Labour government had led to a dramatic decrease in the popularity of the government (this was to be short term). For these reasons, the October 2000 Conservative Party Conference was regarded by Hague as "the most successful, the most determined and the most upbeat conference we have had in years".

The theme of the conference was 'Compassionate Conservatism' with Michael Portillo, the Shadow Chancellor, appealing to his Party to show tolerance, respect and support for all people, whatever their background, gender, race or sexual orientation. Only by doing this could the Party go beyond its core vote he claimed. Many delegates were taken aback by Mr Portillo's transformation from 'right-wing ideologue' to the 'Tory voice of liberal inclusiveness'.

Anne Widdecombe, the popular Shadow Home Secretary and the darling of the Party faithful, created a public and political storm when she announced to the Conference that anyone caught in possession of even a small amount of cannabis should be subject to an automatic minimum fine of £100. Her remarks damaged the credibility of the Party and reinforced the viewpoint that it was a party out of touch with public opinion. Members of the Shadow Cabinet quickly distanced themselves from Widdecombe's proposal. Her humiliation was complete when a newspaper revealed that seven members of the Shadow Cabinet had confessed to taking cannabis.

THE LABOUR PARTY: FROM 'OLD' TO 'NEW'

In the 1980s and early 1990s Labour was beset by internal battles over ideology and organisation. In particular Labour faced the problem of what to do about its socialist commitment. The choices were to move more radically to the left in pursuit of socialism, or to redefine socialism by moving in the direction of less ideological social democratic parties. Such parties in Scandinavia maintained traditional socialist objectives of social justice and equality of opportunity while accepting a strongly market-oriented economic system.

The period following election defeat in 1979 was one of internal argument for Labour as left and right struggled for control of the Party against a background of failure in government in the 1970s. In October 1980 James Callaghan resigned as leader and was succeeded one month later by Michael Foot. At this time there was a significant ideological conflict between the 'left' and the 'right' of the Party. The 'left' preferred the radical socialist vision. The 'right' preferred the social democratic option. It was hoped that Foot would be able to bring together the Party's warring factions.

The battle between left, centre and right focused on two critical areas of the Labour Party Constitution. The first of these concerned Party rules relating to the leadership, the selection of parliamentary candidates and decisions about election manifestos. The second area was that of Party policy, especially the Party's socialist commitment in the celebrated Clause IV.

Swing to the Left

In 1980–81 Labour's left wing achieved two significant organisational reforms and changed the Party's policy direction. An Electoral College was established which decentralised the process for selecting the leader and deputy leader who, until then, had been elected by Labour MPs only. The Electoral College had three sections, illustrating the federal nature of the Labour Party: the trade unions with 40% of the vote, the Parliamentary Labour Party or PLP (the MPs) with 30% and the Constituency Labour Parties (CLPs)with 30%. For most of the post-war period the sections of the Labour Party outside Parliament had been much more left wing than Labour MPs and Labour governments who had to face the realities of power, especially the electoral realities. The right wing of the Party believed that left-wing leadership candidates would benefit from the Electoral College which gave the sections outside Parliament a say in the election of the leader.

The second organisational reform was mandatory reselection of MPs before every general election. Proposals that the Labour Manifesto should be decided by the National Executive Committee rather than by the leader alone were not accepted.

The Labour left wing also won decisive policy battles when the Annual Conference reversed Labour government policies of maintaining Britain's nuclear deterrent and remaining within the European Community. These organisational and policy victories for the left led to some leading right-wingers leaving the Party to set up the Social Democratic Party (SDP). The gang of Four (Roy Jenkins, Shirley Williams, David Owen and Bill Rodgers) decided to continue the struggle for their beliefs outside rather than inside the Labour Party. The choice of name for the new party, whose aim was to 'break the mould' of British politics, was significant—social democratic rather than socialist.

Change of direction

Labour's internal strife and Foot's allegedly weak leadership contributed to the re-election of the Thatcher government in 1983. The first use of the Electoral College for the election of the Labour leader led to the selection of Neil Kinnock from the centre left of the Party. Kinnock won easily over Roy Hattersley who won the post of deputy leader almost as easily. Kinnock realised that Labour had to change its image if it was to have any chance of electoral success and he began the process of organisational and policy reform which took more than a decade, survived two more election defeats in 1987 and 1992 and culminated in the record-breaking electoral success of 1997.

The 1987 Conference agreed to a review of Party policy. The left wing of the Party, now on the defensive realising what was likely to emerge from the policy review, responded by challenging Kinnock's leadership. In the leadership election held at the 1988 Conference, Neil Kinnock and Roy Hattersley easily saw off the left-wing challenge from Tony Benn and Eric Heffer. Benn received almost no support from the unions and only about 20% of constituency and PLP votes. The so-called 'dream ticket' of the 'soft left', Neil Kinnock and the centre-right Roy Hattersley, could now preside over major policy changes. The 1989 Conference agreed to several recommendations of the policy review process. Firstly, it abandoned unilateral nuclear disarmament. Secondly, it accepted most of the Conservatives' industrial relations legislation which reduced the power of union leaders. Thirdly, it committed the Party not to undo the privatisations which had been a major feature of Thatcherism.

The Labour Party's change of direction seemed to be working when it went ahead of the Conservatives in the polls in 1990. The change in the Tory leadership as Thatcher gave way to Major marked the beginning of a Conservative revival. Nonetheless, Labour approached the 1992 Election in a much more optimistic frame of mind.

John Smith, leader of the Labour Party 1992–1994

The Arrival of New Labour

In the event, Labour did improve its share of both votes and seats in 1992 but the Conservatives were re-elected. Once again electoral defeat was followed by a change of leadership. Kinnock and Hattersley stood down. In the leadership election held on 18 July 1992 John Smith, MP for Monklands East and the Shadow Chancellor, a clear centre-right candidate, easily won in all three Party constituencies (Trade Unions, MPs and Constituency Labour Parties) against Bryan Gould. Margaret Beckett was elected deputy leader.

Smith continued the reform process, concentrating on organisational rules. He was particularly concerned to strengthen the Party's democratic credentials which suffered from a popular belief that the unions had too much power within the Labour Party. Smith persuaded the Party to accept the principle of 'One Member, One Vote' (OMOV) which required unions and CLPs to ballot individual members to decide who they would support in leadership elections. The three units in the leadership electoral college were made equal with unions, constituency parties and MPs each casting one-third of the votes.

Tragically, in 1994 John Smith died. In the ensuing leadership election the centre right of the Party, now popularly known as 'New Labour', won handsomely in the person of Tony Blair who defeated Margaret Beckett and John Prescott, winning over 50% of the vote in all three parts of the electoral college. John Prescott won the contest for deputy leader, defeating Margaret Beckett. Although Prescott represented 'Old' Labour through his working-class and trade union background, he was by no means on the Party's hard left.

Rewriting Clause IV

Tony Blair set about implementing further reforms to ensure that Labour's past failures and image would not lead to a fifth Conservative victory. Blair was determined to change Labour's policy image. His principal achievement was the removal of the famous, or notorious, Clause IV from the Labour Party Constitution. (See page 42.)

Clause IV symbolised a commitment to socialism, to public ownership and to an interventionist state. It was an article of faith for the majority of Labour Party members for most of the twentieth century and it was printed on every individual Party membership card.

In April 1995 a special Party Conference voted by a two to one majority to replace totally Clause IV with a new statement of Labour's core values. Constituency Associations were particularly favourable suggesting that the left-wing activists who had been dominant there in the early 1980s had given way to enthusiastic supporters of the new leader. The unions, whose political ideology had been clear in the original Clause IV, supported the change by 55% to 45%.

The Labour Party of 1980 was hardly recognisable in the Party which won the 1997 Election so decisively. Indeed, the cartoonist's depiction of 'Tony' as 'Tory' Blair was merely a humorous way of stating a widespread belief that Labour had moved significantly to the right. Blair himself denied the cartoonist's view, preferring to emphasise that New Labour was attempting to establish a "Third Way" in between the socialism of Old Labour and the selfish individualism of Thatcherism. Many Labour supporters still believe in core values which they claim to be compatible with 'socialism' such as equality of opportunity, equity, and a more even distribution of wealth.

'THE CONTROL FREAKS'

A major criticism of Blair's leadership and New Labour has been its dictatorial behaviour in trying to control both the views of party members and the selection of Labour candidates to serve the public. Below are four examples of this development.

The European experience

The introduction of proportional representation for the 1999 Elections to the European Parliament led to a greater degree of central control (through the National Executive Committee) over candidate nomination and rankings. Tony Blair had not forgotten or forgiven the thirty two Labour MEPs who, in 1994, had signed an advertisement in *The Guardian*

41

"To secure for the workers by hand or by brain the full fruits of their industry and the most equitable distribution thereof that may be possible upon the basis of the common ownership of the means of production, distribution and exchange, and the best obtainable system of popular administration and control of each industry or service".

The Constitution of the Labour Party Clause IV (4)

Labour Party membership cards. The card above contains the original Clause IV. Today the card has an extract from the reformed Clause IV.

604/2K Published by The Labour Party
Millbank Tower London SW1P 4GT

The Labour Party is a democratic socialist party. It believes that by the strength of our common endeavour we achieve more than we achieve alone, so as to create for each of us the means to realise our true potential and for all of us a community in which power, wealth and opportunity are in the hands of the many not the few, where the rights we enjoy reflect the duties we owe, and where we live together, freely, in a spirit of solidarity, tolerance and respect.

Labour

www.labour.org.uk

CLAUSE IV REVISED

The new Clause IV is much longer than its predecessor. Its main points are summarised below.

1   Labour is proclaimed to be a "democratic socialist party". This is an intriguing claim because in the early eighties, leaders of the Labour right defected to form the 'Social Democratic Party'. This term 'softens' the socialist commitment without jettisoning it altogether. It emphasises the democratic component which might have been obscured by charges of trade union dominance.

2   It also reflects the political philosophy associated with Blair— 'communitarianism'. In addition to calling for "power, wealth and opportunity" to be "in the hands of the many not the few", the new Clause IV also emphasises the "duties we owe" to the whole community. This community emphasis contrasts sharply with the individualism associated with Thatcherism.

3   Whereas the old Clause IV stressed "common ownership" and "popular administration and control of each industry or service", the new version refers to "a thriving private sector and high quality public services" and, unlike the old version, to "the enterprise of the market" and to the "rigour of competition".

4   Core values compatible with 'socialism' are retained: a "just society", an "open democracy", a "healthy environment".

5   The trade union link is not rejected. Labour is pledged to "work with trade unions and other affiliated organisations".

which criticised the Party's proposals to reform Clause IV of the Party's constitution. A new code of practice was introduced in September 1997 which required members to support Party policy including the Party's future candidate selection process for MEPs. In October 1997, four Labour MEPs (Ken Coates, Alex Falconer, Michael Hindley and Hugh Kerr) were suspended from membership of the European Parliamentary Labour Party for criticising Labour's policy in public. Two of these MEPs (Coates and Kerr) were subsequently expelled from the European Parliamentary Labour Party in 1998 for failing, once again, to abide by the new disciplinary code.

The Welsh experience

In October 1998 Ron Davies resigned as Secretary of State for Wales in political disgrace. (He admitted an error of judgment in going with a stranger to his flat, having met him at night in a London park.) Blair interfered in Welsh politics and blocked the selection of the popular Rhodri Morgan by persuading Alun Michael to stand for the leadership of the Welsh Labour Party. Rhodri Morgan was seen as being too independently minded

Rhodri Morgan was opposed by the Laboiur leadership in the election for the Welsh Labour Party Leader

while Michael would be a pliable puppet.

In the February 1999 election for the Welsh leadership, Rhodri Morgan won 65% of the votes of Welsh Labour Party members to 35% for Michael. However, the votes of the MPs and Welsh Assembly candidates, alongside the block votes of three trade unions, ensured that Michael was elected by a margin of 53% to 47% over Morgan. Michael was not even standing as a candidate for the Assembly. He was quickly added to the top-up list of candidates in the only region where Labour was likely to achieve a top-up Assembly member. In the election that followed, in May 1999, Labour just failed to win a majority of the seats, gaining twenty nine of the sixty seats. Michael's period as leader of Labour's minority administration was a disaster. He appointed a vegetarian to be in charge of agriculture and a non-Welsh speaker to be in charge of Welsh language teaching. Within a year Michael had resigned just before losing a motion of no confidence. He was replaced by the Welsh people's real choice, Rhodri Morgan.

The London experience

Blair's experience of London Labour politics in the early 1980s explains why he made a major error of judgment in trying to prevent Ken Livingstone from becoming the democratically elected London Mayor. In a candid moment, Blair stated, "Sometimes I think the experience in the Labour Party in the early eighties almost sort of scared me too much."

The new Labour government carried out its manifesto pledge of holding a referendum to confirm popular demand for an elected London Mayor. A referendum was held in May 1998 and, while there was a 72% 'yes' vote, the turnout was only 34%. The hunt was on for New Labour to find a winning candidate. Mo Mowlam had the populist appeal that could reli-

Denis Cananvan challenged and defeated the Labour Party after spending his political life fighting for the Party. The voters put the individual before the Party.

The Scottish experience

The sleaze in local government affairs in Scotland, involving Labour councillors especially in the West of Scotland (see page 152), was used to justify vigorous selection procedures for the selection of Labour candidates for the new Scottish Parliament. However, the Party members in charge of selection procedures used their powers to exclude several MPs and leading activists who displayed a left-wing (and independent) record. Denis Canavan, the popular MP for Falkirk West, was rejected as being "unsuitable". This infuriated Canavan and the electorate of Falkirk West. After much soul-searching, Canavan stood as an independent in the Scottish Parliament Elections and won the largest majority of any candidate.

Ken Livingstone (right) shakes hands with the defeated official Labour candidate Frank Dobson in the election for London Mayor.

ably see off Livingstone, but she declined. Frank Dobson, the then Health Minister, reluctantly agreed to stand in the May 2000 election. The Labour leadership did not choose a one member, one vote ballot of Party members. They tried to fix the election of the mayoral candidate by using a three section electoral college which had worked successfully in Wales.

Dobson won the Labour candidacy by 51.5% to Livingstone's 48.5%. A breakdown of the votes indicated the strength of Ken Livingstone's support. He won 60% of the vote among Party members and 72% among the trade unions but was obliterated by the 86% vote for Dobson among MPs and Euro-MPs. Blair's personal involvement was, as stated, a political mistake. His statements, calling Livingstone an extremist and a disaster waiting to happen if elected Mayor, alienated the London public.

The inevitable happened—Livingstone decided to stand as an independent candidate. In the first stage of the election, Livingstone won 39% of first preference votes over Steven Norris (the Conservative candidate) on 27%. Frank Dobson came third with a humiliating 13%. Livingstone won by 58% to 42% in the run-off against Norris. By trying to fix the Labour Party's selection of its candidate, Blair ensured Livingstone's success. In a straight one member, one vote election, Frank Dobson may well have won the Labour Party nomination.

THE LIBERAL DEMOCRATS: REFORMING THE CENTRE

The Liberal Party, the forerunner of today's Liberal Democrats, has been classified as a 'minor' political party since the 1920s. It last won a parliamentary majority in 1906, last won more seats than Labour in 1923 and its vote was reduced to less than 3% in the 1950s. The Liberals won only a handful of seats, usually less than ten, from 1945 until the 1970s when they enjoyed a 'revival' which suggested that the two-party system was weakening. However, the Liberals were the perennial 'victims' of the electoral system as their share of seats

failed to match their share of votes. The party was electorally strongest in or near the 'Celtic fringes'. Its leadership has come from Scotland (Jo Grimond, David Steel and Charles Kennedy) and south-west England (Jeremy Thorpe and Paddy Ashdown).

The Liberals were perceived as the party of the centre—not socialist but not conservative either. The close election of February 1974 demonstrated that the Liberals were closer in spirit to Labour than to the Conservatives. The Liberals indicated that they would rather support a Labour government than the continuation of Heath's Conservative Administration when neither of the two major parties won an overall majority in the Commons. When the Labour government lost its overall majority in the Commons in 1976, it survived with the support of the Liberals who participated in an informal 'Lib-Lab Pact' which gave the Party some influence but no positions in the government. The Conservative victory in 1979 ended the period of Liberal influence.

The Alliance

The 1970s were thus a frustrating time for the centre party which was unable to achieve major party status. The political centre received a big boost when a number of right-wing Labour MPs left

the Party in order to establish the Social Democratic Party (SDP). Their stated intention was to "break the mould of British politics". The SDP was not socialist and its members had been long-term opponents of the Conservatives, so there were obvious similarities in policy beliefs between the Liberals and the SDP.

These similarities led to the formation of the Alliance between the two parties which fought the Elections of 1983 and 1987 with considerable success. The Alliance was essentially an electoral pact which allowed the two parties to maintain their separate identities and policy preferences. In 1983 the Alliance won twenty three seats and a quarter of the popular vote, coming less than 3% behind Labour. However, the Conservatives increased their overall majority and thus deprived the Alliance of any hope of influencing the government. In 1987 the Alliance fell back slightly and it was clear that neither the SDP nor the Alliance had 'broken the mould'.

Liberal Democrats

Conservative electoral success effectively broke up the Alliance in the same way as it forced Labour into a major policy review. David Steel, the Liberal leader, called for a complete merger of the two Alliance parties as the way forward. Steel's aim was to strengthen

WHAT DOES IT MEAN TO BE A LIBERAL?
"Three simple words—freedom, justice and honesty—sum up what the Liberal Democrats stand for.
FREEDOM – because everybody should have the opportunities they need to make the most of their lives.
JUSTICE – because freedom depends on fairness.
HONESTY – because where fairness has a cost, like investing in schools, hospitals and pensions, we explain how it will be paid for.

Liberal Democrats believe that the role of democratic government is to protect and strengthen liberty, to redress the balance between the powerful and the weak, between rich and poor and between immediate gains and long-term environmental costs. We believe in a society in which every citizen shares rights and responsibilities."
(Adapted from Liberal Democrat election literature)

PADDY ASHDOWN
LEADER OF THE LIBERAL DEMOCRATS 1988 – 1999

- The most successful leader of the Party since Lloyd George. Under his leadership the number of MPs increased from twenty two in 1987, to forty six in the 1997 Election.

- Experienced the taste of power by entering Cabinet committees to discuss the constitution and other issues of 'mutual interest'.

- In Scotland and Wales the Liberal Democrats form part of the Executives in coalition with Labour.

- Liberal Democrats achieved some of their aims regarding a fairer electoral system. Proportional representation systems are now used for elections to the Scottish Parliament and to the Welsh Assembly and the European Parliament.

- Liberal Democrats won ten seats in the 1999 European Parliament.

- Paddy Ashdown's and the Liberal Democrats' relationships with the Labour Party were based on 'constructive opposition'. In 1992 the Liberal Democrats abandoned their policy of 'equidistance' between the two major parties, effectively declaring themselves an anti-Conservative party.

- The Commission on Electoral Reform was chaired by Lord Jenkins, a former leader of the Liberal Democrat peers.

the political centre. His proposal received considerable support from both parties but there was opposition from influential minorities in each camp. David Owen, the charismatic SDP Leader, opposed the proposed merger and resigned his position. After negotiations a new party emerged in January 1988. This was the Social and Liberal Democratic Party (SDLP). About one-third of the SDP refused to join the new party and they continued to operate independently under Owen's leadership.

The SDLP had a short life. David Steel retired as leader and Paddy Ashdown won the contest to replace him in July 1988. The SDLP performed poorly in the 1989 Euro-Elections, and there was considerable discontent with the new party's name. Old Liberals were unhappy even though they predominated within the SDLP; indeed the merger was described as "a Liberal takeover of the SDP". A postal ballot of the SDLP membership revealed strong support for 'Liberal Democrats' as a name

consistent with the traditions of the 'old' Liberal Party and the aspirations of individuals who had opted for 'Social Democracy'. In June 1990 the SDP was disbanded though some of its MPs continued as independent Social Democrats until 1992 when David Owen decided not to seek re-election.

In 1992 the Liberal Democrats, in winning 18.3% of the vote and twenty seats, were clearly much stronger than the Liberals had ever been in the post-war period. Nevertheless, there was still an enormous gap between their support in the country and their representation in the House of Commons.

Radical Liberals

The Liberal Democrats, like Labour, had to adjust to Conservative electoral success. With Labour moving into the centre ground under Smith and Blair, the Liberal Democrats sought ways of redefining their old 'radical' image. Their chosen strategy was to stand aside from Labour's "we shall not raise income tax" platform.

Instead, the Liberal Democrats took the bold step of promising to raise income tax by a penny in the pound in order to increase spending on education. The Liberal Democrats also retained their radical stance on constitutional issues, joining with Labour in the Scottish Constitutional Convention in support of devolution.

In 1997 the Liberal Democrats benefited from a concentration of effort and resources in seats they had a realistic chance of winning. They enjoyed their most successful election of the post-1945 era, winning forty six seats—more than double their 1992 total—in spite of not raising their share of the popular vote. This was the most successful third party performance since 1929. Ironically, the size of Labour's majority meant that the new government would be unlikely to have any need of Liberal Democrat support in order to survive in office.

The Liberal Democrat gains were almost all from the Conservatives. Their objective, which was established by the 1997 result, was to continue the process of replacing the Conservatives as the second major party. This objective was achieved in Scotland in 1997 at the parliamentary level.

CONSTRUCTIVE OPPOSITION

Prior to Labour's landslide victory in the 1997 General Election, Tony Blair had planned to offer Paddy Ashdown a seat in the Cabinet. The extent of the victory changed the relationship between Blair and Ashdown. The Liberal Democrats were invited to sit in a 'talking shop' which was given the elevated status of a Cabinet Committee chaired by the Prime Minister. This was a bitter blow to Ashdown who had been in secret talks with Labour's previous leaders, Neil Kinnock and John Smith. In 1992 Neil Kinnock had been prepared to concede electoral reforms as the price of a coalition with the Liberal Democrats in the event of a hung parliament. The election of Blair as Labour leader in 1994 led to further secret discussions about possible forms of cooperation. In October 1996, Robin Cook, Labour, and Robert MacLennan, Liberal Democrat, held a news conference where they announced the formation of a joint committee of both parties to work on a common programme of constitutional reform.

Joint Cabinet Committee

The Joint Consultative Committee, a sub-committee of the Cabinet chaired by the Prime Minister, included five Liberal Democrats. The remit of the committee was "To consider policy issues of joint interest to the government and the Liberal Democrat Party". The Committee examined constitutional issues such as Scottish and Welsh devolution and House of Lords reforms. It also considered changes to the electoral system.

A significant number of Liberal Democrats displayed scepticism about Ashdown's policy of 'constructive opposition' to Labour and were afraid of being labelled

Kennedy—a new Leader

In August 1999, Charles Kennedy, the 39-year-old MP for Ross, Skye and Inverness, defeated Simon Hughes to become the new leader of the Liberal Democrats. It had been a hard-fought contest with Kennedy winning on the fourth count by a margin of 57% to 43%. The new leader continued Ashdown's policy of cooperation with Labour, for example he endorsed Labour's NHS plan in July 2000.

At the Party Conference in September 1999, Mr Kennedy endorsed the strategy of constructive opposition and claimed that such a strategy had persuaded Labour to support proportional representation in the elections for the Scottish Parliament. The impact of PR on the Liberal Democrats' search for power was immediate. Despite coming fourth in the Scottish Parliament elections in August 1999, the Liberal Democrats entered into a coalition government with Labour—their first peacetime experience of government since 1932. The year 2000 was also a good one for the Liberal Democrats. They won the Romsey by-election taking what had been a safe Conservative seat, and they joined a coalition with Labour in Wales, thus becoming part of the Welsh Executive.

LIBERAL DEMOCRAT LEADERSHIP CONTEST 1999

FIRST ROUND

	Votes
Jackie Ballard	3,978
Malcolm Bruce	4,643
Simon Hughes	16,233
Charles Kennedy	22,724
David Rendel	3,428

Rendel, Ballard and Bruce were eliminated at the first, second and third rounds respectively, and their second preference votes were redistributed.

FOURTH ROUND

Simon Hughes	21,833
Charles Kennedy	28,425

The leader is elected by every paid-up member of the Party on a one member, one vote basis, using the Single Transferable Vote system.

Powers of the Party Leader
While the federal conference must give formal approval, the Party leader has a great deal of influence over the formulation of policy. Most major Party proposals stem from the federal policy committee which is dominated by the Party leadership. The policy committee and the Party leadership are responsible for drawing up the Party's election manifesto.

'Labour's poodle'. Ashdown urged his party to consider the benefits of close links with Labour, such as the setting up of an independent commission under the Liberal Democrat peer, Roy Jenkins, "to recommend a proportional alternative" to the existing voting system for the House of Commons. (See page 12.)

By the end of 1998 it was clear that no action would be taken by the government over the Jenkins proposals for electoral reform. Blair's enthusiasm for cooperation with the Liberal Democrats was not shared by his Cabinet. John Prescott was totally against electoral reform and any referendum on the issue, and Gordon Brown refused to attend meetings of the Joint Cabinet Committee. It was clear to Ashdown that his dream of the re-alignment of British politics, with the Liberal Democrats involved in government, would not happen for many years. Three months after the Jenkins report was published he announced, in a letter to his party, that he would retire as leader of the Liberal Democrats.

THE ORGANISATION OF POLITICAL PARTIES

The study of party organisation focuses attention on where power lies within a political party. Who controls the major parties? This is a vital question because whoever controls the majority party also controls the government.

There are several levels of party organisation common to most major parties. Logically, one starts with individual, dues-paying, card-carrying members. Individual members belong to and participate in the activities of local organisations which are formed around the basic electoral unit in Britain, the parliamentary constituency. In the case of the Labour Party one has to add 'affiliated organisations' to the membership list. These include trade unions, socialist societies, fabian societies and young socialists.

MAKING LIBERAL DEMOCRAT POLICY

The Federal Conference
The supreme policy making body is the Federal Conference. Representatives from every local party are elected to attend the federal conference where policy decisions are made on national and 'English' issues. The English Party delegates its policy making powers to the Federal Conference. The Conference can make decisions about foreign affairs and English domestic issues such as transport and education but the Scottish Conference deals with Scottish domestic issues.

The Federal Committees
(The executive, policy and conference committees)
Membership comes from members of the Parliamentary Party, the three 'state Parties' and councillors. At least a third of each committee must be women.

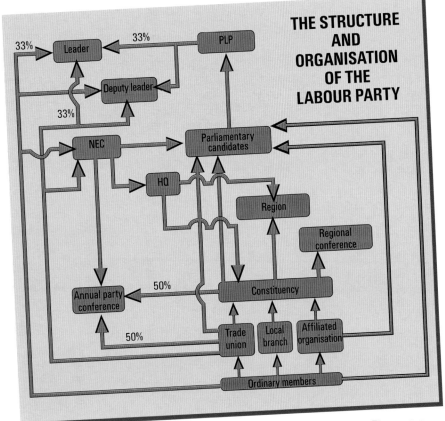

Figure 3.2

Individual members, constituency associations and affiliated organisations constitute the grass roots of the party, sometimes known as the 'party in the country'. The main function of party members is to select the parliamentary candidate who will become the local MP if the party wins the constituency in the general election.

One might expect that the mass membership would be in charge of what a democratic political party does in terms of policy making and governing the country. However, that expectation ignores the need for 'organisation' both at the grass roots and in Parliament. In common with other large groups, political parties must be extremely well organised in order to promote efficiency. This is essential for any group whose members are drawn from all parts of Britain and is especially important for political parties whose members may disagree with each other over important political points. The need to be organised

47

in the interests of efficiency extends to the party's successful parliamentary candidates. Thus the parliamentary parties are organised into leaders (the Cabinet and the Shadow Cabinet) and backbench supporters. Conservative backbench MPs belong to the 1922 Committee; Labour MPs are members of the Parliamentary Labour Party (PLP).

Constituency Organisation

What are the links between grass roots organisations in the country and the parties in Parliament? At this point it is worth emphasising that the Conservative Party was established about seventy years before the Labour Party. The reasons behind the origins of each party were completely different and their contemporary organisation reflects these differences in origin.

The Conservative Party proper, consisting of Conservative MPs only, can trace its origins back to the 1830s. Conservative MPs were organised within the House of Commons before the great nineteenth century reforms of the electoral system and the consequent extension of the franchise made it essential that parliamentary candidates be supported by party organisations in the country. Constituency parties were necessary to encourage the Party's supporters within the increasing number of voters to come out on polling day. Conservative Party Associations were created to serve the Parliamentary Party.

The Conservative Central Office was established as long ago as 1871 to give some degree of coherence to Conservative electoral efforts across the country. Because the Constituency Associations and the Central Office were established to serve the Parliamentary Party before the onset of fully-fledged democracy, they have remained, for the most part, subservient to the Parliamentary Party. The reforms introduced by William Hague have made the

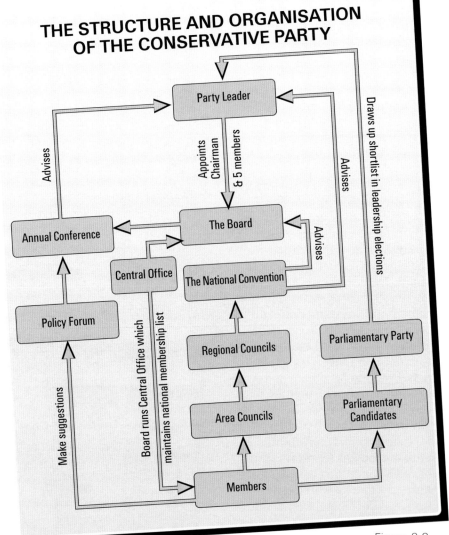

THE STRUCTURE AND ORGANISATION OF THE CONSERVATIVE PARTY

Figure 3.3

Party structure more democratic. (See Figure 3.4 and page 38.)

The Labour Party was established in 1900 as the Labour Representation Committee as a result of a Trades Union Council resolution in 1899. In other words, it was organised by political forces outside Parliament. The objective was to ensure that the labour movement and the working class were represented in Parliament. At this time more and more working-class men were becoming eligible to vote. However, the two major parties, Conservative and Liberal, were middle-class parties. Labour Party membership could be acquired through individuals joining the Party directly or through membership of an affiliated trade union. These historical events explain why important Labour Party decisions are taken by MPs, CLPs and trade unions and also why Labour has

a more complex and decentralised organisational structure than the Conservative Party.

The conventional wisdom has been that the Conservative Party is more centralised and easier to control than the Labour Party. Such a claim might have been true of the Conservative Party under Margaret Thatcher and the Labour Party under Michael Foot, yet few would claim that it accurately portrayed the Conservative Party under John Major or the Labour Party under Tony Blair.

Both major parties have a number of organisations and procedures which give the grass roots some say in decision making but allow the leaders to control the party as a whole most of the time. MPs are the most obvious links between the parties in the country and their party in Parliament. MPs

Delegates to the Labour Party Conference represent the constituency parties, the trade unions and various socialist societies. It is an opportunity for the leadership to communicate with the public as there is extensive television coverage of the debates.

tend to be loyal to the parliamentary leadership, partly because loyalty may lead to promotion and partly because disloyalty would weaken the party in the fight for political supremacy.

Party Conference

The next link is the national party conference which is common to all parties, major and minor. The major parties hold annual party conferences in the early autumn. These act both as a rally of the faithful and as decision making bodies. The Conservative Conference, which is heavily stage-managed, is usually devoted to demonstrating support for the leader and for the policies decided by the Cabinet or Shadow Cabinet.

Until recently, the Labour Party Conference was much less subject to control by the leadership. The Labour Party Constitution stated that Party policies making up

the Labour Programme should be approved by the Conference, subject to receiving two-thirds support. The election manifesto, which consists of policies from the programme, has to be agreed between the parliamentary leadership and the National Executive Committee of the Party. The Labour leadership submits its policy programme to the Conference and both CLPs and affiliated organisations may submit resolutions which may or may not agree with the leadership's point of view. Voting on resolutions is carried out by delegates from both CLPs and affiliated organisations such as trade unions who cast a number of votes determined by the size of their respective memberships. This means that the trade unions dominate voting as there are many more Labour members through trade union membership than through individual members joining the Party directly.

Labour retains a federal organisation in that despite the introduction of 'one member, one vote', various posts are decided by an electoral college of trade unions, constituency associations, MPs, and others. The federal organisation limits the power of Labour leaders compared to their Conservative counterparts. Once elected, the Conservative leader in Opposition has a free hand in relation to choosing the Shadow Cabinet and deciding Party policy. The Labour Shadow Cabinet is selected by a vote of the PLP. Labour Prime Ministers are not subject to such limitations, since they select their own Cabinet colleagues. However, the organisational and policy reforms accomplished by Labour leaders since the mid-1980s strongly suggest that in the long run the Parliamentary Party prevails over the Party in the country and the affiliated organisations.

Partnership  in Power

A discussion of Tony Blair's first Prime Ministership, 1997–2001, is covered in Chapter 6. The section which follows concentrates on Blair's relationship with the Labour Party and his determination to weaken the influence of Old Labour.

Blair used the euphoria of the May 1997 victory to push through a series of Party reforms called 'Partnership in Power' (PIP). At the October 1997 conference, PIP set up new machinery for agreeing Party policy which strengthened the leadership's position. Under the old system the National Executive Committee (NEC) had formal responsibility for policy making between conferences and Party policy was determined largely by votes at conference. Partnership in Power has created new bodies to work within a two-year 'rolling programme'. After two years of discussion, policies are presented to the NEC and then passed on to the Conference for a final decision. Officials highlight that previously local parties would have been offered a three-minute slot at conference to argue their case. Now they are able to feed their viewpoints to the policy commission throughout the year. Critics argue, however, that the policy reports are written from the government's point of view and spend more time praising current policies than discussing future ones.

Margaret McDonagh was appointed the General Secretary of the Party in October 1998 representing the change in style between Old and New Labour.

All previous Labour General Secretaries had been men, usually from a trade union background. McDonagh, a Party organiser since the early 1980s, had campaigned for Blair in his quest for the Labour leadership in 1994 and in the successful bid to rewrite Clause IV in 1994-95. She claims that PIP makes the Party more democratic: "We have a party whose members, from bottom to top, are involved in its decisions".

The structure of the NEC ensures that the left will be outvoted. Only six of the thirty three NEC seats are directly elected by constituency activists who tend to support the left of the Party. Most of the rest of the seats are, in reality, controlled by the Party leadership or the trade unions. NEC members are allowed to vote only when they are on a relevant sub-committee. Left-wingers, such as Mark Sedden, argue that "this control-freakery goes beyond the Labour Party. It presents a major potential danger to democracy if it continues". (See the 'Control Freaks', pages 41–44.)

Nevertheless, the actions of New Labour to ensure 'unity' led to the creation of a strong economy and a raft of moderate, some would say Conservative, policies, ensuring that Labour approached the June 2001 Election high in the opinion polls. In contrast, William Hague approached the Election with a disunited party, and a large number of unpopular party policies.

SELECTING THE PARTY LEADERS

Both parties have reformed the leadership selection process in recent times, Labour in 1981 and the Conservatives in 2001. Both parties allow for challenges to be made to the incumbent leader. Leadership elections provide an indication of the degree of ideological or policy conflict within the major parties.

The Labour Party

The Labour leader used to be elected by the PLP with only a simple absolute majority being required for victory. Michael Foot was the last Labour leader to be chosen only by MPs. He defeated Denis Healey in November 1980 in a contest which has been compared with the 1997 Tory leadership contest. Foot, a left-winger, defeated Healey who was regarded as the representative of the centre-right leadership which had failed by losing the 1979 General Election.

The Labour leader is now chosen by an electoral college representing three elements of the Party inside and outside Parliament—Labour MPs, the membership organised in Constituency Parties, and members of trade unions affiliated to the Party. This reform was carried out in 1981 when the left wing of the Party, which was in favour of extra-parliamentary controls over the leadership in the House of Commons, was dominant. The CLPs and the unions, the Party outside Parliament, were each given a 'constituency' within a tripartite electoral college. MPs and the CLPs were each given 30% and the unions received 40% of the votes in the college. In 1992 the three electoral college constituencies were made equal. It was also decided at that time to make the leadership election process more democratic by requiring both CLPs and trade unions to consult with their individual memberships in accordance with the principle of 'one member, one vote' (OMOV). The operation of the electoral college may be explained by examining the result of the 1994 contest which established Tony Blair as the leader.

Within the constituency section, every CLP has one vote which is assigned to the leadership candidate who wins the ballot of individual members. Within the trade union section, every affiliated union is assigned a share of the overall trade union vote (one-third of the total electoral college) based on the size of its membership. Every affiliated union holds a postal ballot of its members and its electoral college votes are divided between the candidates according to their share of the postal ballot. Tony Blair won a majority in each section of the Party. John Prescott was the runner-up. His strongest support came from the trade union membership which reflected his own working-class and trade union background.

Blair's comprehensive victory symbolised the change in the Labour Party since electoral defeat in 1979. One commentator summed up the change thus:

> "The Labour Party has deliberately chosen a leader whose image and style appeal to a younger generation and whose association with class politics and fundamentalist socialism is almost non-existent."

The Conservative Party

The Conservative leadership election process has been much more competitive and controversial than Labour's in recent decades. The Conservative leader has been elected only since 1965 when Edward Heath succeeded Sir Alec Douglas Home who stood down following Labour's victory in the 1964 General Election. Until then the Conservative leader was said to 'evolve' from a consultation process held within the Party. However, the absence of a clear-cut electoral procedure led to difficulties in 1957 and 1963 when the Conservative leader resigned while holding the office of Prime Minister. In controversial circumstances on both occasions, the leadership issue was settled when the Queen appointed the new Prime Minister. It was argued that the Conservative Party was unnecessarily involving the Monarch in the political process which was held to be contrary to constitutional principles.

The Conservatives adopted a complicated election procedure confined to MPs. In order to ensure that the elected leader would enjoy strong support after the election, a sizable majority was required to win on the first ballot—an absolute majority plus 15% more of the vote than the runner-up. This majority was accomplished only once in the five contests using this system since 1965. This was in 1989 when Mrs Thatcher was opposed by a virtual unknown in what amounted to a protest against her leadership style. In 1990 Mrs Thatcher was forced out of office after failing by only a single vote to attract the 15% margin over Michael Heseltine. In the second ballot new candidates were allowed to enter the contest. At this stage an overall majority was required for victory. A third ballot may have been held if necessary. This third ballot was confined to the leading three candidates in the second ballot. At

this stage preferential voting was used if there were more than two candidates.

Margaret Thatcher challenged and defeated Edward Heath in 1975. Thatcher herself was opposed by Sir Antony Meyer in 1989 and then forced out of office in 1990 as a result of the challenge from Michael Heseltine, though the winner was John Major who entered the contest after Mrs Thatcher's withdrawal. John Major resigned immediately after the 1997 Election defeat to be succeeded, after three ballots, by William Hague.

The election of William Hague

The 1997 contest took place within an environment dominated by electoral defeat and a party badly divided by the issue of European integration, especially the single currency question. Four of the candidates had served under John Major until the Labour victory. John Redwood had resigned from the Cabinet to contest the leadership against Major in 1995. The policy divisions ran from Kenneth Clarke on the centre-left of the Party to John Redwood on the right. Michael Howard and Peter Lilley were also regarded as right-wingers while the youngest candidate, William Hague, was considered to be the centrist candidate whose views were not as well known as those of the others.

The greatest divide was on 'Europe'. Clarke was the only 'Europhile', favourable to a common currency though open to persuasion about when Britain should join. Redwood was opposed to the common currency under any circumstances. Howard and Lilley were also opposed to a common monetary policy for the EU. Hague's view on the single currency was hostile, but less hostile than that of the three right-wingers. Clarke's disadvantage was that the small number of Conservative MPs was more Eurosceptic than Europhile.

The contest turned on three issues: leadership, Party unity and the European question. Although Clarke was ahead on the first ballot, this was due to the right-wing vote being divided at least three ways. Hague did better than expected. It had been anticipated that Howard, Lilley and Redwood would unite behind whichever one of them did best in the first ballot. However, when this surprisingly turned out to be Redwood, who was the furthest to the right, Howard and Lilley withdrew and called for their supporters to vote for Hague as the best strategy to ensure the defeat of Clarke, the common enemy. In the second ballot Clarke was still ahead but narrowly. At that point the unexpected happened. Clarke and Redwood, the two furthest apart on most policy issues including Europe, reached an agreement which saw Redwood standing down in favour of the former Chancellor. In the final ballot Hague won by a surprisingly wide margin.

Conservative Party leader William Hague with members of the shadow cabinet and prospective parliamentary candidates for the 2001 General Election.

THE SELECTION OF CANDIDATES

One of the potential battlegrounds of internal party conflict is the process of candidate selection. Whoever controls the selection of candidates, and the process of reselection of sitting MPs, could be expected to control the party. The reason for this is that candidates represent the constituencies which elect them and democratic theory assumes that there should be an element of local control over who should be selected to represent both party and constituency.

There are elements of local and central control in the candidate selection procedures of the two major British parties. The Conservatives maintain a list of candidates approved by a committee under the control of the Party leader. Would-be candidates are subjected to interview before they can get onto the approved list. They are then eligible to be selected by a constituency party. A short list of candidates is drawn up by committees before the full membership of a local Conservative Constituency Association meets to listen to the candidates and to select one in a vote of the individual members of the Party present.

Labour Party organisation at the constituency level is more complex than Conservative organisation. A CLP (Constituency Labour Party) may include a number of branches based on local government wards and some affiliated organisations such as trade unions. Both the branches and the affiliated organisations may propose individuals as candidates. Labour Party headquarters in London maintains lists of candidates who may be approached by CLPs. A short list is determined by the CLP's executive committee and the candidate is then chosen by a vote of the individual members of the constituency party.

The two major parties have experienced internal conflicts over candidate selection, especially at the stage of the reselection of sitting MPs. If an MP's general ideological position or his/her position on a particularly divisive policy issue is at odds with the majority of members in the constituency party then the MP may be in trouble. In the early 1980s when Labour required the mandatory reselection of sitting members it was feared that this would lead to the deselection of right-wing and centrist MPs out of step with left-wing majorities among the party activists who would turn up and vote at CLP meetings. In the event, although there have been a number of deselections, these fears were unrealised. Labour has acted to deselect left-wing Militant candidates who caused problems during the 'modernisation' of the Party under John Smith and Tony Blair.

52

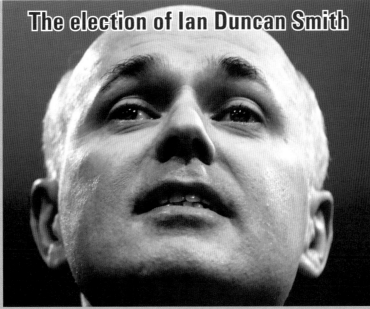

The election of Ian Duncan Smith

William Hague immediately announced his resignation in the aftermath of the Conservatives' disappointing electoral performance in 2001. The campaign to elect a new leader was to last eight weeks and open up the deep divisions within the Party. Victory in the end went to the relatively unknown and inexperienced Iain Duncan Smith.

The Campaign

Under the new election rules for electing the Party leader, MPs would decide which two candidates would go forward to the second stage, whereby the 300,000 Party members would choose the new leader. Five candidates entered the contest and, as expected, Michael Ancram and David Davis dropped out. In the third round, Michael Portillo just lost out to Iain Duncan Smith, by one vote, for second place, with Ken Clarke leading at this stage. (See Table 3.3.) Michael Portillo had been the front-runner and had the backing of nearly two-thirds of the Shadow Cabinet. A poor campaign and prejudice within the Party towards Portillo ensured his defeat. Por-

tillo had argued that the Party must be less rigid and conservative in its own social attitudes and should be more tolerant of people whose sexual and social choices differed from their own.

The removal of Portillo left the Party with a clear choice between the leftist, pro-European and highly experienced Ken Clarke and the right-wing inexperienced Eurosceptic, Iain Duncan Smith. Ken Clarke had held the offices of Chancellor of the Exchequer, Home Secretary and Health Secretary and had lost the last leadership election because of his unwillingness to compromise his pro-European views. It was clear that Iain

Duncan Smith, a former captain in the Scots Guards, appealed to the party's grass roots with his opposition to Europe and his right-wing views on social issues.

The campaign was bitter and exposed the fault lines within the Party. Ken Clarke called Smith a "hanger and flogger", and the revelation that one of Smith's local organisers was the father of the leader of the racist British National Party (BNP) reinforced this viewpoint. Edgar Griffen was quickly removed from Smith's campaign team when it further emerged that his wife was an active member of the BNP.

Former Party leaders also entered the fray, with Mrs Thatcher, the former Prime Minister, describing Clarke as a "political has-been" and a "disaster for the Party if elected". Not to be outdone, John Major endorsed Ken Clarke and accused Iain Duncan Smith of doing "immense damage" to his government by voting against his European policies.

On Thursday 14 September, Iain Duncan Smith was declared the leader of the Conservative Party, beating Ken Clarke with a majority of 2:1. In a short acceptance speech, he paid tribute to Ken Clarke and signalled his intention to focus on the state of the country's public services. The shadow front bench team displayed its right-wing credentials with the appointment of Eurosceptic David Davis as the new Party chairman. The bookmakers immediately lengthened the odds on the Tories winning the next election from 3/1 to 7/2.

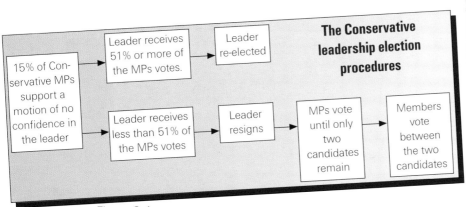

The Conservative leadership election procedures

Figure 3.4

Round Three : July 2001 Votes by Conservative MPs	
Ken Clarke	59
Iain Duncan Smith	54
Michael Portillo	53

Table 3.3

Votes of Party Members September 2001		
	Number	%
Iain Duncan Smith	155,933	61
Ken Clarke	100,864	39

Table 3.4

Labour Party Policies – *2001 General Election*

The Labour Manifesto reflected the Party's status as the governing party since 1997. It included five "achievements".

- Economics: lowest inflation for thirty years and a typ-ical mortgage lower than under the Conservatives.
- Education: the best ever results in primary schools.
- Health: 17,000 more nurses in the NHS.
- Crime: crime rate down 10%.
- Families: a new Children's Tax Credit and one million more people in work.

Labour's policies were detailed under five headings:

1 Prosperity for All (the Economy)

Children's Tax Credit of £1,000 for new parents. Guarantee of a minimum family income of £225 for a 35-hour week. National minimum wage to rise to £4.20 in October 2002. ISA £7,000 pa contribution limit to be maintained for the next Parliament. A ten-year Transport Plan costing £180 billion to compensate for past under-investment; increased expenditure on railways and roads.

Labour's policy on joining the 'Euro' is summed up as: "in principle, we are in favour of joining a successful common currency" as long as five economic tests are passed. The government is to decide whether the tests have been passed "early in the next Parliament". The issue, if the government recommends joining, is to be decided by the people in a referendum.

2 World-Class Public Services

The government has more or less admitted that it will be judged at the next election in relation to its ability to "deliver" effective public services. Education is established as "Labour's top priority".

In education Labour is committed to a target of 50% of school leavers going on to higher education. Expenditure on education went up from 4.7% to 5% of national income; the target for 2003–2004 is 5.3%. Expenditure of almost £8 billion on school buildings and equipment is promised.

In health, spending is to rise by an average of 6% per year. A major objective is to bring "UK health spending up to the EU average". Waiting times are to be reduced to forty eight hours to see a GP by 2004; maximum time for outpatient appointments from six to three months and for inpatients from eighteen months to six months.

3 A Modern Welfare State

Pensioners to be targeted to eliminate poverty: "within two years, no pensioner need live on less than £100 per week". National Childcare Strategy to provide places for 1.6 million children by 2004. Disability Rights Commission to ensure full civil rights for the disabled. Winter Fuel Payment to be retained.

4 Strong and Safe Communities

Crime to be tackled so that burglary rate is halved. Claim of a 7% decline in recorded crime since 1997, 20% decline in car crime and 28% decline in domestic burglary. Repeat of slogan "tough on crime and its causes". More police to be deployed in the community.

Aim of making "Britain a model of a multicultural, multiracial society". Implementation of the Macpherson Report recommendations following the Stephen Lawrence murder.

Constitutional reform to include "directly elected regional government to go ahead where people decided in a referendum to support it". No need for an English Parliament but devolution hailed as "preserving the union". Parliamentary reform to include encouragement to parties to increase the representation of women. Reform of electoral systems to be "reviewed" but any proposed changes to House of Commons electoral system to be subject of a referendum. House of Lords reform to be completed including removal of remaining hereditary peers.

5 Britain Strong in the World

Europe seen as "an opportunity not a threat". "British ideas" to "lead a reformed and enlarged Europe". Maintenance of NATO commitments but the EU to "act where NATO chooses not to".

Ambitions for Scotland
Labour's manifesto 2001

Conservative Party Policies – *2001 General Election*

The Conservatives' Manifesto represented their attempt to recover from the major electoral setback of 1997 and to overcome Labour's comfortable lead in public opinion polls for most of the subsequent four years. The key words in a short introduction by William Hague were "free" and "freedom": "We want to set people free so that they will have greater power over their own lives." The Manifesto provided a list of what common sense requires: strengthening the family; enough police to keep the streets safe; less tax and regulation of people and businesses; ending political interference in medical judgments; respect and independence for older people; valuing what makes us distinctive as a nation; valuing the distinctiveness of both town and country; fewer politicians and more local decision making.

1 Raising a Family
Claim that tax bills of "typical families" had increased by £670 pa under Labour. Conservatives to "give families a break" by cutting taxes by a £200 pa Children's Tax Credit and the introduction of a Married Couples Allowance of £1,000 per year.

Educational policy to be decentralised ;education not to be run from Whitehall. Basic aim of giving "parents choice and head teachers freedom". Parents to be given right to call for a special Ofsted inspection if school is thought to be failing. Student loans not to be repaid until income reaches £20,000 per year.

2 Living Safely
Number of police on streets to be increased to reverse Labour's cuts. Persistent young offenders to be "taken off the streets" by a ten-fold increase in places in Secure Training Centres. Victims of crime to be treated fairly. Suspension of Labour's early release scheme.

3 Earning a Living
To be "a tax-cutting government". £8 billion to be saved after two years by improving performance of government, this money to be used to fund tax cuts including raising personal allowances for pensioners by £2,000 pa; abolishing taxes on savings and dividends; cutting petrol tax by 6p per litre; business rate reductions. The Manifesto include a list of where the saving were to be made.

Channel 4 to be privatised and the proceeds to be allocated to cultural institutions such as museums and art galleries.
"We will keep the pound".

4 Staying Healthy
NHS in "a state of permanent crisis". Conservatives to match Labour's spending on NHS but would ensure that money went further. Build a new partnership between the state and independent sectors. Waiting List Initiative to be replaced by a Patient's Guarantee. Commitment to "a comprehensive NHS free to all its users" but tax penalties on private medical insurance to be abolished. Emphasis on giving patients choice e.g. to decide in which hospital to be treated and GPs to decide "how to organise themselves".

5 Growing Older
Comprehensive package including tax cuts, higher pensions, abolition of compulsory annuities at age 75, the option to take a higher pension in place of "perks" such as winter fuel allowance etc., and a commitment to "protect savings and homes of those needing long-term care".

6 A World Leader
"In Europe but not run by Europe". Choice is between a "fully integrated superstate with nation states and the national veto disappearing" and "a network Europe" which is based on flexibility and member states being allowed to opt out of EU decisions if their national interests so dictate. Keeping the pound reiterated as a firm policy commitment.

Britain's independent nuclear deterrent to be maintained.

7 A Proud Democracy
Opposed to Labour's regional assemblies proposals; Section 28 of the Local Government Act to be retained. Only English and Welsh MPs to vote on bills on exclusively English and Welsh matters. Prime Minister to answer parliamentary questions twice a week as before. No reform of general election voting system. Reform of House of Lords to be proposed by a Joint Committee of Commons and Lords.

time for **common sense in Scotland**

55

MEMBERS OF PARLIAMENT

A general election is organised around individual candidates along with the voters in constituencies. The 2001 Election returned 659 men and women to the House of Commons to represent the various interests of the single-member constituencies which preferred these candidates to their rivals. It used to be the case that only the names of the individual candidates were listed on the ballot paper, but now the candidates' parties are also listed.

MPs are elected by voters in individual constituencies. These constituencies vary enormously in terms of size, socio-economic composition and economic activity (how constituents make their living). A constituency might be concentrated in a very small inner city area with a high population density (Glasgow Kelvin has 47.2 individuals per hectare) or spread across a vast rural territory running from one side of Scotland to the other (Ross, Skye and Inverness West has a population density of 0.1 people per hectare). The individuals elected to represent the 659 localities are known by the name of the constituency which elects them—the Right Honourable Member for Glasgow Springburn or the Right Honourable Member for Edinburgh Pentlands, for example.

REPRESENTATIVE DEMOCRACY

MPs are, above all, representatives. Britain is often called a 'representative democracy'. How do MPs carry out their representative function? How far can they go on behalf of their constituents? Members of Parliament have considerable powers. Collectively, through the right to vote in the House of Commons, they possess the powers to legislate and to hold the government to account. Once in the Commons it might appear natural that each MP would decide how to vote according to the interests and wishes which are predominant among and sometimes unique to her/his constituents and supporters.

Divided Loyalties

However, MPs experience divided loyalties—to individual constituents, especially those who voted for them, to their local constituencies, to their party, to region and to nation, to individual conscience and to ideological beliefs. Predominant among these loyalties is the MP's political party. MPs do get the opportunity to be true to all of these loyalties but to vastly differing degrees. Elections and the House of Commons are organised by political parties, as we saw in Chapter 1. Indeed, both major parties have been at pains to strengthen party control because lack of unity and discipline cost Labour dearly in elections from 1979 to 1987 and helped to cause the Conservatives' downfall in 1997 and 2001.

The proper role of the MP has long been the subject of debate. The classic case for allowing an MP to act primarily as an individual at Westminster was made in 1774 by Edmunde Burke, a celebrated political theorist. Burke had just been elected to the Commons as MP for Bristol. He informed the people who had returned him to Parliament that MPs should not be considered to be merely constituency delegates or agents. Rather, the MP should first be considered to be a Member of Parliament before being thought of as member of a particular con-

56

stituency. In Parliament he (there were no female MPs until 1919) should represent the 'one interest' of the 'one nation' which he would define according to his own individual judgment of the issues to be decided by Parliament. Burke was the originator of 'One Nation Conservatism', the idea that the British nation as a whole has identifiable interests. During the 1990s this became a rallying cry of Conservatives opposed to Thatcherism on the grounds that it was dividing rather than unifying the country.

The formation of the Labour Party at the very beginning of the twentieth century by organisations outside Parliament suggested that MPs should be subservient to the people and the interests which they represented. The widening franchise (the right to vote) and the resulting development of party organisation spelt the end of Burke's independent MP who had used his judgment to decide what was best for the nation. MPs were now expected to toe the party line. Rebellious MPs are unlikely to advance through the ranks to hold governmental office.

MPs are still expected to represent their constituents and the nation, but there are strict limits on how far they may go as constituency representatives. (See 'The viewpoint of an MP' on page 60.) MPs of the governing party are expected to support their party leaders in government so that

THE WHIP SYSTEM

The task of maintaining discipline among MPs lies with the Party Whip. Each party has a Chief Whip and a number of assistant Whips. The Chief Whip is also an important link in communicating the mood of MPs to the leadership of the party.

Each week, the Whips issue MPs notes giving the order of business for the following week. Each item to be discussed will be underlined once, twice or three times according to its importance. A debate underlined once indicates no division (vote) is expected; one underlined twice indicates there will be a division which MPs are expected to attend unless they have organised to 'pair' with a member of the other major party; a three-line whip indicates that the division is of vital importance and all members are requested to attend.

Hilary Armstrong arriving at Downing Street after the 2001 General Election to be appointed as Labour's Chief Whip

Whips have an important say in the appointment of party members to select committees, and to the post of junior minister. If an MP defies the Whips, he/she will be warned and if he/she persistently fails to support the party the Whip can be withdrawn. This means that the party disowns the MP and he/she serves the rest of that term as an independent. At the next election the party will select a new candidate to fight the seat leaving the 'rebel' to contest the seat as an independent.

Whips also act as tellers when a vote takes place. At least one Whip is always present at the debate, keeping an eye open for trouble. Whips seldom speak in the House and are discouraged from expressing any political opinions outside it.

Adjournment Debates in the House of Commons: Week of 16 July 2000

At the end of each parliamentary day a motion is put that 'this House do now adjourn'. A backbencher then speaks on an issue which he/she has chosen and a Government Minister replies. Backbenchers frequently select issues which are significant to their constituents, perhaps pointing out problems which their constituents believe are in need of attention. The range of topics which come up in Adjournment Debates is illustrated below.

	BACKBENCH SPONSOR	TOPIC OF DEBATE
Monday 16 July	John McDonnell (Hayes & Harlington) Labour	Issues of concern to the Punjabi community in Britain, e.g. Operation of the Visitor Visa System, support for Punjabi culture.
Tuesday 17 July	David Amess (Southend West) Conservative	Economic problems of Southend; need for regeneration.
Wednesday 18 July	Martin Caton (Gower) Labour	British bases (Kenya), people being killed by unexploded bombs on ranges used by the British army.
Thursday 19 July	Sir Patrick Cormack (South Staffordshire) Conservative	Proposed takeover of Wolverhampton & Dudley Brewery by foreign-owned company.
Friday 20 July	George Mudie (Leeds East) Labour	Deterrent effect of fees levied on appeals to obtain overseas visitor permits/visas.

their common objectives may be achieved. Opposition MPs are expected to unite behind their leaders who form an alternative government in waiting. Perceptions of party loyalty and unity may play a decisive role in determining general election results.

THE ROLES OF THE BACKBENCHER

Members of Parliament are not equal in status in spite of their common representative function. There are two types of MP-frontbenchers and backbenchers. The seating arrangements in the Commons emphasise its partisan nature as does the presence within the legislature of the political executive—Prime Minister and Cabinet—which is a central feature of the parliamentary system. The two major parties sit confronting one another. Members of Her Majesty's Government and of Her Majesty's Opposition sit at the front (the front benches)and their supporters who do not hold office sit behind them (backbenchers). Thus each party has its frontbench leadership and its supporting backbenchers. Backbenchers are also known as Private Members.

The 'record breaking' 1997 General Election returned 419 Labour MPs, including the Speaker, to Westminster. The new government, the Labour frontbench, comprised seventy three MPs (fourteen women), and fifteen members of the House of Lords

Parliamentary Timetable
1990-1991

	% of Time
Government legislation	24.6
Government Motions & Debates	11.1
Opposition Motions	8.6
Ministerial Statements	8.3
Question Time	8.4
Backbenchers' Bills	4.2
Backbenchers' Motions & Debates	16.0
Miscellaneous (eg. debate on Queen's speech)	18.8

Table 4.1   Source: Bill Jones et al, *Politics UK* (Harvester Wheatsheaf, 1991) page 330.

(five women). Another sixteen MPs (two women) were appointed as Whips, and another forty one were appointed as parliamentary private secretaries (PPSs) to Ministers. The PPSs are on the fringe of government, hoping for promotion to ministerial status when the Prime Minister decides to reshuffle her/his government team. For example, when Martin Chisolm resigned as Undersecretary of State at the Scottish Office in protest at his government's proposed cuts in welfare benefits, he was replaced by Calum MacDonald who was serving as PPS to the Secretary of State for Scotland, Donald Dewar. These government appointments left 290 Labour MPs on the backbenches. The Conservative frontbench in the Commons comprised forty MPs; another ten Conservatives were appointed Whips. This left just over 100 Conservative backbenchers. This chapter looks primarily at the role of backbenchers. Chapter 6, The Executive, examines the role of frontbenchers.

The backbench 'class of '97' included 260 MPs new to the House of Commons, a post-war record. This was due to Labour's larger than expected majority and to a large number of retirements (117) prior to the Election. New MPs made up 44% of the Parliamentary Labour Party (PLP) and a majority (twenty nine out of forty six) of theLiberal Democrats' parliamentary representation. The size of the Labour majority and the large proportion of 'fresher' MPs stimulated speculation about how disciplined the new intake would be. Large majorities are sometimes thought to encourage indiscipline because the government is very unlikely to be defeated if a few of its backbenchers defect or abstain on issues about which they feel strongly.

Representation, which is one of the central functions of the British Parliament and its members, may be looked at from two distinct viewpoints.

➡ MPs 'represent' both their constituents and their constituencies.

➡ MPs are also representative of some sections of British society.

To what extent are they representative of society as a whole? In other words, we are interested in what our Members of Parliament do and in who they are.

Backbenchers and voting

The first duty of the MP is observed in the division lobbies of the Commons. MPs have little option but to toe the party line, especially if they are politically ambitious and hope one day to be part of the leadership of their party and be a member of the government. British parliamentary parties are strongly centralised and disciplined. Thus MPs have frequently been scornfully described as 'lobby fodder'—as mere supporters of their frontbench leaders who are expected to be like good children 'seen and not heard'. A government with a comfortable working parliamentary majority controls the business and the timetable of the Commons and allocates the great majority of the parliamentary timetable to enacting its own legislative policies and debating issues of its choosing.

Table 4.1 indicates the relative shares of frontbench (including Opposition frontbench) and backbench time in the 1990–91 parliamentary timetable. Backbenchers are allocated about 20% of the timetable for their two major contributions to the work of the Commons: Private Members' legislation and debates on topical issues which they select. Backbenchers also play a leading role at Question Time, though the focus is more on how Ministers perform under the pressures of interrogation and the televising of parliamentary proceedings. MPs do participate in debates on government legislation and on issues selected by both frontbenches, though such debates are

(continued on page 61)

The Wild Mammals (Hunting with Dogs) Bill

The issue of banning fox-hunting has dogged the Labour government since the introduction of the Wild Mammals Bill in November 1997. It was a Private Member's Bill put forward by Michael Foster, Labour MP for Worcester.

The Bill, which received its second reading in November 1997, did not reach the Statute Book in the 1997–98 parliamentary session because the government did not allocate adequate time for the Bill to complete its parliamentary stages. Significantly, on 1 March 1998 a massive Countryside March organised by a pressure group called the Countryside Alliance was held in London with 200,000 people attending to demonstrate their opposition to the proposed ban on fox-hunting and to demand restrictions to the right to roam on private land. The Bill was 'talked out' on 13 March 1998.

The government was uneasy about the Bill for several reasons even though Labour backbenchers were solidly in favour as was even rural public opinion. The Home Secretary Jack Straw was unsympathetic, fearing that a ban could be difficult to apply and would lead to a breakdown in public order if rural hunts attempted to defy a statutory ban. The govern-

ment did not welcome the prospect of mass arrests at a time when claims were being made that Labour was essentially an urban party looking to ride roughshod over rural interests. The supporters of the Countryside Alliance are overwhelmingly Conservative and upper middle class.

The Bill was reintroduced in the 1999–2000 session by Ken Livingstone after the Prime Minister and the Home Secretary, mindful of overwhelming support in the PLP for the Bill, both promised that this time sufficient parliamentary time would be made available. There have been twenty two Private Members' Bills on this subject in the last twenty years. This time the Bill lapsed in the Commons on 7 April 2000 because there was not a quorum when it came up for its second reading. A quorum of one hundred MPs is required to give a Bill its second reading; only seventy four MPs voted.

The government decided to bring matters to a head by introducing a Bill which would leave it to Parliament to decide how to solve the problem. This was an unusual piece of legislation in that it was introduced by the Home Secretary, Jack Straw, who declared that "it was not determined principally by the

government." The Bill comprised three options developed in discussions between the government and three opposing political factions on this emotive issue. Parliament was to choose one of the options.

The Countryside Alliance representing those in favour of fox-hunting with dogs proposed self-regulation by hunts by means of a newly established Independent Supervisory Authority on Hunting. An organisation called Deadline 2000, comprising the RSPCA, the League Against Cruel Sports and the Fund for Animal Welfare, proposed a total ban on hunting with dogs. This would 'criminalise' fox-hunting. The third option was proposed by the Middle Way Group represented by three MPs, one from each of the three largest parties in the Commons. The 'middle way' would be to permit fox-hunting to continue but only if consent was given by a new independent public body to be called the Hunting Authority which would issue licences to individual hunts.

On 18 January 2001 the House of Commons voted in favour of the Deadline 2000 option. Some publicity was given to Mr Blair flying off to Belfast before the vote was taken, suggesting that the

Prime Minister would have preferred the 'Middle Way' option because that would avoid the threat of public disorder that criminalising fox-hunting might bring about.

Even this 'government' Bill did not reach the Statute Book in the 2000–2001 session. It ran foul of opposition in the Lords, where there were many hunt supporters who ensured that passage of the Bill would take a long time. The calling of the General Election in June meant that there was not time to complete parliamentary scrutiny of the proposed legislation.

By that time responsibility for this matter in Scotland had devolved onto the Scottish Parliament. The Labour MSP Lord (Mike) Watson (Life Peers may sit in the Scottish Parliament) introduced a Bill calling for a total ban on hunting with dogs in Scotland. His Bill originally ran foul of the Committee on Rural Affairs which refused its support because Watson's Bill would have outlawed all hunting by dogs, by farmers as well as by hunts. The Bill did not focus exclusively on blood sports such as fox-hunting and hare coursing.

The Rural Affairs Committee was chaired by a Conservative MSP and it appeared to be more favourable to 'rural interests' than the Scottish Parliament as a whole. When the Bill was reported back from the Committee to the Parliament in September 2001, a clear majority, 84–34, decided in a free vote to allow the Bill to proceed to the next stage of the legislative process. This decision was overwhelmingly supported by Labour and SNP members while most Conservatives and Liberal Democrats opposed it.

Local Representative

I speak to the government and the country as the voice of Grimsby, articulating the needs of its people, its industries, its council, its development. I am required increasingly to be the town's public relations booster. This is a right to be heard but not to get. Normally, governments listen—and then explain why nothing can be done. Occasionally they concede, though usually only to wider causes espoused with others. Recently, helping to win belated redundancy pay and compensation for trawlermen who lost their jobs when Icelandic fishing stopped in 1976 was a rare local triumph.

Local Ombudsman

Status and the local representative role give MPs access to the top, to the chief executive officer on consumer matters, the Minister on policy or the local departmental head on individual cases. This isn't an ability to exert influence or change correct decisions but to remedy failures. An MP's complaint gets a full explanation, which often satisfies the constituent. The threat of publicity in the press or by questions and adjournment debates allows MPs to bully both private and public organisations and that occasionally helps.

Most MPs hold weekly surgeries and a minority of MPs finance offices in the constituency to serve local needs. To pay for all this, as well as telephones (rural MPs often provide one number at local rates to cover several exchanges, which is an expensive business) and staff in Westminster to service parliamentary work, MPs get an allowance of £51,572.

Party Representative

Most MPs are in Parliament on a party ticket. Party is a career ladder to climb, a substitute for thought and a whirl of the obsessive. In Parliament, the party is a framework of control, ensuring that MPs tramp through

VIEWPOINT OF A MEMBER OF PARLIAMENT

Austin Mitchell has been Labour Member of Parliament for Grimsby since 1977. Here he identifies the different roles of an MP which centre around three masters—Parliament, party and constituency. He also highlights the reforms which he believes are necessary to improve the effectiveness of MPs.

the lobbies, feeding party points every day, providing yah-boo fun, and trundling them out to every by-election as unpaid door knockers. The policy role of MPs is largely gone, handed to policy forums guided by Ministers. The Parliamentary Labour Party (PLP) is seldom used by Ministers to gauge Party or public opinion. Ministers only trust focus groups and pals, so the MP's role is being reduced to campaigning and transmitting messages from on high down to the faithful.

Legislator

All-powerful in theory, MPs are impotent in practice. Laws cannot be passed without them, yet what the government wants goes through, largely unaltered—even when it should be. Legislation, which takes around 45% of parliamentary time, is the job worst done. Government gives backbenchers ammunition for the defence but prefers them to shut up so as not to consume time. In opposition, effective arguments depend on individual research and help from interested parties. Government backbenchers are on standing committees to vote, not speak.

Controller of the Executive

Most members of the governing party see their role as supporting the executive, however bad its case. Many may grumble, a few may vote against their party and more may abstain. Yet the premium is on maintaining unity. Dissent is never taken to the point of endangering the government. Question Time typifies the problem. The opposition attacks everything, while the government backbenchers rally loyally, even sycophantically, particularly at Prime Minister's Question Time. Select Committees are better: they can examine the intellectual basis of government policy. They provide a forum for detailed questioning of Ministers and access to the specialised information which makes MPs influential.

Trainee Minister

Most MPs want to become Ministers, to hold power and change things, and the House of Commons is the ministerial recruiting and training ground. MPs hope to be noticed. Being in opposition trains shadow Ministers, while 150 juniors and trainees on both sides learn the techniques of the dispatch box, master specialised fields and develop the tactics of debate and giving nothing away. Apprenticeship gives no influence on policy and can be a dead-end street but it is an experience all MPs want.

Austin Mitchell's views on the reforms needed to improve the effectiveness of MPs

- Constituency and London offices with staff and sufficient money to pay for them.
- A career path other than becoming a Minister.
- A greater role in the legislative process.
- A change in the role and power of the Whips.
- Joint parliamentary committees to tap the expertise of the Commons and the Lords.
- Better television coverage to bring current affairs to a wider audience, e.g. a current affairs channel.

led by government and Opposition spokespersons.

The most significant parliamentary procedures from the backbench viewpoint are adjournment debates, questions both oral and written, and Private Members' legislation. These procedures permit backbenchers to represent their constituents, to introduce Bills of their own, and to compete for promotion to the front benches.

Backbenchers in the legislative process

Although the primary function of a legislature might appear to be to legislate, the legislative process in the Commons is dominated by the government of the day. Backbench MPs have very few opportunities to introduce legislation. Rather, they are expected to support or oppose the government's legislative programme which dominates the parliamentary timetable.

Backbenchers are given two procedures by which they may introduce Bills which they have initiated themselves or put forward on behalf of the interests of their constituents or pressure groups to which they are sympathetic—the Private Members' ballot and the 'ten minute' rule. Every parliamentary session a ballot is held which awards twenty backbenchers the opportunity to introduce Bills for which time is allocated on Fridays. The lucky MPs have a fair chance of seeing their proposals enacted—in 1990–91 ten of the Bills introduced in this way reached the statute book. MPs may also introduce Bills under the ten minute rule which permits an MP to explain the purpose of a Bill without any guarantee that space will be available in the parliamentary timetable to take the Bill through the full legislative process.

HOW REPRESENTATIVE ARE OUR MPs?

MPs represent, but how representative are they? Who are the MPs we elect in terms of their social characteristics? The conventional wisdom has long been that MPs have been predominantly 'male, middle class and white'. Nonetheless, there have been changes over the years and the 1997 General Election may have been a significant landmark in gender representation. In the fifty six years since the Commons elected in 1945, the Conservative Party in Parliament has become less elitist in educational terms and the Labour Party has become less working class and more middle class.

Educational background

MPs are highly educated individuals; just over two-thirds of those elected in 1997 had been to university. The 165 Conservative MPs in the 'class of '97' were still distinctive in terms of educational background. Two-thirds had been to public school, though only fifteen (9%) had been to Eton. Over 80% were university graduates, just over half having been to 'Oxbridge' (Oxford or Cambridge). The proportion of Labour MPs with a university education had increased since 1974 from 53% to 66%. However, the Parliamentary Labour Party was less elitist than the Conservative Party in the Commons; only 15% had been to Oxbridge. Only one Labour MP had been educated at Eton though sixty four (16%) had attended (lesser) public schools. The educational profile of Liberal Democrat MPs was almost mid-way between that of their major party rivals.

Occupational background

The occupational backgrounds of the parties in the Commons did differ but all three were almost exclusively middle class. Only fifty six MPs, nearly all Labour, came from manual occupations. The proportion of Labour MPs from manual occupations had fallen from 28% in October 1974 to 13% in 1997. The teaching profession was strongly represented in the PLP with no fewer than 111 having been employed in schools or higher education institutions. The PLP also contained representatives of other public sector workers such as civil servants, local

The Class of 1997: MPs' Education & Occupation

	LABOUR (%)	CONSERVATIVE (%)	LIBERAL DEMOCRATS (%)
Education*			
MPs who attended:			
University	66	81	70
Oxford & Cambridge	15	51	32
Public School	16	66	41
Occupation*			
Percentage of MPs in:			
Professions	45	37	50
Business	9	39	24
Manual Workers	13	1	2

*The educational and occupational categories are not exhaustive and so do not add up to 100%.

Table 4.2   Source: *Times Guide to the House of Commons,* May 1997

government officers and social workers. Thirty Labour MPs and only five Conservative MPs had worked in the civil service or in local government. Conservative MPs were strongly representative of the business community and the professions, especially the law. Over fifty Conservative MPs, compared to sixteen Labour, were company directors or executives. The smaller Liberal Democrat representation in the Commons was closer to Labour in its number of MPs from the professions and closer to the Conservatives in its members from the business community.

Ethnic Representation

The number of candidates from an ethnic minority background almost doubled between 1992 (twenty three) and 1997 (forty two). The Liberal Democrats led the way with nineteen such candidates followed by Labour with thirteen and the Conservatives with ten. Labour's ethnic minority representation increased from five in 1992 to nine in 1997. Glasgow Govan elected the first Muslim MP, Mohammed Sarwar. The only Conservative Asian MP, Nirj Deva, was defeated. Two more MPs of Asian ethnicity, both Labour, were elected in 2001

Mohammed Sarwar MP, elected as the first muslim MP in 1997.

Gender Representation

As noted earlier the 1997 General Election marked an important breakthrough in the representation of women in Parliament. The first woman to sit in the Commons was Nancy Astor in 1919. However, female representation at Westminster remained under 5% of the total membership of the Commons until the 1980s when it started to rise from a low point of only nineteen MPs in 1979.

The trend in the number of women candidates and MPs is illustrated in Table 4.3. There was very little change in the number of women candidates and women MPs between 1945 and 1970 with fewer than 100 candidates and thirty MPs throughout this period. Then the number of women candidates doubled between 1970 and 1979. By 1992 there were over 500 women candidates with the number elected rising to sixty in 1992 and 120 in 1997. However, if 1997 represented a major breakthrough in gender representation, the 2001 Election was characterised by the maintenance of the 1997 achievement rather than a further advance, though the number of women appointed to government office did increase significantly. (See Table 4.4.) The number of women MPs actually fell back by two to 118 in 2001. In spite of the large increase in women MPs in 1997, the proportion of women in the House of Commons, 18%, remains much lower than the proportion of women in the British population as a whole which is just over half (52%).

The considerable variation in the number of women candidates and MPs by party is illustrated in Tables 4.3–4.6. By 2001 Labour was well ahead of the other major British parties with women MPs making up almost a quarter of the Parliamentary Labour Party. Table 4.3 emphasises Labour's greater success in getting women candidates elected to the Commons in 1997 and 2001. There were two reasons for this achievement. Firstly, Labour took positive measures to encourage Constituency Labour Parties (CLPs) to adopt female candidates. The 1993 Labour Conference set an objective of selecting women in at least half of the Labour-held seats where the sitting MP intended to retire at the next election. Labour went even further by encouraging women-only short lists at the candidate selection stage. By early 1996 thirty five CLPs had used this device. However, some disgruntled male Labour members complained to an Industrial Relations Tribunal that such lists contravened the *Sex Discrimination Act*. They argued that being an MP constitutes employment, that the selection of candidates amounts to competing in the job market and that therefore the Act outlawing sex discrimination in em-

	Number of Women Candidates	Number Elected	% of House of Commons	Conservative	Labour	Liberal	Other
Number of Women MPs: Selected Elections 1945–2001							
Election							
1945	87	24	3.8	1	21	1	1
1964	89	28	4.4	11	17	0	0
1979	206	19	3.0	8	11	0	0
1983	276	23	3.5	13	10	0	0
1987	327	41	6.3	17	21	2	1
1992	568	60	9.2	20	37	2	1
1997	NA	120	18.2	13	102	3	2
2001	NA	118	17.9	14	95	5	*4

* 3 Northern Ireland and 1 SNP

Table 4.3   Source: *Times Guide to the House of Commons*

ployment practices should apply to the selection by parties of parliamentary candidates. The Tribunal found in their favour in August 1996. Thereafter women-only short lists were not permitted but the candidates already selected by this method were allowed to stand. Many other CLPs selected women candidates without resorting to women-only short lists. The result in 1997 was that there were 150 women in Labour's total of 641candidates in Great Britain. (Labour, like the other major British parties, put up no candidates in Northern Ireland.) Secondly, Labour's landslide victory meant that no fewer than 64% of Labour's women candidates were elected.

Gender representation did not advance in 2001. The Labour total fell by seven and the SNP total by one; the Conservatives' and Liberal Democrats' totals increased by one and two respectively. The most significant advance in female representation occurred in Northern Ireland where three women were elected—one each for the UDP, the UUP and Sinn Fein. They were the first women elected in Ulster in over quarter of a century.

The main reason for the 2001 standstill in the representation of

WOMEN IN BRITISH GOVERNMENT 1997 AND 2001

| | 1997 | | 2001 | |
	TOTAL	Nº. OF WOMEN	TOTAL	Nº. OF WOMEN
Cabinet	22	5	23	7
Ministers of State	31	6	33	11
Junior Ministers	32	8	34	10
Totals	85	19	90	28

Table 4.4 Source: HM Government listed in *Hansard*

women in the House of Commons is that the major political parties, apart from Labour prior to the 1997 Election, have not got into the habit of 'voluntarily' selecting women candidates to fight winnable seats. Only four of the thirty eight new Labour MPs elected in 2001 were women because the great majority of CLPs where the sitting MP stood down selected male candidates. The 2001 Labour Manifesto included a commitment to introduce legislation "to allow each party to make positive moves to increase the representation of women." The aim here will be to provide "positive moves" which will not suffer the fate of Labour's 'women only' lists in 1996.

The disappointment of the failure to advance the representation of

women in Parliament in 2001 was compensated to some extent by the Prime Minister's appointment of more women to all levels of executive office. (See Table 4.4.) Following the 2001 Election 30% of Cabinet members and of government posts overall were women. The principal promotions were Estelle Morris, once a teacher in a comprehensive school, first elected in 1997, to Secretary of State for Education; Patricia Hewitt as Secretary of State for Trade and Industry; Tessa Jowell as Secretary of State for Culture, Media and Sport; and Hilary Armstrong as Chief Whip. Margaret Beckett, Helen Liddell and Clare Short retained their Cabinet posts. Two of the three law officers are women: Harriet Harman as Solicitor General and Lynda Clarke as Advocate General for Scotland.

GENDER REPRESENTATION IN SCOTLAND

Scotland's Women Candidates & MPs by Party, 2001

	Women Candidates Nº.	%	No. of Women Elected	Success Rate (%)	% of Women MPs in Scottish Party
Labour	15	21	10	66.6	18.2
Conservative	7	9.8	0	0	0
Lib. Dems.	15	21	0	0	0
SNP	13	18	1	7.7	20.0
SSP	24	33.3	0	0	0
Total			11		15.3

Table 4.5 Source: 2001 General Election results reported in the press

Note: The Labour, Conservative and Liberal Democrat Parties each put up seventy one candidates in 2001, not 72. This is because the Speaker, David Martin, Springburn, holds a Glasgow seat where he stood as 'the Speaker'. It is customary for the major parties not to oppose the Speaker. The SNP, and the SSP, did not respect this tradition.

The number of women Scottish MPs remained the same in 2001 at 11 which is 15.2% of Scottish representation at Westminster compared to 23% in the House of Commons as a whole. Labour's total went up by one to ten by virtue of East Lothian CLP selecting Ann Picking to succeed the retiring John Home Robertson who had held the seat since 1978. Maria Fyfe was succeeded in Maryhill by another woman, Ann McKechin. The SNP lost one female MP as a consequence of the decision of five of the six MPs elected in 1997 to stand down from Westminster to concentrate on the Scottish Parliament where they also held seats. Winnie Ewing's daughter, Annabelle Ewing, succeeded Roseanna Cunningham in Perth but her daughter-in-law Margaret Ewing was succeeded in Moray by Angus Robertson. The Liberal Democrats lost their one female MP when Ray Michie was succeeded in Argyll and Bute by Alan Reid.

The SSP selected the highest proportion of women candidates but won no seats. The second party in Scotland in terms of seats won, the Liberal Democrats, did not select women in their winnable seats.

The impact of the new women MPs 1997-2001

The number of women elected to the House of Commons doubled from sixty in 1992 to 120 in 1997. Out of this total, seventy one were new MPs and forty nine were in the 1992 Parliament. Five of the new MPs were Conservative, one was a Liberal Democrat and sixty four were Labour. The media characterised this change as a "seismic shift in politics." The picture of Prime Minister Tony Blair with his 101 women MPs was predictably entitled as "Blair's Babes." The newspaper headlines predicted confidently that this significant intake of women would storm the male citadel of Westminster. With the election of a new Parliament in 2001, the question being asked is, what has been their impact in creating a new, modern House of Commons more sympathetic to the needs of women and family life?

A SIGNIFICANT IMPACT

✔ The attention from the media and the modernisation campaign by women's groups has lifted the profile and influence of women MPs.

✔ Women MPs have obtained important posts in Tony Blair's Cabinet. Until 1997, there had been only one female Prime Minister and eight Cabinet Ministers. In 1997, Tony Blair included five women in his first Cabinet (Ann Taylor, Clare Short, Mo Mowlam, Margaret Beckett and Harriet Harman). Mo Mowlam, for example, held the high-profile post of Northern Ireland Secretary. Kate Hoey entered a predominantly male arena by becoming Minister of Sport in 1999 and, in January 2001, Helen Liddell became the first woman Secretary of State for Scotland.

In the Parliament of 1992–97, Betty Boothroyd became the first woman Speaker of the House, a position she retained until her retirement from the House in 2000.

✔ Eight of the new women who entered Parliament in 1997 received junior ministerial posts.

✔ A Cabinet sub-committee was set up, chaired by Harriet Harman, to discuss women's issues.

✔ A modernisation committee, chaired by Margaret Beckett, was set up and has achieved some reforms.

In November 2000, Parliament agreed to a programme of modernisation which means that all business, debates and voting should be concluded by 10.30 pm save for exceptional circumstances.

A LIMITED IMPACT

✘ One of the first social policy actions of the Labour government in 1997 was to cut extra benefit payments to single parents, the vast majority being women.

✘ Sexist barracking in the Chamber still continues. When Jane Griffiths stood up to deliver her maiden speech, Conservative backbenchers opposite were weighing melons with their hands. According to one woman MP, "they (male MPs) would often not just tackle what she was saying in a debate, they would make remarks about her clothes, her hair and her make-up. You know, all very disgusting."

✘ There are still no crèche facilities (but fourteen bars). Women MPs do not receive maternity leave.

✘ Many male MPs have not yet adjusted to the notion that the House is no longer a 'man's club'. One Labour male backbencher commented about women Labour MPs, "I don't know what they do to the Tories, but, by God, they frighten me."

The assertive and challenging nature of this new group of women MPs partly explains the deplorable behaviour of some male MPs. Margaret Beckett, Leader of the House, made the valid comment, "When I first came here, there was a gentlemanly respect for women members."

✘ The refusal to change the hours of Parliament or to introduce electronic voting creates frustration among many women MPs. However, Margaret Beckett suggests caution and highlights the uniqueness of a politician's working life. She argues that there will never be a total regulation of hours, "Some people say there won't have been any modernisation until the House sits from 9.00 – 5.00, but this will never happen, because politics is a way of life."

Women Candidates & MPs by Party: 1997

Party	No. of Women Candidates	No. of Women Elected	Success Rate (%)	% of Party in Commons
Labour	159	102	64.0	24.4
Conservative	67	13	19.4	7.9
Liberal Democrat	142	3	2.1	6.5
Nationalist	23	2	8.7	20.0
Total	391	120	30.0	18.2

Table 4.6

The euphoria of entering Parliament and becoming part of the historic force to change the male atmosphere of the Commons has evaporated for many of the new intake. Three female MPs, Jenny Jones, Judith Church and Tess Kinghorn, announced, in 2000, that they would not stand again and were leaving politics. Below are the comments of some of the women MPs who make no attempt to hide their contempt for the 'archaic' traditions of the House.

Tess Kinghorn, MP for Gloucester

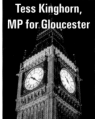

"The whole place is organised for men working in the city and popping into the club for dinner and a vote. We're lecturing Britain on being a modern, dynamic country and we ought to be leading from the front."
(Tess gave birth to twins during her time as an MP)
"We tell the public they have a right to up to forty weeks maternity leave and I started work four days after a Caesarean section because there were things I couldn't pass on."

Julia Brown, MP for Swindon South

(Reprimanded by the Speaker, Betty Boothroyd, for requesting permission to breast-feed in the committee rooms.)
"This is ... a terrible place to work. Women aren't as good at tub-thumping, dispatch box speeches and it's childish. I don't want to be like that."
"For parents of young children, the late hours are a problem because you can't get twenty four hour childcare. Westminster needs to let us give our children all the time and love they deserve while working to make the world a better place for them."

Lorna Fitzsimmons MP for Rochdale

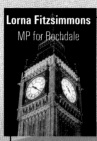

"If you are saying you have to choose between having a family and being an MP, this place will be white, male and middle class for another 700 years. I want to have a family but how can I have a baby without some sort of childcare in the House?"

Jenny Jones MP for Wolverhampton

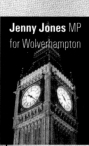

(Left the Commons to pursue her interests in the Council of Europe.)
"What worries me about my own party is the rampant 'laddism'. It's New Labour, new sexism, as far as I can see. You get it in the younger male MPs and the constituency parties. I won't be sorry to leave this place."

Anne Campbell MP for Cambridge

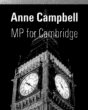

(protested about overlong hours)
"The Tory view is that it's such a privilege to work here, we should put up with everything. I have been told if I can't stand the heat to get out of the kitchen – and by other women! They are always the worst."

In April 2001 The Guardian newspaper asked every MP what they were proudest of achieving since the 1997 Election. More than 200 replied. The Guardian, which had described MPs "as legislators living in an odd obscurity", praised the work of MPs and stated: "What emerges from this sample of a third of all MPs is that notions of public service are hearteningly alive in the House of Commons. It would appear that they do a great deal of good which goes unnoticed.

David Amess MP
Conservative, Southend West

My proudest achievement was to pilot successfully through Parliament the Warm Homes and Energy Conservation Act. This should improve the lives of up to five million people, taking them out of fuel poverty by ensuring their homes are properly insulated.

Harry Barnes MP
Labour, North East Derbyshire

Major aspects of my two Private Member's Bills have been turned by Labour into improved rights for disabled people and a more modern system of electoral registration.

Siobhain McDonald MP
Labour, Mitcham and Morden

London Electricity threatened a local charitable trust, which houses elderly people, with a bill for £60,000 for the installation of central heating. After I had managed to get an adjournment debate and the London Evening Standard had picked up the story, London Electricity backed down and installed the heating for free.

Mohammed Sarwar MP
Labour, Glasgow Govan

The successful campaign I led with shop stewards to win orders for Govan shipyard. We lobbied Cabinet Ministers and campaigned across Scotland, gathering 80,000 signatures on a petition supporting the yard. The government listened and delivered vital work. We fought for Govan and won.

Teddy Taylor MP,
Conservative, Rochford and Southend East

As democracy has declined, the main achievements of MPs today are either as social workers or community interventionists. Among my achievements since 1997 is inviting a young man who was about to commit suicide to give me a week to solve his problems, and contacting him after six days to say those problems had been solved.

Simon Burns MP
Conservative, Chelmsford West

Successfully piloting through Parliament my Private Member's Bill— the Football (Offences & Disorder) Act 1999—to tighten up the law on football hooligans, and pressuring the government to strengthen legislation further by giving the courts the power to withdraw hooligans' passports to prevent them from causing trouble abroad.

43 MPs mention passing legislation—eighteen of introducing their own legislation (Private Members' bills etc.).

27 MPs mention securing a new hospital or health investment (or saving an old hospital from closure).

25 MPs are proud of having been a member of a Select Committee.

19 MPs mention helping to create or safeguard jobs.

18 MPs mention helping individual constituents.

13 MPs mention securing educational investment (school building, nursery places, etc.) for their constituency.

9 MPs mention securing substantial money for regeneration in their constituency.

9 MPs mention securing a new road or road improvement for their constituency.

7 MPs mention helping to establish the Scottish Parliament or the Welsh Assembly.

6 MPs mention supporting the creation of the minimum wage.

5 MPs mention securing peace for Northern Ireland.

4 MPs mention securing flood defences for their constituency.

4 MPs are proud that former Far East POWs received compensation.

Richard Burden MP
Labour, Birmingham Northfield

As the local Labour MP, I am proud to have played a part in saving the Longbridge car plant from closure. More than 20,000 jobs were at stake. The experts said Rover could not be saved. The community came together and we proved them wrong. Under new ownership, MG Rover is now doing well.

PARLIAMENT

What you will learn:

1   The role of the Monarch – the 'Queen in Parliament'.

2   The debate over House of Lords reform.

3   The functions and procedures of the House of Commons.

Parliament is the centrepiece of the British political system. It is in Parliament that the policies proposed by Her Majesty's Government arc debated and then transformed into the law of the land. It is in Parliament that Ministers of the Crown carry out their democratic responsibilities to the elected representatives of the British people. In other words, the British system of government is first and foremost a parliamentary system.

To most people the British 'Parliament' means the elected House of Commons. This is where we see the major party leaders in action. This is where the major legislative powers are located. The MPs we elect sit in the Commons as do most government Ministers. Nonetheless, 'Parliament' goes beyond the Commons; it also includes the House of Lords and the Monarch. Indeed the full formal title of the British legislature is the 'Queen in Parliament'. Under the formal legal provisions of the Constitution, the Monarch and the House of Lords are required to assent to the legislative proposals passed by the Commons before they become the law of the land as Acts of Parliament. The formal powers of the Monarch and the Lords have been deprived of political significance over the centuries. Their use is now governed by conventions of the Constitution although many of the formal powers remain.

The process of parliamentary change is not yet complete. Both the Monarchy and the House of Lords have been subjected to calls for further reform, though for different reasons. The cost of the Monarchy (for example, the controversy in Janu-

The business of Parliament ranges from highly ceremonial occasions such as the State Opening, when the Queen's Speech is read by the Monarch in the House of Lords, to present-day political spectacles such as Prime Minister's Questions in the House of Commons when the leaders of the two major political parties indulge in the modern political equivalent of hand-to-hand combat. 'Parliament' therefore combines long-standing formal traditions associated with the celebrated evolutionary character of British political history and modern political dramas such as Sir Geoffrey Howe's speech in the Commons on 13 November 1990 which led to the resignation of the most powerful Prime Minister of modern times. (See page 91.)

67

ary 1997 about whether to finance a replacement for the royal yacht Britannia) and the behaviour of the present Queen's children and their spouses have, on occasion, put the Monarchy on the front pages of the tabloids. Questions have been raised about the suitability of Prince Charles to succeed to the throne. The Labour government elected in 1997 reformed the composition of the House of Lords, drastically reducing the number of hereditary peers who are allowed to sit in the Upper House.

THE BRITISH CONSTITUTION

A 'Constitution' is a set of rules which lay down the powers and duties of the institutions of government and establish the rights and liberties of citizens.

It is frequently claimed that the British Constitution is unwritten but this is misleading. What is true is that the British Constitution, unlike the American, does not consist of one comprehensive document most of which was laid down at one historical moment (such as 1787 in the case of the USA) and subsequently amended to meet changing circumstances. The American Constitution is to be found at the back of every textbook on American politics. It is impossible to produce a copy of the British Constitution as it has 'evolved' over many centuries. Nevertheless, one can describe its major sources which are

➡ parliamentary statutes,
➡ the common law and
➡ 'conventions'.

Parliamentary Statutes

Acts of Parliament which are 'constitutional' in nature include the *Act of Settlement* of 1700 which requires that the Monarch is a member of the Church of England and the *Parliament Act* of 1911 which limited the legislative powers of the House of Lords. Various *Representation of the People Acts* lay down the law relating to who has and who does not have the right to vote. The controversial

Police Powers Bill, which passed into law immediately before the 1997 General Election increased the powers of the police in relation to arrest and search.

Common Law

Many principles of the Constitution lie in the common law and not in parliamentary statutes. The 'common law' is to be found in judicial decisions, many of which are centuries old. The formal powers of the Monarch are essentially common law powers. Individual rights often exist in the common law.

Conventions

Conventions are accepted constitutional rules which do not have legal status (they are not enforceable by the courts) but which are obeyed because most people believe that they should be obeyed. The best way to explain 'conventions' is to give an example. It is now a constitutional rule that the Prime Minister must be a member of the House of Commons. The reason is that in a democratic age the chief executive politician should be accountable to the people's elected representa-

(continued on page 70)

CONVENTIONS: CHOICE OF SPEAKER

Michael Martin in the Speaker's chair

Conventions are accepted constitutional rules which do not have legal status. For over thirty years convention has dictated that the position of Speaker in the House of Commons should alternate between the two main parties. In October 2000, the House of Commons abandoned this convention when it elected Michael Martin, a Labour MP, to succeed Betty Boothroyd, also a Labour MP, as Speaker. The Prime Minister and most of the Cabinet supported the Conservative (and convention) candidate, Sir George Young. This, ironically, provoked Labour backbenchers to defy the wishes of the government by electing a 'genuine representative' of the working class to the post of Speaker.

The election was also significant as Mr Martin, a former shop steward from Glasgow, became the first Roman Catholic Speaker since the Reformation. In retrospect, the decision by Labour backbenchers to assert their independence over this issue was a perverse one. Political commentators argue that it further weakens Parliament's ability to hold the government to account with its large Labour majority. An 'independent' Speaker can protect the prerogatives of the House of Commons against a dominant government, as Betty Boothroyd did when she complained about the government's habit of telling the media what it intended to do before informing Parliament.

PREROGATIVE FUNCTIONS

The British Monarch still holds some long-standing common law powers known as royal prerogatives. These play a very visible part in British politics even though the Monarch no longer wields such powers personally but must exercise them on the advice of members of the government.

Opening Parliament

The parliamentary year runs from the date when the Queen 'summons' (opens) Parliament until the date when it is 'prorogued' (closed). Parliament actually chooses these dates, the Monarchy simply having a ceremonial function. The reading of the 'Queen's Speech', containing the government's major policy proposals, marks the beginning of the parliamentary year.

Dissolution of Parliament

The maximum term of any Parliament is five years, at the end of which the Monarch declares that Parliament has terminated and gives the date of the general election which has been decided by the Prime Minister. When the Prime Minister decides to go to the country before the five years are up, he/she must request the Monarch to dissolve Parliament before a general election can be held. The Monarch also dissolves Parliament when a government resigns after losing a vote of confidence in the House of Commons.

Appointing the PM

The Monarch still 'appoints' Ministers of the Crown, including the Prime Minister. By convention all Ministers are effectively appointed by the Prime Minister who 'advises' the Monarch of his/her

The Constitutional Monarchy

choices as Foreign Secretary, Chancellor of the Exchequer, Home Secretary etc. The Prime Minister is responsible for these appointments. However, a Prime Minister cannot choose his/her successor because he/she cannot be held responsible after leaving office. The possibility that the Monarch might have a real say in the appointment of the Prime Minister forced the Conservative Party in the 1960s to change its method of selecting its leader to one of election by its MPs.

The Monarch's choice of Prime Minister after an election and when the existing Prime Minister resigns or else dies in office is automatic provided that one party in the House of Commons has a majority. In such circumstances the Monarch 'appoints' the leader of the majority party. However, if there was no majority party in the Commons, the Monarch's choice of a new Prime Minister could be a difficult one. Should proportional representation (PR) be introduced at some future date, elections might routinely fail to produce a majority party in the Commons. In such circumstances

the selection of a Prime Minister supported by a Commons majority could become more difficult and a much more political process. It would be harder to abide by the constitutional principle that the Monarch must not be involved in politics.

The Royal Assent

A Bill which has passed through the required legislative process in the Houses of Parliament must still receive the Royal Assent before it becomes an Act of Parliament. By convention the Monarch grants such assent.

SYMBOLIC FUNCTIONS

Head of State

It is the Monarch rather than the Prime Minister who is the Head of State. Unlike France and the USA, the British Head of State is above party politics.

Head of the Commonwealth

The Monarch heads this multi-racial 'Family of Nations' and in this capacity usually opens Commonwealth Conferences.

The Crown

The Monarch's role as Head of State is reinforced by the fact that Ambassadors, Judges, government Ministers and so on all carry out their normal functions in the name of the Crown.

Awarding Honours

The Monarch can only personally award a few honours, for example the Order of Merit, the Garter and the Thistle. All other honours awarded by the Monarch are, in fact, decided by the government.

tives. In the nineteenth century it was commonplace for Prime Ministers to be members of the House of Lords, but the last Prime Minister in the Lords was Lord Salisbury who left office in 1902. Now politically ambitious members of the House of Lords give up their peerage if they wish to compete for the highest political office in the land. Lord Home gave up his peerage in 1963 when the Conservatives selected him to succeed Harold Macmillan who had resigned as Prime Minister. Sir Alec Douglas-Home was, for a short time, Prime Minister without being a member of either House of Parliament. However, he entered the Commons by winning a by-election in Perthshire in a seat left vacant by an obliging Tory MP.

Some of the most important constitutional rules in Britain take the form of conventions as we shall see in the next chapter when we look at the rules determining the relationship between government and Parliament, such as the conventions of ministerial responsibility. Conventions are also vital to the conduct of modern politics in that they dictate how some common law powers which have great historical significance, are applied in an age when they are no longer appropriate. This applies particularly to the prerogative powers of the Monarch.

THE MONARCHY

The British parliamentary system includes a Constitutional Monarchy which has no effective political power. The royal prerogatives—personal powers which the Monarch still holds such as the power to dissolve Parliament—are, by convention, held by others such as the Prime Minister and other Ministers of the Crown. (See page 69.) They in turn are responsible to an elected House of Commons. Therefore, although he or she carries out certain prerogative functions which suggest some royal influence over political decisions, there is, in practice, no choice available to the Monarch of the day.

In spite of its lack of real political power, the Monarchy's proper role in the British political system has become an emotive and widely debated issue in recent years. Often, people hold strong opinions about the Monarchy, either feeling that it is doing a wonderful job or else questioning the need for it at all in a democratic society in the twenty first century. Some critics even questioned the fitness of Prince Charles as the heir apparent in the light of his 'going public' over his marital problems with Princess Diana. In January 1997 a poll organised by ITV as part of a television programme on the Monarchy found that two-thirds of the British people still supported the existence of a Monarchy. There were intriguing regional variations. Only in Scotland was there a majority supporting the view that the Monarchy had outlived its usefulness.

Do We Need the Monarchy?

Many people feel that the Monarchy should claim its place in history. Since we live in a democratic society where political power lies with our elected representatives rather than with the Monarch, the whole extended Royal Family is seen by many as a drain on the nation's resources.

In September 2000, Demos, a Labour think tank, set out a programme to 'modernise' the Monarchy. Three central reforms were proposed.

- ☞ The removal of all the Monarch's constitutional powers, such as the power to dissolve Parliament and to appoint the Prime Minister.

- ☞ The introduction of a referendum at times of succession to the throne for the public to decide who should be the

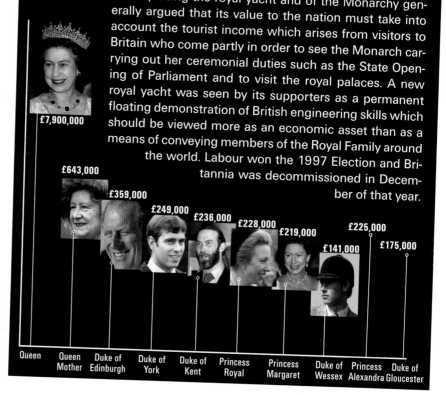

The Civil List The Royal Family receives an annual sum of money (known as the Civil List) from Parliament but, in addition, other expenses are incurred as palaces must be maintained. In 1997 the Conservative government announced that it would fund the building of a replacement for the ageing royal yacht Britannia. This sparked a political controversy. Labour said that it would not contribute public funds to such an enterprise in the first two years after the 1997 General Election which it expected to win. Supporters of replacing the royal yacht and of the Monarchy generally argued that its value to the nation must take into account the tourist income which arises from visitors to Britain who come partly in order to see the Monarch carrying out her ceremonial duties such as the State Opening of Parliament and to visit the royal palaces. A new royal yacht was seen by its supporters as a permanent floating demonstration of British engineering skills which should be viewed more as an economic asset than as a means of conveying members of the Royal Family around the world. Labour won the 1997 Election and Britannia was decommissioned in December of that year.

£7,900,000 — Queen
£643,000 — Queen Mother
£359,000 — Duke of Edinburgh
£249,000 — Duke of York
£236,000 — Duke of Kent
£228,000 — Princess Royal
£219,000 — Princess Margaret
£141,000 — Duke of Wessex
£225,000 — Princess Alexandra
£175,000 — Duke of Gloucester

Monarch (and, by definition, whether there should be a Monarchy).

☞ The disestablishment of the Church of England as the State's official religion, and the removal of the Monarch's role as head of that Church.

In December 2000, *The Guardian* newspaper added its voice when it called for a referendum to be held on whether the Head of State should be elected after the present Queen's death. The newspaper also backed a legal challenge of the *Act of Settlement* in the High Court in London on the grounds that the Act clashes with the *European Human Rights Act*. The Act institutionalises religious discrimination as it states that a Roman Catholic cannot become the Monarch of the United Kingdom. Michael Forsyth, the former Tory Scottish Secretary, described the 300-year-old *Act of Settlement* as "the grubby little secret of the British constitution". The Scottish Parliament has called for this section of the Act to be repealed.

There are those who argue that the Monarch's constitutional role is a more effective safeguard of British democracy than any replacement, such as an elected president, could be. The Monarch's reserve powers may encourage politicians to abide by the constitutional rules of the game. In future, if the first-past-the-post system is replaced by a more proportional system, then the power to appoint Prime Ministers in the event of a hung Parliament will become more important. If this power was taken from the Monarch and given to the Speaker it would lead to partisan decision making. Part of the reason why the Monarch is popular is because the Queen is not a politician and is an independent arbitrator in any political crisis.

THE HOUSE OF LORDS

The House of Lords, like the Monarchy, has survived the transition to democracy because its powers have been cut back and its composition modified to meet democratic expectations. During the nineteenth century the hereditary membership of the Upper House and its equality of power with the Commons were increasingly seen as being incompatible with the gradual extension of the franchise to every citizen, a process which itself took a century to complete. The powers and composition of the House of Lords were reformed in the nineteenth century by constitutional convention and in the twentieth century by statute. (See page 72).

In its 1997 Manifesto, the Labour Party declared that "The House of Lords must be reformed" and promised as a "first stage of reform" to end by statute "the right of hereditary peers to sit and vote in the House of Lords". This objective was duly achieved with the passage of the 1999 *House of Lords Act*.

The constitutional debate over reform of the Lords focuses on two key questions:

1 Does Britain still need a second legislative chamber?

2 If the answer is Yes, what should be the powers, functions and composition of the second chamber in a modern democracy?

There are a few countries, for example New Zealand and Sweden, with unicameral legislatures—only one legislative chamber. Most countries have bicameral legislatures although the relationship between the two legislative chambers varies. The Upper House in the USA, the Senate, is as powerful as the House of Representatives because both are directly elected. As a result the process of making new laws in the American Congress is more difficult.

In most countries the Lower House is stronger than the Upper House. The fact that almost every country in the world has a bicameral legislature explains why most commentators answer 'Yes' to the first question above. Upper chambers, however they are set up, are useful for three main reasons.

➡ Firstly, they can carry out essential tasks which the Lower House does not have the time to perform fully.

➡ Secondly, they can both debate themes of public interest and give representation to sections of public opinion.

➡ A third, more controversial, reason for an upper chamber is that it can act as a constitutional 'fail safe' device against

Reducing the powers of the House of Lords in the twentieth century

The 1911 Parliament Act

In 1909 the Lords rejected the Liberal government's budget which had secured the consent of the Commons. Under the 1911 *Parliament Act*, the Lords could no longer reject financial legislation submitted to it by the Commons. In terms of non-financial legislation, the Act limited the Lords to a delaying power of just over two years.

The 1949 Parliament Act

This Act, which was itself passed under the terms of the 1911 Act against the wishes of the House of Lords, reduced the power of the Lords to delay legislation to one year. One exceptional power was retained by the House of Lords. The Upper House can still veto any Bill which seeks to extend the life of a Parliament beyond the five years currently permitted by statute. This power provides a constitutional safeguard against a Commons majority which might be tempted to behave undemocratically.

The Life Peerages Act 1958

This Act, introduced by a Conservative government, gave prime ministers the power to create peers whose titles die with them. The impact of life peerages has been to reduce Conservative domination of the Lords and to widen its social representation.

The Peerages and Renunciation of Titles Act 1963

This Act gave hereditary peers, who were not allowed to be members of the Commons, the right to renounce their peerage and stand for election to the Lower House. The Labour MP, Tony Benn, campaigned for the right to renounce his peerage when he inherited it on the death of his father, Viscount Stansgate. Since under the law at the time Benn, now Viscount Stansgate, was disqualified from sitting in the Commons, a by-election was held. Benn stood and won but was refused entry to the Commons. In the light of the publicity generated by Benn's crusade, the Conservative government introduced the 1963 Act. In 1963, Lord Home renounced his peerage and became leader of the Conservative Party and Prime Minister after the resignation of Prime Minister Harold Macmillan. In 1994, Lord James Douglas Hamilton, MP for Edinburgh West and Minister of State at the Scottish Office, renounced his peerage when his father, the Duke of Hamilton, died.

The 1999 House of Lords Act

The Act changed the composition of the House of Lords.
- 92 hereditary peers were retained
- the transitional chamber consists of 92 hereditary peers, 527 life peers, 26 bishops and 28 current and former law lords.

At the beginning of the twentieth century the House of Lords was the location for the speech by the Monarch which opened a new session of Parliament.
The various reforms of the Lords over the century did not affect this ceremony. At the beginning of the twenty first century the first event of Parliament's new session is still the Monarch's speech

a lower chamber which might be taken over by political extremists.

FUNCTIONS OF THE HOUSE OF LORDS

Although the House of Lords usually gives way to the will of the House of Commons, many believe that it carries out a number of useful and indispensable functions which are listed below.

Legislation

Most Bills are passed by the Lords before becoming law. However Money Bills, like the Finance Bill which contains the Budget, cannot be rejected by the House of Lords and other Bills may only be held up for about one year. If the House of Lords rejects a Bill which has been passed by the Commons in two consecutive parliamentary sessions, it automatically becomes law even if the Lords rejects it a second time.

The bulk of the government's legislative programme is introduced in the Commons. Consequently, the legislative business of the Lords has to await the passage of Bills in the Lower House. The government does introduce a few Bills in the Lords, usually, though not exclusively, of the non-controversial variety. In session 1990–91, eighteen of the sixty eight Acts of Parliament passed began life in the Upper House. The Lords acts as a cleaning up agency for the government which often introduces amendments in the Lords in response to improvements suggested as Bills pass through the legislative processes in the Commons.

Public Debate

The more leisurely, less confrontational style of the Upper Chamber allows it to function as a debating chamber for issues which are of public interest. The Lords has the time to devote to such debates unlike the Commons. This also applies to the 'tidying up' function of the Lords in respect of govern-

ment legislation. Consequently, the very existence of the Lords is often said to depend on its ability to perform useful tasks which cannot be fitted into the current organisation and timetable of the Commons.

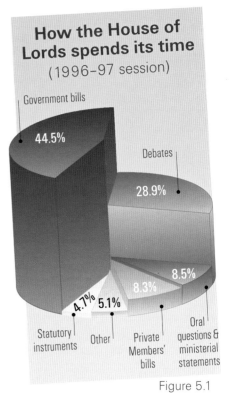

How the House of Lords spends its time (1996–97 session)

Government bills 44.5%
Debates 28.9%
8.5%
8.3%
4.7%
5.1%
Statutory instruments
Other
Private Members' bills
Oral questions & ministerial statements

Figure 5.1

Scrutiny

The primary function of a legislature in a system which is dominated by the executive branch is often said to be to find out and publicise what the government is doing. In this way the executive branch may be held to account for its actions by Parliament and ultimately by the electorate. The Lords possesses the various scrutiny procedures available to the Commons such as Question Time, Select Committees and debate. The Lords makes a special contribution through Select Committees in two areas: European Communities and Science and Technology. The Select Committees on these two topics in the Lords are acknowledged to be more expert than their parallel Committees in the Commons.

Adjudication

The highest court of appeal in Britain is located in the House of Lords, though this function is performed only by the small band of Law Lords. About five to ten of the Law Lords form a judicial committee which considers appeals.

THE HOUSE OF LORDS ACT

It was not until Labour was elected in 1997 with a massive working majority in the Commons that it could set about radically reforming the membership of the Lords, an aim which the Party had tried but failed to achieve in the late 1960s. Labour's Manifesto commitment to abolish the hereditary principle as the major qualification for membership was achieved with the passage of the 1999 *House of Lords Act*. Conservative peers threatened to obstruct the passage of the necessary legislation although they could have done so for only one year. The government prevented a major conflict between Lords and Commons by allowing ninety two hereditary peers to sit in the Lords until it could come up with a scheme for deciding membership of the Lords on a permanent basis. A Royal Commission under Lord Wake-

COMPOSITION OF THE LORDS *before and after* **THE 1999 HOUSE OF LORDS ACT**

	1996	(Women)	2000	(Women)
Lords Spiritual	26		26	
Law Lords	21		28	
Life Peers	398	(16)	549	(107)
Hereditary Peers	762	(65)	92	(4)
Total	1207	(81)	695	(111)

Table 5.1

POLITICAL COMPOSITION of the House of Lords: 1996 & 2000

	1996	2000
Conservative	481	232
Labour	116	200
Liberal Democrat	57	63
Crossbenchers	320	164
Others	111	

Table 5.2

ham was established to make recommendations. The impact of the 1999 *House of Lords Act* is illustrated in Table 5.1.

The 1999 Act left the 'spiritual' and judicial membership of the Lords untouched. The Lords Spiritual are the two Archbishops (Canterbury and York) and twenty four Bishops of the Church of England who represent the relationship between Church and State. The Lords Spiritual are entitled to attend the House of Lords only when they hold Church office. The Law Lords, twenty eight in 2000, enter the Lords by virtue of their appointment to high judicial office. The Law Lords retain their seats until death so there are more Law Lords than are required to perform the judicial function of acting as the highest court of appeal in Britain.

Table 5.1 shows the elimination of the hereditary majority in the Lords—the proportion of hereditary peers fell from 63% in 1996 to 13% in 2000. The decline in hereditary membership also accounts for the rise in the proportion of women in the Lords from 6.7% to 16%. There was also a slight rise in

the proportion of women among life peers.

Table 5.2 illustrates the decline in Conservative support in the Upper House. In 2000 there were still more Conservative than Labour or Liberal Democrat peers but the margin of superiority had been drastically reduced. Neither in 1996 nor in 2000 did the Conservatives enjoy an overall majority in the Lords, partly because of the large numbers of crossbenchers who did not admit to any party allegiance. The current membership of the Lords is much more in accord with Labour's 1997 Manifesto claim that "No one political party should seek a majority in the House of Lords".

The 1999 Act ended the hereditary basis of membership of the House of Lords as part of the legislature but it did not establish an alternative. In the short term, membership consists of life peers, spiritual and law lords and ninety two hereditary peers who were elected by their aristocratic colleagues on a party basis.

The Royal Commission chaired by Lord Wakeham reported in Janu-

(continued on page 76)

THE WAKEHAM COMMISSION

In January 1999 the government set up a Royal Commission on Reform of Britain's Upper House under the chairmanship of Lord Wakeham. It identified four main roles for the reformed Lords.

- ➡ It should bring a range of experience and expertise into the chamber.
- ➡ It should be more representative of modern British society.
- ➡ It should be a formal voice in Parliament for the nations and regions of the United Kingdom.
- ➡ It should work with the House of Commons to hold the executive more effectively to account.

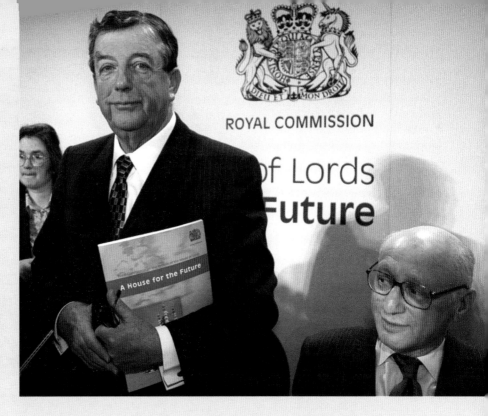

ROYAL COMMISSION

of Lords Future

A House for the Future

The *Economist* magazine criticised Lord Wakeham's proposals as being too timid, especially the Commission's rejection of the voters choosing most Lords. *The Economist* stated:

"It is not beyond the wit of the reformers through staggered elections and longer terms of office, to produce an elected Lords with a different complexion from the Commons. An elected Upper House would, at last, enjoy the democratic legitimacy it needs in order to make full use of these powers."

Opinion was divided within Lord Wakeham's committee. While some members called for a wholly elected second chamber others, supported by senior Labour Cabinet Ministers, argued for it being filled exclusively by appointees. It was also clear that the Prime Minister did not support the creation of elected peers with the right to exercise their democratic legitimacy against Labour's Commons majority. Lord Wakeham would argue that his proposals represented a compromise position.

Much of the year 2000 was spent appointing new Life Peers. In April 2000, for example, thirty three new peers were appointed. In terms of party affiliation, twenty of the

new peers supported Labour, nine supported the Liberal Democrats with four for the Conservatives. Surprisingly, five of the newcomers were hereditary peers who had lost their seats in Autumn 1999 and were brought back to take the Labour Whip. Only eight were women and only one was from an ethnic minority background. The major criterion for selection was not based on a balanced representation of gender and ethnic origin; it was based on rewarding individuals who had contributed to party funds.

The 'interim' House of Lords, even without a 'Conservative majority', still challenges government legislation on bills which are controversial in the country (such as the government's attempt to repeal the law preventing local authorities from 'promoting' homosexuality or the law to privatise the National Air Traffic Service (NATS). The 'interim' House of Lords still respects the Salisbury convention which states that the unelected House should not block a manifesto item which the elected majority in the Commons has passed.

THE WAKEHAM COMMISSION'S MAIN PROPOSALS

- ☞ A new, largely appointed House, comprising between 450 and 550 members.
- ☞ Members would serve for a fixed term of fifteen years rather than for life, as happens at present.
- ☞ A minority of the members to be elected, ranging from 65 to 195.
- ☞ Elected members to be elected on a regional basis, using proportional representation.
- ☞ A minimum of 20% of crossbenchers (no party affiliation) to avoid domination of the new House by any one party.
- ☞ An independent Appointments Commission (rather than the Prime Minister as now) with the responsibility of ensuring balance in terms of political parties, gender and ethnicity.
- ☞ Representatives of other faiths, in addition to Church of England bishops, should be included. The proposal is sixteen Church of England bishops (down from twenty six), five representatives of other Christian denominations in England, five from Christian denominations in Scotland, Wales and Northern Ireland, and five from non-Christian communities.
- ☞ Present powers to be retained but increased power to delay secondary legislation for up to three months by sending it back to the Commons.

75

ary 2000. It suggested three alternative methods of making up the Upper House comprising different combinations of selection and election. Direct election of even a limited proportion of the Upper House carries with it the possibility of members so elected taking any dispute they might have with a majority in the Lower House to the electorate. This is why the simple solution of directly electing the entire House of Lords is not attractive to party leaders in the Commons. On the other hand, an entirely appointed Upper House might command little public respect because it would be regarded as the creature of those who appointed it—mainly the Prime Minister and party leaders in the Commons.

PEOPLE'S PEERS?

In April 2001 the House of Lords welcomed fifteen new 'People's Peers' selected by the Appointments Commission from 3,141 hopefuls. Labour had maintained its pledge of modernising the House of Lords by allowing ordinary members of the public to apply for membership. The only problem was that those appointed were all 'establishment figures'.

The inclusion of seven knights and three professors was attacked as 'a sick joke' by a Labour MP. The appointments created a further political row when the chairperson of the Appointments Commission, Lord Stevenson, insulted the ordinary British public by stating that they were not fit to sit in the Lords. He stated, "… before we were to nominate someone from an ordinary background, with an outstanding achievement in his or her chosen way of life, we would have to be very confident that they would feel comfortable standing up in debates and talking and cutting it". John Cryer, the Labour MP for Hornchurch, stated, "These aren't people's peers, they are members of the elite, just like peers were in the past … (it) is appalling".

WHITE PAPER REFORM OF THE HOUSE OF LORDS

In November 2001, the government published its White Paper which confirmed the removal of the ninety two remaining hereditary peers from the House of Lords. Robin Cook, Leader of the Commons, declared that "These proposals will produce far-reaching reforms … They will put the appointment of independent members outside political patronage". Supporters of a more democratic second chamber were disappointed that only 120 members would be elected by the public and that membership would not be the fifteen years recommended by Wakeham but based on one or two electoral cycles. The government's insistence on shorter terms and reappointment is seen as a move to ensure that the Chamber is dependent on patronage and to strengthen party control.

Criticism was also made that the political appointees would be appointed by the political parties and not by an Independent Appointments Commission. Nick Cohen, in *The Observer* newspaper, declared: "Party donors and trustees will apply, as ever, to the Prime Minister, or to the opposition parties, which, like small-time gangsters, will continue to receive a piece of the action from the capo."

MAIN PROPOSALS

☞ The ninety two hereditary peers to be removed. Members of the Lords will no longer be called peers, but will have ML after their name.

☞ 30% of the new members will be women and there will be a more representatives from ethnic minorities.

☞ 120 directly elected members to represent the nation and regions.

☞ 120 independent members appointed by the Appointments Commission.

☞ A balance of not more than 332 members nominated by the political parties (in proportion to their share of votes in the general election). The final number to be decided by the Appointments Commission.

☞ Number of Bishops to be reduced to sixteen. Rejection of the Wakeham Commission's proposal to include other Christian denominations.

☞ At least twelve Law Lords will remain in the Lords.

☞ Size will be capped at 600 in statute, with an interim House of about 750.

THE HOUSE OF COMMONS

The House of Commons consists of 659 Members of Parliament, each representing a single constituency. At present, Scotland sends seventy two members to Parliament, a figure which will decrease in the future as Scotland is over-represented in the House of Commons.

THE MAJOR FUNCTIONS OF THE HOUSE OF COMMONS

1 Supporting or opposing Her Majesty's Government.
2 Legislating—passing Bills sponsored by the government or by backbench MPs.
3 Scrutinising and publicising the work of the government and thereby influencing what the government does.
4 Representing constituents and expressing the views of the country.

The Chancellor of the Exchequer delivers his Budget speech from the Dispatch Box. This is the Second Reading of the annual Finance Bill.

SUPPORT AND OPPOSE THE GOVERNMENT

The reality of British politics is that the first function of the Commons is not to legislate but to sustain the government. While it is true that the British Constitution assumes that the executive is responsible to the House of Commons (see Chapter 6), the impact of elections and party discipline has been to give the executive more power over the Commons than the other way round. The executive only has this power if the electorate returns a government with a comfortable working majority. Thus the first function of the Labour majority returned in the May 1997 General Election was to maintain the government of Prime Minister Tony Blair.

While Labour MPs have been characterised as being Blair's 'poodles', there has been significant backbench opposition on two occasions. In December 1997 the cut in lone parent benefits led to forty seven Labour MPs voting against the government and to Malcolm Chisholm, a Scottish Office Minister resigning his office. The largest rebellion took place in May 1999, when sixty seven Labour MPs voted against the government over cuts in incapacity benefits.

Supporting the executive is, of course, the primary function of the MPs of the majority party. The first function of MPs of other parties is to oppose the government. Unless there is a government with a very small majority or no majority at all, there are severe limits on the 'Power of Parliament'. Nevertheless, proceedings in the House of Commons above all provide the public with often dramatic information about the behaviour of government and Opposition.

THE LEGISLATIVE PROCESS

Legislative proposals (Bills) may be introduced in either the Commons or the Lords. However, the government introduces most of its legislation in the Commons. Government legislation expressing its policies takes up most of the parliamentary timetable. A limited amount of time is made available for Private Members' legislation. There are six main stages in the legislative process.

1 White Paper
A legislative proposal may begin as a 'White Paper' which contains the government's thinking on the issue in question. White Papers are really written to allow consultation. The government will consider comments from interested parties before firming up its policy by drafting a Bill to be introduced in Parliament.

2 First Reading
The Bill is introduced by its title being read. There is no debate. The Bill is then printed in full and distributed to MPs.

3 Second Reading
A debate is held on the floor of the House on the general principles of the Bill. The debate on government Bills may last from half a day to a two day debate on major Bills such as the Bill to ratify the Maastricht Treaty in 1992. The debate commences with the government Minister responsible for the Bill explaining and defending its contents. The Opposition 'shadow' frontbencher then gives what is usually the case against the Bill. The critical moment is the vote at the end of the debate. If it is rejected, the Bill is withdrawn, although this happened only three times in the twentieth century. In 1986 the Conservative government was defeated at the second reading stage of the Shops Bill (Sunday Trading). Usually the two major parties impose a 'three line Whip' to ensure maximum turnout and therefore victory for the majority governing party. (See the Whip system, page 57.)

4 Committee Stage
The Bill is now referred to a standing legislative committee for a detailed clause-by-clause examination. The committee stage of Bills of constitutional significance such as the European Communities (Amendment) Bill which led to acceptance of the Maastricht Treaty may be taken on the floor of the House of Commons. This is also where the committee stage of money Bills such as the Finance Bill (the budget) takes place, thus allowing all MPs to examine it in detail. Standing committees are made up for each Bill, with usually about twenty MPs sitting on the committee. The parties are represented according to their strength in the Commons as a whole, so the government normally has a majority. Amendments are made, many of which the government accepts because they will improve the Bill.

5 Report Stage
The Bill as amended by the committee is 'reported' back to the House when further amendments, often introduced by the government, are debated and put to the vote.

6 Third Reading
Once again the principles of the Bill, now as amended, are debated. Usually the debate is shorter than it was on the second reading.

If the Bill is approved by the Commons it then goes through a similar process in the House of Lords (unless it is a finance Bill) before receiving the Royal Assent. (The Monarch has not given the Royal Assent personally since the middle of the nineteenth century.) The Bill is now an Act of Parliament and enters the Statute Book as part of the law of the land.

The legislative process takes up about one-third of the time of the Commons, most of it on government Bills. In 1994–95, fifty four Acts of Parliament were passed including nineteen which were introduced in the House of Lords and sixteen by backbench MPs.

SCRUTINISING THE WORK OF GOVERNMENT

As long as the government has a majority it will succeed in getting its legislative proposals accepted. It is often argued that even more important than legislation is subjecting the actions of the government to close examination so that the business of government is in the open. Scrutiny also allows interested voters to judge the performance of the government on the basis of fact rather than guesswork. Such close study gives the House, in spite of its partisan framework, opportunities to 'influence' what the government does. Some commentators use the phrase 'control of the executive' to describe the impact of various scrutiny procedures though that may be going too far except when a government loses its majority or comes close to doing so.

The main scrutiny procedures are debates on the floor of the House, Select Committees and Question Time.

Debates
Debates include the second reading stage of the legislative process, adjournment debates, and substantive motions. Most debates involve the government having to explain, defend and justify both its actions and its policies. The executive is forced to account for its actions to Parliament.

Formally the executive is accountable to Parliament. However, party politics and the electorate usually ensure that the government controls Parliament rather than the other way round. For this reason debates do not normally end up with the government being defeated. In the last three months of the Major government, when it lost its overall Commons majority, the opposition parties attempted to force a general election by bringing motions of confidence before the House. The government survived all of these motions because the Opposition parties could not unite. The Ulster Unionist parties frequently came to the government's rescue.

The opposition parties are allowed twenty days per session (seventeen for the major opposition party and three for the third largest party) when they can choose the issues to be debated. Labour selected the BSE crisis as the topic to be debated on 17 February 1997 in the hope of moving a vote of no confidence against the Agriculture Minister Douglas Hogg. This tactic failed, even though the government no longer had a majority in the House, because Ulster Unionist MPs refused to join in the attempt to bring down the government.

Backbench MPs are given the opportunity to force the government to explain and defend its policies through the procedure of adjournment debates which are held at the close of each parliamentary day. The issues which are chosen for debate by backbenchers often concern matters of interest to their constituents. On 17 December 1996, Mr Peter Kilfoyle (Labour, Liverpool Walton) used the adjournment debate procedure to seek a reopening of the inquiry into the Hillsborough Tragedy in which scores of Liverpool football fans died. The Home Secretary, Michael Howard, replied to the debate and promised to consider all the issues brought up before reaching a decision. On 25 June 2001 Archie Kirkwood, Liberal Democrat MP for Roxburgh and Berwickshire, used the adjournment debate procedure to focus attention on the EU Cod Recovery Programme, a matter of major concern to the fishing industry in Scotland and other parts of Britain. Over-fishing has depleted fish stocks in the Atlantic and in the North Sea forcing EU member states, through the Common Fisheries Policy, to take steps to halt the over-fishing and to encourage the recovery of fish stocks. Kirkwood asked for information about the effectiveness of EU measures to encourage the regeneration of fish stocks, particularly cod. He also expressed

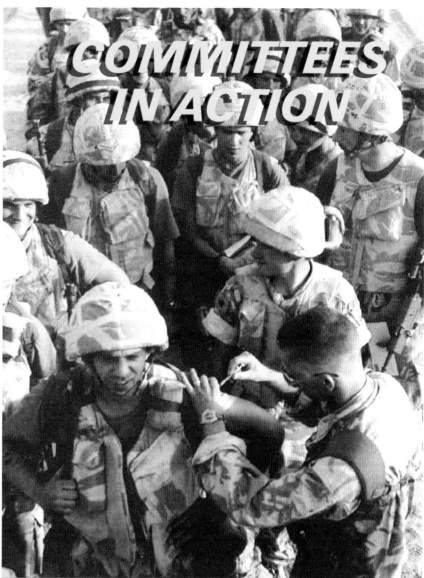

COMMITTEES IN ACTION

Committee proceedings often generate publicity which influences decision making. On 26 February 1997 the Defence Select Committee interviewed Nicholas Soames, the Armed Forces Minister, about Gulf War Syndrome. About 1,200 British soldiers who had fought in the Gulf War in 1990–91 subsequently experienced a wide range of illnesses. Claims were made that their ailments were the result of the use of organophosphate pesticides to combat the effects of insect borne disease and the possibility of Iraq using germ warfare. Government spokespeople, including Mr Soames in the House of Commons, denied that organophosphates had been used. This denial turned out to be untrue. Soames had to explain to the Defence Select Committee that gross errors had been made by civil servants in a particular section of the Ministry of Defence. Labour called for Soames's resignation amid claims that the Minister should have known the facts in spite of misleading advice from civil servants and army doctors. A key participant in the processing of the Defence Committee interview with Soames was a Conservative MP who expressed the opinion that he smelt a cover-up. Soames claimed that there had been "major errors" but no cover-up. The Select Committees often take a bipartisan line in their investigations.

concern that EU policy seemed to favour Spanish fishermen much more then British fishermen.

Question Time

Question Time begins the business of the Commons four days a week. It lasts for about thirty minutes and now plays a dramatic part (proceedings are often televised) in securing the redress of constituents' grievances, representing the people and ensuring the responsibility of the executive to Parliament.

Question Time allows MPs to 'grill' Ministers about their policies and actions. MPs must put questions (of which Ministers are informed in advance); they must not attempt to debate. Questions may be designed to elicit information to embarrass the government (if the question is put by an Opposition MP), or to allow a government Minister to release a particularly favourable piece of information (if the question is put by a government backbencher). Ministerial reputations can be made or lost at Question Time.

One of the first parliamentary actions of the new Labour government in 1997 was to reform 'Prime Minister's Questions'. The Prime Minister had, since 1960, been present to answer questions for fifteen minutes on Tuesdays and Thursdays. Labour decided to schedule 'Prime Minister's Questions' on Wednesdays for the full thirty minutes. Such a move was justified on the grounds that it would permit more in-depth questioning of the Prime Minister and that it would thus improve the ability of the Commons to hold the country's most powerful politician responsible for his/her own actions and also his/her government's actions. Others argued that the reform merely added to the cult of the personality and to the forces making for 'Prime Ministerial government' at the expense of 'Cabinet government'.

The Prime Minister has to account for his government's actions at Question Time in the House of Commons.

Select Committees

Debates on the floor of the House of Commons are grand occasions which, through television and the press may catch the public eye and influence public opinion. A less dramatic but more detailed scrutiny of government is provided by a comprehensive Select Committee system covering the major government departments. This system has been in place in its present form since 1979. These committees have an investigative or supervisory function, which means that they were set up "to examine the expenditure, administration and policy of individual departments". They can look into how public policy is worked out or formulated and also how such policy is implemented or put into practice. The committees have the power to request the presence of both government Ministers and civil servants for questioning and representatives of outside bodies may also be asked to give evidence.

The purpose of the scrutiny function of the Select Committees is twofold: to keep government departments on their toes and to make sure that government is open to the public eye. The parties are represented according to their strength in the House as a whole. Each Committee has about eleven members.

There are currently seventeen departmental Select Committees including one each for Scottish, Welsh and Northern Ireland Affairs. When the Select Committee on Northern Ireland Affairs was established in 1994, it was claimed that the decision was influenced by the government's need to retain the votes of Ulster Unionist MPs when it was in danger of losing the support of Eurosceptic Conservative MPs.

Criticisms of Select Committees

The example on page 79 support the viewpoint that Committees have improved the scrutiny of government. The requirement of government Ministers and their officials to give evidence has often resulted in changes of policy.

Nevertheless, criticism has been made of the Select Committees. A May 2000 report, by the Liaison Committee which coordinates the work of Select Committees highlighted their shortcomings. The Liaison Committee states that the government, "has been too ready and has found it too easy to thwart the work of the Select Committees in holding Ministers to account". The Liaison Committee highlighted two major areas of concern, namely the influence

Select Committee on the Modernisation of the House of Commons

This Committee, chaired by the Leader of the House, was set up in June 1997 with the remit "to consider how the practice and procedures of the House should be modernised and to make recommendations thereon." The Committee was very active and by the summer recess of 2000 it had published twelve reports. Below are some of the changes introduced.

- The wearing of a collapsible opera hat to raise points of order during a division was no longer required.
- The Grand Committee Room off Westminster hall was converted into a mini, or parallel, chamber to discuss issues on which a vote would not be taken.
- Bills to be allowed to be carried over from one session to another

To many of the new Labour (female) MPs who entered the House in 1997, modernisation meant changing the hours of Parliament and the 'male' culture which dominates the Commons. (See page 65). However, addressing MPs in July 2000, Betty Boothroyd, the then Speaker, declared:

"Let us start by remembering that the function of Parliament is to hold the Executive to account ... It is the core task of members ... Furthermore, the House must be prepared to put in the hours necessary to carry out effective examination of the government's legislative programme. If that means long days, or rearrangement of the parliamentary year, so be it. Of course, I have been here long enough to recognise the importance of enabling parliamentarians to enjoy a domestic life; it should not be impossible to meet both objectives—but where there is a clash, the requirements of effective scrutiny and the democratic process must take priority over the convenience of Members."

Commons motion calling for greater independent scrutiny of the executive attracted more than 200 signatures, including 127 from Labour backbenchers.

- With the exception of the Public Accounts Committee, Select Committees suffer from a lack of resources. There are only 107 staff, assisted by 145 part-time specialist advisers, to service twenty five committees.

Government Interference

Further evidence of the arrogance and interference of the executive occurred in July 2001 when the new Chief Whip, Hilary Armstrong, removed two Labour colleagues, Donald Anderson and Gwyneth Dunwoody, as chairpersons of two House of Commons Select Committees. As respective chairpersons of the Foreign Affairs and Transport Committees they were occasionally "troublesome" to the government.

Tony Blair's 'poodles' decided to bite and MPs voted to reinstate Donald Anderson and Gwyneth Dunwoody. This was an embarrassment to Tony Blair and reinforced the "control freakery" allegations against his government. Robin Cook, the Leader of the House accepted that the government had made a mistake and that the action of the MPs was correct.

A Conservative MP, Sir George Young, declared that the Leader of the House, the Cabinet Minister responsible for getting the government's business through should not be the chairperson of the Commons 'modernisation' Committee.

of the party Whips and lack of resources.

- Party Whips play a crucial role in the appointments to the Select Committees and can veto any MP whose opinions do not suit. Frank Field, an independent-minded MP and a former Labour Minister, was unable to get a place on the Public Accounts Committee, and Anne McIntosh, a Conservative MP and a former member of the European Parliament, was denied membership of the European Scrutiny Committee.

The Liaison Committee's proposal to introduce a new method of selection which would ensure that Whips do not interfere in appointments to Select Committees was welcomed by Parliament. A

THE EXECUTIVE

THE TRADITIONAL VIEW

What you will learn:

1 *The organisation of the executive branch.*

2 *The relative powers of the Prime Minister, Cabinet and civil service.*

3 *The conventions of ministerial responsibility.*

4 *The limits of executive power.*

The traditional view of political theory assumes that there are three institutions of government:

→ a legislature to pass laws

→ an executive to implement these laws

→ a judiciary to interpret the meaning of the laws passed by the legislature

This traditional view of government, which puts the legislature at the beginning of the policy making process, is generally consistent with describing the British political system as a parliamentary system. Nevertheless, it has long been inaccurate as a description of the relative powers of the legislature and the executive. It is certainly true that the British executive, led by the Prime Minister and his or her Cabinet colleagues, has the responsibility of implementing the laws passed by Parliament. However, as in most countries today, it is the executive branch of government which is the most powerful source of the policy proposals debated in, and accepted or rejected by, Parliament. It is the executive branch which decides how much to spend on the NHS or whether to hold a referendum on the issue of a common European currency, the 'Euro'. It remains true that Parliament must give its consent to executive proposals, but that consent is rarely withheld. The secret of executive dominance lies in comfortable working majorities supporting the government in the Commons, in strong party discipline and in the 'first-past-the-post' electoral system.

The radical reforms achieved by the post-war Labour government, 1945–51, and by the Thatcher governments in the 1980s and the presidential style of Blair illustrate the considerable strength of the British executive. Nonetheless, there have been significant exceptions to the normal practice of executive dominance. The Labour governments led by Harold Wilson and James Callaghan from 1974 to 1979, and the Conservative government of John Major from 1992 to 1997, were weakened by small and eroding parliamentary majorities and went down to electoral defeat in 1979 and 1997 respectively. The Labour government could not 'deliver' devolution in the 1970s and the Conservative government could not enforce party unity on European issues in the 1990s. The strength of the British executive depends ultimately upon electoral support reflected in parliamentary majorities. When that support weakens, the executive is weakened.

There are three areas of interest in relation to the role of the executive in British politics.

❶ How is power organised and distributed within the executive branch itself? The main issue here is whether Britain now has Prime Ministerial rather than Cabinet government.

❷ What are the constitutional and political relationships between the executive and legislative branches of government? This question focuses attention on the conventions and practices of ministerial responsibility and on the role and status of the civil service.

❸ What changes to the executive branch have followed from membership of the EU and from the introduction of devolution for Scotland and Wales and the reintroduction of a Northern Ireland executive? Some areas of decision making have been removed from the central British executive in Whitehall and Westminster and assigned to executives in Brussels, Edinburgh, Cardiff and Belfast. This aspect of executive government in Britain will be dealt with in Chapters 8 and 9 on Scotland.

The British executive branch divides into three parts:
● the Prime Minister
● the Cabinet and
● the civil service.

The Prime Minister and the Cabinet are politically partisan whereas the civil service is politically neutral and performs administrative tasks.

THE POWERS OF THE PRIME MINISTER

The modern Prime Minister possesses three principal powers:
☛ the power of appointment commonly known as 'patronage'
☛ majority party leader
☛ chairperson of the Cabinet

Power of Appointment

The Prime Minister's power to appoint the members of the Cabinet and a long list of non-Cabinet Ministers is his/her most powerful weapon within the executive branch. The Prime Minister, in taking over the office, decides which politicians to include in the Cabinet and which subsequently to demote or promote. The power to 'hire and fire' includes the right to 'reshuffle' the membership of the Cabinet and government at any time and for whatever reason. The Prime Minister also decides the size of the Cabinet. Prime Ministers are strongly tempted to

THE STRUCTURE OF GOVERNMENT 2001

Below is a description of the several layers of seniority within the Labour government appointed after the General Election in 2001.

PRIME MINISTER AND CABINET (23)
(16 men; 7 women; 21 MPs; 2 Lords)
Almost all are heads of individual government departments
e.g. Stephen Byers, Secretary of State for Transport, Local Government and the Regions

MINISTERS OF STATE (33)
(22 men; 11 women; 26 MPS; 7 Lords)
e.g. 2 Ministers of State within the Health Department
John Hutton: Minister for the NHS and Delivery
Jacqui Smith: Minister for Mental Health and Social Care

LAW OFFICERS (3)
Lord Goldsmith QC, Attorney General
Harriet Harman QC MP Solicitor General
Lynda Clarke QC MP Advocate General for Scotland

JUNIOR MINISTERS (34)
(Parliamentary Secretaries and Under-Secretaries)
(24 men; 10 women: 24 MPs; 10 Lords)
e.g. 3 Under-Secretaries in Health Department
Yvette Cooper Public Health
Lord Hunt Performance and Quality
Hazel Blears Emergency Care and Public Involvement

PARLIAMENTARY PRIVATE SECRETARIES (53 MPS)
(Serve as personal assistants to government Ministers)
(36 men; 17 women)

GOVERNMENT WHIPS
[House of Commons (16) House of Lords (7)]
Government Chief Whip Hilary Armstrong MP Parliamentary Secretary to the Treasury

[142 Labour MPs are government Ministers of various degrees of seniority or on the fringes of government as Whips or Parliamentary Private Secretaries, which leaves about 270 Labour MPs on the back benches.]

exercise such powers when their government is doing badly in the opinion polls and is believed therefore to be in need of a little 'freshening up'.

The power to appoint is known as 'patronage' and extends far beyond the 'hiring and firing' of members of the government. The Prime Minister has the final say in the appointment of life peers, of archbishops and bishops in the Church of England and members of the judiciary. In exercising these appointment powers, the Prime Minister is essentially the heir to the personal prerogative powers of the Monarch who now has no influence over appointments, although newly selected Ministers still have to go to Buckingham Palace to be formally ushered into office by the Monarch of the day.

On 8 June 2001, Robin Cook entered 10 Downing Street as the Foreign Secretary and left as the Leader of the House of Commons. He had been demoted by the Prime Minister in the Cabinet reshuffle following the General Election.

Party Leader

The Prime Minister reaches the top political position in British government by virtue of his/her leadership of the majority party in the House of Commons. Formally the Monarch appoints the Prime Minister. All the parties have made it clear that the Monarch should send for their elected leader when the opportunity to appoint a Prime Minister arises. In effect, then, it is the majority party which chooses the Prime Minister when it elects its leader. Such elections may take place when the party is in office (John Major was elected to replace Margaret Thatcher in November 1990) or in opposition (Tony Blair was elected leader of the Labour Party when John Smith died in 1994).

As leader of the majority party, the Prime Minister enjoys the support of Parliament. As long as there is a working majority in support of the Prime Minister and Cabinet in the Commons, the Prime Minister can rely on Parliament to adopt the policies of his/her government. The loss of such a majority and possible revolt within the governing party can weaken the power of the Prime Minister and government as the Major administration discovered in the run-up to the 1997 Election. John Major had to devote much more time than Margaret Thatcher to the business of party management because of a smaller parliamentary majority.

Cabinet Chairperson

The Prime Minister chairs Cabinet meetings and is the political head of the civil service. As Chairperson of the Cabinet the Prime Minister may, in practice, dominate Cabinet meetings. The Prime Minister usually controls the agenda, leads the discussion and sums up the 'sense' of the meeting. The Prime Minister is the one member of the Cabinet with a 'global' view of the business of government. Cabinet Ministers who are in charge of large government departments are too busy with their own departmental responsibilities to be concerned with the work of other departments. The Prime Minister is a member of the most important Cabinet Committees which do much of the work of the Cabinet. However, there are other powerful Cabinet members who may be able to limit the power of the Prime Minister. It was widely believed that the Chancellor of the Exchequer, Kenneth Clarke, a supporter of monetary union

within the European Union, prevented John Major adopting a more 'Eurosceptic' position in discussions about whether and when, if ever, Britain should accept a common European currency.

The Cabinet

The role of the Cabinet seems to have diminished as both the frequency and the length of its meetings have been reduced. The frequency of Cabinet meetings reached a peak in the early 1950s with over 100 meetings annually; the Cabinet met twice a week and for two hours at a time. By the 1970s the number of meetings was down to sixty annually. Thatcher and Blair further reduced the time Ministers spend in Cabinet. Blair held about forty meetings per year, many of which lasted for an hour or less. (See page 90.)

The Prime Minister's position may also be strengthened by the emergence of an 'Inner Cabinet' which may be formal or informal. This 'Inner Cabinet' may be no more than the leading Departmental Ministers among whom there is an acknowledged 'pecking order'. The Foreign Secretary and the Chancellor of the Exchequer hold the two most most prestigious offices after the Prime Minister. The Deputy Prime Minister may or may not be significant. Mrs Thatcher reluctantly appointed Geoffrey Howe as Leader of the House of Commons and Deputy Prime Minister in 1989 but 'froze' him out of important decision making because they disagreed on the European issue. John Major appointed Michael Heseltine as Deputy Prime Minister in 1995 in order to secure the support of a senior Cabinet member. Michael Heseltine and Kenneth Clarke were in a pro-European Union minority in the Cabinet towards the end of the Major administration when they limited the Prime Minister's options in this policy area which was tearing the Conservative Party apart. John Prescott, the Labour Deputy Prime Minister since 1997, represents the

As chairperson of the Cabinet, the Prime Minister decides what is to be discussed and how often the cabinet will meet. He/She also summarises the view of the cabinet which all government members then have to support in public.

'soul' of the Labour Party and its links to its working-class roots.

Cabinet Committees

Before the full Cabinet meets to discuss the most significant issues facing the government, preliminary decisions will have been reached in Cabinet committees. The Cabinet often can do little other than formally approve the decisions of these committees which are composed of the departmental Ministers who are the 'experts' on the subject matter dealt with in committee. In 2000 there were twenty four standing (permanent) and seven ad hoc (temporary) Cabinet committees. Of the twenty four standing committees, the Prime Minister and the Chancellor of the Exchequer (Gordon Brown) each chaired five, the Deputy Prime Minister (John Prescott) and the Lord Chancellor (Lord Irvine) each chaired four. The Prime Minister chaired committees dealing with sensitive political and constitutional issues such as Northern Ireland, Constitutional Reform, consultation with the Liberal Democrats, and Defence and Overseas themes. The Chancellor chaired committees dealing with economic issues such as welfare to work, produc-

tivity and competitiveness, energy and public expenditure.

The Conventions of Ministerial Responsibility

The convention of collective responsibility has two elements.

- The first relates to the executive branch. Members of the government, no matter how low they are in the pecking order, for instance Parliamentary Private Secretaries, must support publicly the policies arrived at in Cabinet or else they must resign.

- The second element relates to the links between the executive and the legislature by requiring that the executive resigns if it is defeated on a motion of confidence in the House of Commons. The Major government had some narrow escapes on issues such as the Scott Report (see page 93) but survived to call an election in May 1997.

Cabinet Ministers are, in theory, bound by the convention of collective ministerial responsibility. Every Minister is considered to have agreed to Cabinet decisions, even those which are not unanimous. Cabinet Ministers and all

other members of the government not of Cabinet rank are bound by collective responsibility to support the agreed policies in public, even if they voted against the decision. If they publicly disagree with the decision, they must resign. In 1986 Michael Heseltine, then Secretary of State for Defence in the Thatcher administration, resigned when he disagreed with the government's policy on the 'Westland Affair'. Mrs Thatcher refused to allow a decision reached by a Cabinet Committee, with which Heseltine disagreed, to be discussed in the full Cabinet. Heseltine resigned because he would not support the decision in public and because he objected to the Prime Minister's handling of the matter in Cabinet. (See the Downfall of Margaret Thatcher, page 91.)

Ministers are also individually responsible to Parliament for their own actions and for the work of their departments. This means giving Parliament full information about the policies and actions of the executive branch on occasions like Question Time and during debates. Over the years the extent of individual responsibility has been narrowed as it has become clear that Ministers are personally acquainted with only a small proportion of departmental decisions and actions. Ministers remain responsible for the major policies of their departments, although collective responsibility may take over in order to shield Ministers who are under attack. When Lord Carrington resigned as Foreign Secretary over the events leading up to the Falklands War, Mrs Thatcher tried to persuade him to carry on. The Prime Minister was prepared to protect her Foreign Secretary by, in effect, assuming that the entire Cabinet was responsible for those events.

The extent of ministerial responsibility is illustrated in two case studies on pages 93 and 94.

The conventions of ministerial responsibility have a crucial impact on British politics. Because a government could be forced to resign if defeated on a major issue in the House of Commons, the government's backbenchers will normally be loyal in the voting lobbies in order to prevent the opposition from taking over the powers of government. Similarly, opposition MPs usually toe the party line in order to put maximum pressure on the government. As a consequence, the constitutional rules of ministerial responsibility tend to produce centralised and disciplined political parties, especially when two parties predominate.

The Power of Dissolution

The Prime Minister enjoys other powers over the the Cabinet and his/her party. The Prime Minister alone decides when to ask the Monarch to dissolve Parliament and, consequently, decides the date of the general election. The Prime Minister is, by convention, exercising one of the prerogative powers of the Monarch and it can be used to hold general elections whenever opinion polls suggest that the government will be re-elected. For this reason Margaret Thatcher successfully called general elections in 1983 and 1987 with one year of the five-year Parliaments still to run. John Major, on the other hand, had to wait out

the full five-year term before holding elections in 1992 and 1997. James Callaghan, Labour Prime Minister from 1977 to 1979 was criticised for not calling a general election in the autumn of 1978 when Labour might have won. Instead Callaghan waited in the expectation that Labour would do even better in the spring or summer of 1979. However, the 'winter of discontent' intervened and Labour was forced into an election in June 1979 which produced the first of three Conservative election victories under the leadership of Margaret Thatcher.

The power to dissolve Parliament is regarded by some as a weapon which may be used to discipline rebellious elements within the ranks of the governing party. However, the threat to call an election may not be credible if the government is behind in the opinion polls. Not long after the 1992 Election, when the Conservative Party was trailing behind Labour in the opinion polls, John Major threatened to call a general election if the Tories did not back his stance on the Maastricht Treaty. This threat could obviously not be carried out and merely served to make Mr Major look weak, especially when he had to withdraw the threat, stating that he had been misunderstood.

The last two years of Mr Major's reign as Prime Minister and as Tory leader were plagued by internal Party dissension and criticism of his leadership. In 1995, in an effort to reassert his control over the Party, Major resigned as Party Leader but not as Prime Minister. He could not call an election because the polls suggested that the Conservative government would have been badly defeated. Major was opposed by John Redwood, who had been Secretary of State for Wales until he resigned to fight for the leadership of the Conservative Party. Major won the election by 218 votes to 89. This result was interpreted as both a vote of confidence in Major and as an indication that the right wing of the Party was unhappy with

Major's leadership and his stance on European Union issues.

A DOMINANT EXECUTIVE

British government used to be labelled 'Cabinet government'. The Prime Minister's position relative to the Cabinet was described by a famous phrase 'primus inter pares'—first among equals. This suggested that in spite of the Prime Minister enjoying powers denied to other Cabinet Ministers, such as the power of patronage and appointment, the Cabinet reached its decisions collectively on a majority basis, even though the Prime Minister summed up the sense of the meeting. The phrase suggested that the Prime Minister's status as First Minister was of a formal nature with little extra power attached. During the course of the twentieth century, however, the Prime Minister became more powerful so the holder of this office is no longer just 'first among equals'. Indeed, many commentators claim that British government should now be labelled 'Prime Ministerial government' to indicate where the decisive policy making power usually lies.

THE BLAIR PREMIERSHIP 1997-2001

Assessments of Blair's first premiership have concentrated on his alleged 'presidential' style, his relationship with Gordon Brown and the 'control freakery' of his administration. It is significant that Blair regarded Major as a weak Prime Minister who failed to give leadership or to control his own party.

Control from the Centre

Blair came to office with a total lack of experience of government but with a huge parliamentary majority. A major feature of his office has been his determination to by-pass the traditional sources of influence such as senior civil servants in Whitehall. This was achieved through the appoint-

(continued on page 88)

THE PRIME MINISTER'S POWER BASE

There is no Prime Minister's department as the Prime Minister does not have a ministry to run. There is a Prime Minister's office which includes political advisers as well as permanent civil servants. Over the years the number of staff employed in the Prime Minister`s office has increased.

The Cabinet Office has traditionally provided support to the Prime Minister. However under Tony Blair it has developed an even closer relationship with the Prime Minister's office to such an extent that the Cabinet Office is now an extension of the Prime Minister's office. The Social Exclusion Unit and the Performance and Innovation Unit created by the Prime Minister are housed in the Cabinet Office and they report to Tony Blair through Richard Wilson, Cabinet Secretary.

In an answer to a question in 1998 on the future of the Cabinet Office, the Prime Minister gave the following reply, "The role of the Cabinet Office has traditionally been to help the Prime Minister and the government as a whole to reach collective decisions on government policy. Since the election, the three principal parts of the centre —my own office, the Cabinet Office and the Treasury—have worked closely and effectively together, and with other Departments, to take forward the government's comprehensive and ambitious policy agenda."

THE PRIME MINISTER'S OFFICE

The Private Office
The Prime Minister's private office deals with Tony Blair's official engagements and his relationship with Parliament and government departments. The office is mainly staffed by permanent civil ser-vants and convention requires that the head of the private office, the Principal Private Secretary is a civil servant.
A key individual within the office is Jonathan Powell, appointed by Blair as his Chief of Staff. His role is to act as 'gatekeeper'— deciding who should have access to the Prime Minister. The private office is also responsible for filtering the flow of information received from all government Departments.

The Political Unit
The Prime Minister's Political Unit, staffed by Party members, is responsible for maintaining close links with Party members, constituencies and MPs. It creates a bridge between the Prime Minister and his Party.

The Policy Unit
This Unit consists of outside specialists brought in as temporary civil servants to advise the Prime Minister on specific government policy. Head (Director) of the Policy Unit is David Miliband. It offers the Prime Minister an alternative source of policy advice. Staff in the Policy Unit see Cabinet papers and attend Cabinet committees.

The Press Office
The Prime Minister's press office, as the name suggests, looks after the Prime Minister's relations with the media. Under Blair and his Chief Press Secretary, Alistair Campbell, presentation of policy assumed great importance during New Labour's first term in office.

The Strategic Communications Unit
Evidence of the importance of 'spin' was reinforced by the creation of the Strategic Communications Unit serviced by a staff of six (a mixture of civil servants and political advisers). According to *The Guardian* "the unit is intended to spot pitfalls. Coordinating ministerial announcements and thinking well ahead, keeping the big picture in mind."

ment of special advisers, who doubled in number to seventy four over the 1997–99 period. Half the increase took place in 10 Downing Street where the number of special advisers rose from eight to twenty five. (See role of Special Advisers.)

Much was made, especially in Parliament, of an order in council allowing special advisers Jonathan Powell, Chief of Staff, and Alistair Campbell, Chief Press Secretary, to 'manage' career civil servants in the No. 10 private office and press office respectively. Sir Richard Wilson, Cabinet Secretary, denied that this was harmful to the 'independence' of senior civil servants: "I do not think that the senior civil service of 3,700 people is in danger of being swamped by seventy-odd special advisers."

While much is made of the 'control freakery' of Tony Blair and his presidential style, it is based in part on a power sharing agreement with Gordon Brown, his Chancellor of the Exchequer. (See page 89.) One must therefore separate the dominance of the executive from the limitation of Blair's domestic authority, especially in economic affairs. The Blair/Brown administration, through the triennial comprehensive spending review (CSR), tightly controls the direction of spending of all Departments. As David Lipsey puts it in his book *The Secret Treasury*:

"The CSR was a triumph for a strong Prime Minister and a strong Chancellor working together. Nothing illustrates this more clearly than the brutality of its execution. The two

just called in Ministers and told them how much they were getting. There was no appeal."

The Role of Special Advisers

In July 2001 the government published a list of its seventy one special advisers who provide political and strategic advice to Ministers. 10 Downing Street has the services of twenty six special advisers and most Cabinet Ministers have two. Significantly the Treasury, the power base of Gordon Brown, has the greatest number of special advisers after the Prime Minister's office. Brown's chief special adviser is Ed Balls who has been accused of trying to direct the government's policy on entry into Europe during its second administration.

(continued on page 90)

STYLE OF LEADERSHIP

"People have to know that we run from the centre and govern from the centre."

Blair (1997)

"Goodbye Cabinet Government. Welcome the Blair Presidency. The Ministerial Code sets out in a formal code of conduct, to be obeyed by all Ministers, the biggest centralisation of power see in Whitehall in peacetime."

Peter Riddell, Times Newspaper (1997)

"You have got to run an efficient government and you have got to run an effective centre. I want to make sure we are driving (the programme) through. I just think you live with this. You are either a strong Prime Minister, in which case you are a control freak or you are a weak Prime Minister ... and I think in the end I know what I would like to be accused of."

Blair (1999)

"The idea that the Prime Minister is 'primus inter pares' is wrong. The Prime Minister is not pares. He's way above that; like Caesar, he bestrides his world like a collossus."

Senior Whitehall figure, shortly after the end of the Balkans War (1999)

"We do not simply exist to govern. We are there to transform."

Blair (2000)

CABINET DECISION MAKING

"Rather than refer an issue to a Cabinet committee, he sees a problem and sets up a group and he is not very interested in their turf and titles."

Senior civil servant (1999)

"The old days of Labour governments, where, I think the meetings occasionally went on for two days and you had a show of hands at the end of it, well, I mean, I shudder to think what would happen if we were running it like that."

Blair speaking on Television (2000)

"You may see a change from a feudal system of barons to a more Napoleonic system."

Blair insider (1997)

"The Cabinet is no longer a central organ of government. Cabinet Ministers still matter as heads of Departments, but Cabinet meetings no longer really count. The system is no longer collective. It is a centralised system directed by 10 Downing Street."

Peter Hennessy (2001)

RELATIONSHIP WITH GORDON BROWN

"It is clear that Tony Blair entered 10 Downing Street with the intention of maintaining a 'command premiership' bypassing traditional government structures and working through his inner group of advisers. Blair also made a pact with his greatest Party rival Gordon Brown which enabled Blair to implement a centre driven administration. For the deal at the heart of the Blair style was that a command premier would operate alongside a command Chancellor licensed to dominate across a wide range of economic and domestic policy."

Peter Hennessy The Prime Minister (2000)

"Gordon Brown's ambition was fierce but could only be advanced through loyalty."

John Rentoul Tony Blair–Prime Minister (2001)

COMMENTARY ON THE BLAIR ADMINISTRATION

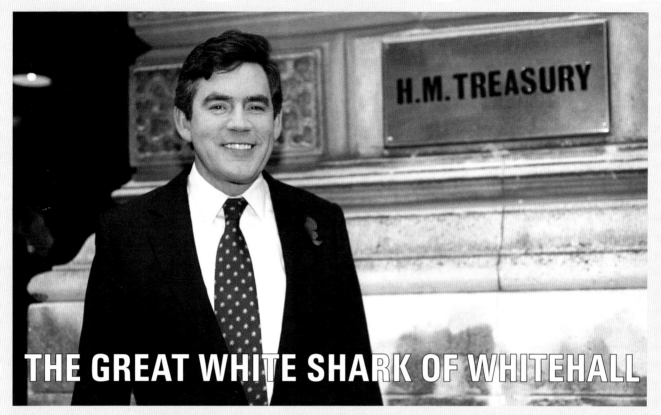

THE GREAT WHITE SHARK OF WHITEHALL

FORGET about Tony Blair's 'presidential' powers. It is HM Treasury that now dominates government. Its role should be diminished argues Stuart Weir.

One of the abiding images of New Labour in power, as described in Andrew Rawnsley's compelling book, is of Gordon Brown being driven away from the Blackpool Party Conference in 1998 and heckling Tony Blair's conference speech as it came over the car radio. "The New Deal is up and running." ("He didn't want that.") "What Tory government would have introduced the first statutory minimum wage?" ("He opposed that.") "The working families' tax credit ..." ("He fought that.") Downing Street wrote the incident off as just another bubble in the froth of Rawnsley's journalism. Froth is pretty insubstantial stuff, but it is also often a sign of agitation below. And so it has been for the relationship between Brown, Blair

and Peter Mandelson. Mandelson's resignation undoubtedly strengthens Brown. But what should concern us is the power of Her Majesty's Treasury, over which he presides. There has been a major power shift within government. The list of achievements that Blair was presenting to Party delegates belonged largely to Brown and the Treasury. Political analysts have concentrated on Blair's creation of a 'secret' Prime Minister's department. But the Treasury, under Brown, has taken on a dominant policy role in Whitehall which is not fully appreciated. It is the great white shark of government, a subterranean but mysterious presence that everyone fears. Peter Kemp, formerly a top Treasury civil servant, has argued that it is taking "a position of power which is dangerous in our society". Its role has increased, is increasing, and ought to be diminished.

It was Sir Terry (now Lord) Burns, Permanent Secretary

until he was cast out by Brown in 1998, who set the Treasury on its new course. He decided that it should stop simply being a finance ministry and move into the wider policy domain across Whitehall. The old-style spending rounds began to evolve into the new fundamental expenditure reviews. The Treasury began to concern itself not just with what Departments got but with how they spent it. Brown has taken this process much further through the new public service agreements (PSAs) with spending Departments. These are supposed to drive through improved services and policies by negotiating commitments and targets with departmental Ministers and officials. The Treasury likes to present this as a 'shared' process. But the Treasury naturally negotiates from a position of strength. First, it determines government priorities, controls the money and decides how much should be spent. Second, it now plays an active role in

creating the departmental policies it pays for. Its public services directorate deploys roughly 200 staff in fifteen spending teams and employs 250 officials in all across the Treasury.

There is no doubt that there has long been a power vacuum at the centre of UK government. There is a genuine need for "joined-up government" in the loose federation that is Whitehall. Blair has been desperately seeking to strengthen prime ministerial control at the centre but, he has very limited executive resources. It is the Treasury under Brown and the present Permanent Secretary, Sir Andrew Turnbull, that have filled the vacuum and become the powerhouse of the British executive. Forget about fears that Blair may assume presidential powers. For the time being, the Treasury steers Whitehall's course and the Cabinet Office rearranges the deck chairs.

Adapted from *The New Statesman* 5.2.01

Andrew Tyrie a Tory MP (and former special adviser) claimed that "they (advisers) are effectively unelected Ministers. They are the people who are really running the country and I don't think that is acceptable."

The Cabinet under Blair

Senior Ministers have privately complained about feeling that they are on the outside and not involved in collective decision making. The change in the role of the Cabinet was made clear in the first week of the Blair government. The crucial decision to transfer responsibility for setting interest rates from the Chancellor/Prime Minister to the Bank of England was made before the Cabinet had even met for the first time.

Cabinet meetings seldom last longer than an hour; a thirty minute meeting just before the 1997 recess may well have been a post-war record. The agenda tends to be informal merely standing items grouped under domestic, foreign and parliamentary decisions. It was not surprising, therefore, that the Cabinet seldom engaged in challenging debate over policy. The postponement of joining the Euro, the reduction of the lone parent benefit and the decision over hereditary peers were not decided at Cabinet meetings. The Millenium Dome was discussed at Cabinet but a decision was pushed through despite the misgivings of the majority of Cabinet members.

Revised Ministerial Code 1997
The publication of the Revised Ministerial Code and its paragraph 88 order(see box), reinforced Blair's centralisation of power and his control over Cabinet colleagues. For Peter Preston of *The Guardian*, adherence to 'Paragraph 88' would reduce any Minister to a "diminished driv-

> **MINISTERIAL CODE PARAGRAPH 88**
> In order to ensure the effective presentation of government policy, all major interviews and media appearances, both print and broadcast, should be agreed with the N°· 10 press office before any commitments are entered into. The policy content of all major speeches, press releases and new policy initiatives should be cleared in good time with the N°· 10 private office.

elling figure" and Peter Riddell in *The Times*, declared "Goodbye Cabinet Government, Welcome Blair Presidency".

Bilateral Meetings

Instead of conducting business at Cabinet meetings or even in Cabinet Committees, Blair prefered "Bilaterals"—two-sided meetings —with his Secretaries of State. While this gave Ministers direct access to 10 Downing Street in matters relating to their own Departments, it ensured that they would not have an overview of strategic government policy or an insight into other Department policies and performance.

In domestic/economic affairs the bilateral model equated with 10 Downing Street and the Treasury agreeing first on policy and performance especially through the CSR agreements. (See page 88.)

LIMITING THE PRIME MINISTER'S POWER

During the twentieth century, Prime Ministers gradually acquired more influence over the decisions which are made by the government. However, the Prime Minister's powers are controlled in various ways.

Powerful Colleagues

The Prime Minister's power in the Cabinet is limited by certain considerations. Theoretically a Prime Minister can promote to Ministerial rank whichever MPs he/she chooses. However, those who display the greatest ability really must be included in the government, even though some of them may represent views to the right or the left of the Prime Minister's own position. Senior party members are more or less guaranteed a Cabinet place, though the Prime Minister may not always give them the government post each desires. It is generally assumed that it is safer for the Prime Minister to include potential rivals in the Cabinet rather than to leave them

(continued on page 92)

Gordon Brown, Chancellor of the Exchequer, has very strong support within the Labour Party which would make it very difficult for the Prime Minister to sack him.

THE DOWNFALL OF MARGARET THATCHER

THE resignation of Mrs Thatcher on 28 November 1990 after more than eleven years in office indicates that there can be limits to the tenure of even the most powerful of Prime Ministers. Her downfall was caused by a combination of factors:

● She had made enemies in the Conservative Party, particularly Sir Geoffrey Howe and Michael Heseltine.

● The provision of a constitutional mechanism for challenging Party leaders.

● The belief of many Conservative MPs that they would not be re-elected if Mrs Thatcher remained as leader.

● The highly emotive influence of the European issue within the Conservative Party.

The crucial element in the story of Mrs Thatcher's exit was provided by Sir Geoffrey Howe, Leader of the House of Commons and Deputy Prime Minister. Howe resigned from the Cabinet on 1 November 1990 due to personal and policy factors.

The next crucial step was Howe's resignation speech in the House of Commons on 13 November. Howe argued that the Thatcher style of abrasive diplomacy would result in Britain, which had joined the European Community fourteen years after its foundation, "being once again shut out" when the Community made vital decisions.

Howe's dramatic speech, which was televised and which dominated the newspaper headlines the following day, gave Heseltine his chance. (He had resigned from the government in 1986 as a protest against Thatcher's autocratic control of the Cabinet.) He announced his candidacy for the Conservative leadership on 14 November. The first ballot was held on 19 November. The Prime Minister, who was in Paris, 'won' by 204 votes to 152 with sixteen Conservative MPs not voting. The margin of victory was 52—two votes short of an outright victory.

In the second ballot an overall majority was required. Heseltine was certainly going to stand. Who would be running against him? The Prime Minister immediately announced her intention to stand. On 22 November came the dramatic announcement that Mrs Thatcher was withdrawing from the contest. Why did she take the decision which brought her 'reign' to an end?

Mrs Thatcher consulted with her Cabinet colleagues. If they had been unanimous in encouraging her to contest the second ballot she would have done so, but most of them told her she would lose to Heseltine in the second ballot. This advice proved to be crucial. Ironically, the collective decision making model of Cabinet government prevailed; the Prime Minister gave way to the majority view. She stood down, releasing Major and Hurd to take part in the contest. On 2 December Major won by 185 votes to Heseltine's 131 and Hurd's

Mrs Thatcher leaves Downing Street for the last time. Although she was a very successful Prime Minister, she was removed by her party's MPs when they felt that she had become a liability.

56 votes. Heseltine did not force a third ballot, preferring to stand down and guarantee himself an important post in the Major Cabinet.

Mr Major's victory was based on several factors:

● Major was Thatcher's preference among the contenders because he was closest to her on policy. Major appealed to many Conservatives because he was perceived as being 'Thatcherite' in policy but not in style. Many Conservatives voting against the Prime Minister were rejecting Thatcher the individual but not the policy side of 'Thatcherism'.

● Major attracted more support than his rivals from both the Thatcher Cabinet and the many Conservative constituency associations which had not been in favour of Heseltine's challenge to the Prime Minister. Thatcher might have survived if the constituency associations had had a vote in the leadership contest.

● Unlike Heseltine, Major did not suffer from the disadvantage of having divided the Party. Consequently, Major was much more likely to be able to unite the Party in time to fight the next election.

The Prime Minister commands attention from the media and so can talk to a mass audience. No other Minister can gain such media attention.

The Power of the Media

Media coverage may strengthen or weaken the Prime Minister's position. The Prime Minister's personal popularity often protects him/her from his/her leading rivals. In spite of critical press comment, John Major remained more popular in the opinion polls than his Party as a whole. Media comments suggested that his most dangerous rival was Kenneth Clarke, the Chancellor of the Exchequer. However, Clarke was even more unpopular than Major with the Tory right wing because the Chancellor was perceived as being a Europhile rather than a Eurosceptic.

on the back benches where they could become the focus of opposition if and when public opinion turns against the government. The convention of collective responsibility forces Cabinet Ministers to support all government policies in public and prohibits the voicing of dissent.

Party Support

Without party backing, the Prime Minister would not be party leader and therefore would not be Prime Minister. Party leaders are subject to re-election annually, though challengers have been rare. Mrs Thatcher became Conservative leader by challenging and defeating Edward Heath in 1975 after the Party had lost the October 1974 General Election. She was challenged on two occasions during her almost sixteen years as Conservative Party leader. The first challenge in 1988 did not pose a serious threat to her leadership, but the second challenge in 1990 led to her stepping down as leader and as Prime Minister. (See page 91.)

The Power of the Electorate

The electorate also exercises some control over the Prime Minister whose party must seek re-election at least every five years. An unpopular party will not be re-elected. Prime Ministers who lose general elections may resign as party leader shortly afterwards (Home in 1964, Callaghan in 1979 and Major in 1997) or they might, (like Heath after the 1974 Elections) lose a party leadership election. Wilson, on the other hand, survived Labour's loss in the 1970 General Election. Most commentators believe that Mrs Thatcher, first elected to 10 Downing Street in 1979, grew more powerful after her re-election in both 1983 and 1987. Her failure to retain the Conservative Party leadership in the 1990 contest was widely attributed to a belief among Tory MPs that the Party would not win the next election if she remained as leader.

The Opposition

The second largest party in Parliament is officially recognised as 'Her Majesty's Loyal Opposition'. Assuming the government has a healthy majority, the opposition has little chance of outvoting it in the House. In terms of providing a check on the government's actions, its powers are very restricted and, in fact, the House of Lords (pages 71–76) and pressure group activity (Chapter 7) have far greater influence.

The role of the opposition parties is a frustrating one. All that they can really do is emphasise the worth of their own policies, attempt to discredit government policies and actions, and 'score points' in the Commons. The main opposition party offers an alternative range of policies and can embark on a long-term campaign of swaying the electorate.

THE CIVIL SERVICE

The executive branch in Britain comprises a political element, who are the elected politicians, and a non-political or neutral administrative element, the civil servants. Theoretically, government Ministers make the policy decisions and civil servants administer those decisions. Constitutionally, Ministers are responsible to Parliament for the policies and administration of their Departments. Politicians are elected on the basis of policy promises which should determine their aims and their approach to the policy issues and problems arising during their term in political office. Civil servants, who are permanent appointees, are expected to be anonymous, being neither 'named nor blamed' in public for departmental successes and failures. They provide Ministers with the advice they need to formulate and supervise the administration of policy decisions.

The dividing line between Ministers and civil servants is difficult to maintain in practice. Civil servants may remain in the same department for many years whereas Ministers, on average, rarely serve more than two years in one department. Accordingly, civil servants acquire an expertise in the types of problems confronting the Minister which may give the bureaucrat considerable influence in the departmental decision making process.

Historically, fears have been expressed that the civil service could frustrate the will of both individual Ministers and entire governments. Senior civil servants are likely to have been educated at Oxford or Cambridge, and they constitute a social elite in strategic positions within the government. However, such fears have not been realised. The radical policy reforms introduced by the 1945–51 Labour government and by the Conservative governments of the 1980s suggest strongly that a determined government should have little difficulty in bending the civil service to its will. The same is true of many individual Ministers.

Civil Service reform

Reform of the civil service has been a consistent governmental objective since the 1960s. Britain's weak economic performance relative to many international competitors gave rise to the view that the efficiency of the government machine could and should be improved. One reform introduced by Labour after its 1964 and 1974 Election victories, in spite of opposition from within the civil service, was the appointment as advisers to Ministers of experts in relevant fields of research and administration from outwith the civil service in Whitehall. It was hoped that this reform would broaden and improve the quality of advice by weakening the burcaucratic tendency to protect the 'departmental interest' at all costs. It broke down the traditional 'anonymous but permanent' character of the civil service because these temporary appointees were often political supporters who were brought into the government in order to strengthen the political and one-sided dimensions in the advice given to the Ministers who take the final decisions. This practice was continued and extended by the Conservatives after 1979.

(continued on page 95)

Arms Sales to Iraq

THE SCOTT REPORT

On 26 February 1996, the Conservative government survived, by a single vote, a motion on the Scott Inquiry Report into allegations that the government knew about and encouraged sales of military equipment from a British firm, Matrix Churchill, to Iran and Iraq in the 1980s. Three executives of Matrix Churchill were originally charged with illegally supplying arms to Iraq— the charges were later dropped. Since this affair hit the headlines after the outbreak of the Gulf War against Iraq, the Scott Inquiry was widely believed to be political dynamite threatening certain Ministers and possibly the government as a whole. The opposition called for the resignations of two Ministers whom they accused of misleading the House on the true nature of the govern-

ment's policy on arms sales to Iraq and Iran. The government was accused of 'running scared'. When the Report was published on 15 February 1996, government Ministers and civil servants were given three days in which to prepare for the inevitable debate in the House of Commons. Opposition MPs were given three hours in which to read the Report's 1,806 pages! The Report did not lead to the resignation of any government Ministers. One of the Ministers most at risk, Mr William Waldegrave, stated that the Report found him not guilty of lying to Parliament and of intending to mislead the public. Scott did indeed clear Ministers of any "duplicitous intent" and of the charge of conspiracy to deny the Matrix Churchill defend-

ants a fair trial. However, the Report was critical of the way in which the Executive used the convention of ministerial responsibility. "Throughout the period that the Inquiry has had to examine there is found to be a consistent undervaluing by government of the public interest that full information should be made available to Parliament. In circumstances where disclosure might be politically or administratively inconvenient, the balance struck by government comes down, time and time again, against full disclosure." Scott also concluded that the government had misled both Parliament and the public into believing that "a stricter policy towards non-lethal defence and dual-use exports to Iraq was being applied than was the case".

THE PHILLIPS INQUIRY

The first known human victim of BSE/CJD died in 1995. By 2000, at least eighty individuals had died, over 170,000 cattle had been slaughtered, British beef had been banned from export to Europe, and millions of pounds had been paid out in compensation to farmers. It is estimated that the BSE/CJD disaster will cost at least £4 billion including compensation and care costs awarded to human victims and their families.

The BSE crisis raises questions about executive accountability, about the relationship between civil servants and government Ministers, about rivalry between government departments, and about open government. It casts light on how governments (politicians and officials) deal with acute and unexpected problems.

The first cases of BSE in cattle occurred in the 1970s but went undetected to begin with. It is still not clear how the disease originated. More cows became infected as the 1970s and early 1980s unfolded as a result of being fed meat and bone meal produced from the carcasses of infected, slaughtered cattle. In this way infection entered the food chain of domestic herds of beef and dairy cattle. Humans were probably infected by eating meat products such as hamburgers, pies etc. produced from infected cattle. Some infection of humans occurred before anyone was aware of the disease in cattle or aware of the possibility of transmission of the disease from animals to humans. Scientific uncertainty was a key feature of the BSE crisis as it developed in the 1980s and became a political and administrative problem as well as a medical and scientific one. These difficulties were intensified by the long incubation period of the disease in both cows and humans which meant that answers to questions about the sources of infection and risks to humans from infected cattle could not be established quickly.

The BSE/CJD crisis became a political and administrative problem in the mid-1980s when the Conservative Party dominated British government. However, it was not until after the 1997 General Election that an inquiry was launched into what had gone wrong with efforts to deal with the problem. In December 1997 the government established a Judicial Inquiry led by Justice Phillips.

Findings of the Inquiry

The Phillips Report was published in October 2000. By then many of the senior officials involved had retired and Conservative Ministers who had been responsible for policy formulation and implementation were now in Opposition. The Report both praised and criticised individuals and the measures they took to deal with the BSE/CJD crisis. Officials and government Ministers adopted "sensible measures" but "they were not always timely or adequately implemented and enforced".

A critical feature of the whole BSE/CJD crisis was that it was not believed for certain until early 1996 that the disease in cattle, spongiform encephalopathy, could be transmitted to humans through the food chain.

The main findings of the BSE inquiry were:

➡ A Whitehall culture of departmental rivalry and unnecessary secrecy exists.

➡ There was a delay in the proper consideration of the risk to humans.

➡ The ban on the use of meat and bone meal in cattle feed was not implemented effectively.

➡ MAFF did not bring in the Department of Health soon enough to consider the risk to humans and that risk was not communicated to the public.

➡ On the crucial question of open government, the Report said that:

"The government did not lie to the public about BSE. It believed that the risks posed by BSE to humans were remote. The government was preoccupied with preventing an alarmist reaction to BSE because it believed that the risk was remote. It is clear that this campaign of reassurance was a mistake."

The Report concluded that, in general, there had been both individual and institutional failings which contributed to the spread of the disease in both cattle and humans. Nevertheless, it cleared all concerned of a deliberate cover-up and of attempting to mislead the public.

No government Ministers resigned, were sacked or were subjected to a vote of censure in the Commons though some serving civil servants are subject to investigation. The Labour Minister of Agriculture, Nick Brown, who informed the House of Commons of the main findings of the Inquiry, did not make any attempt to make political capital out of its criticisms of the Conservative government's handling of the BSE crisis. Some of the Conservative Ministers in departments at the centre of decision making during the crisis are still MPs and some are on the Opposition Front Bench.

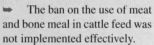

In 1990 the Minister for Agriculture, John Gummer, attempted to reassure the public that British meat was safe by publicly giving his 4-year-old daughter a burger to eat.

TERMINOLOGY

BSE: Bovine Spongiform Encephalopathy

CJD: Creutzfeldt-Jakob disease

MAFF: The Ministry of Agriculture, Food and Fisheries

BSE is a disease in animals which eats away the brain.

CJD is the human variant of BSE.

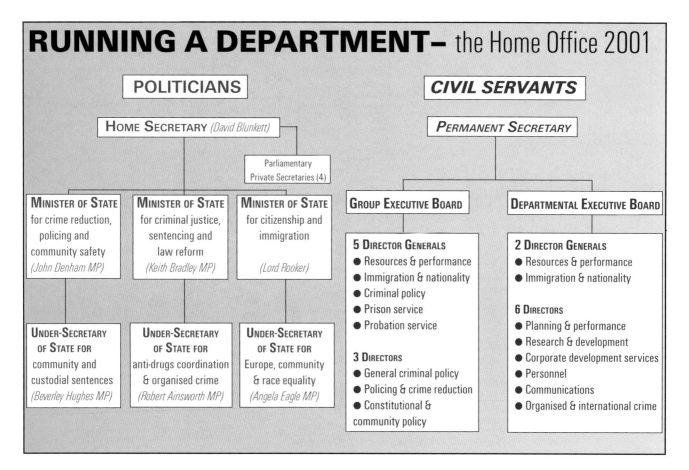

RUNNING A DEPARTMENT– the Home Office 2001

POLITICIANS

CIVIL SERVANTS

HOME SECRETARY *(David Blunkett)*

Parliamentary Private Secretaries (4)

PERMANENT SECRETARY

MINISTER OF STATE for crime reduction, policing and community safety *(John Denham MP)*

MINISTER OF STATE for criminal justice, sentencing and law reform *(Keith Bradley MP)*

MINISTER OF STATE for citizenship and immigration *(Lord Rooker)*

UNDER-SECRETARY OF STATE FOR community and custodial sentences *(Beverley Hughes MP)*

UNDER-SECRETARY OF STATE FOR anti-drugs coordination & organised crime *(Robert Ainsworth MP)*

UNDER-SECRETARY OF STATE FOR Europe, community & race equality *(Angela Eagle MP)*

GROUP EXECUTIVE BOARD

5 DIRECTOR GENERALS
- Resources & performance
- Immigration & nationality
- Criminal policy
- Prison service
- Probation service

3 DIRECTORS
- General criminal policy
- Policing & crime reduction
- Constitutional & community policy

DEPARTMENTAL EXECUTIVE BOARD

2 DIRECTOR GENERALS
- Resources & performance
- Immigration & nationality

6 DIRECTORS
- Planning & performance
- Research & development
- Corporate development services
- Personnel
- Communications
- Organised & international crime

The most profound modern reforms of the civil service were introduced after 1979 when the principles of 'Thatcherism' were applied to government administration. The Thatcherite principle that as much decision making as possible should be taken by the market or according to market principles and the Thatcherite prejudice against the public sector stimulated several major changes in the size, organisation and functions of the civil service.

Next Steps
In 1988 a reform known as Next Steps was introduced. It distinguished between the policy making and the managerial functions of civil servants. Policy making means formulating policy, in other words deciding on solutions to the problems faced by the government, for instance what to do about traffic congestion. Implementing the chosen policy solution, for example ensuring that roads are built cost effectively, is regarded as managerial. Civil service functions deemed to be 'managerial' in character were transferred to 'agencies' such as the Benefits Agency and the

Employment Service Agency. There were almost 750,000 civil servants in the mid-1970s. About half of all civil servants were employed in departments dealing with social security, taxation and defence. By 1994 the number of civil servants had been reduced to just over half a million.

The 'politicisation' of the civil service has continued under Blair. There has been a significant increase in the number of political advisers. (See pages 88 and 90.) However, there has been no attempt by the Blair administration to interfere in the appointment of senior civil servants.

Future reform

The government's vision for the civil service was included in the Modernising Government White Paper. It stated that the civil service faced seven challenges.

- Implementing constitutional reform in a way that preserves a unified civil service and ensures close working between the UK government and the devolved administrations.

- Getting staff in all departments to integrate the EU dimension into policy thinking.

- Focusing work on public services so as to improve their quality, make them more innovative and responsive to users and ensure that they are delivered in an efficient way.

- Creating a culture in the civil service which is more innovative and more willing to take risks.

- Improving collaborative working across departments.

- Managing the civil service so as to equip it to meet these challenges.

- Thinking ahead strategically to future priorities.

The Blair administration maintained the Conservative approach of regarding senior civil servants more as administrators implementing the policies of Ministers rather than as policy advisers. The Blair government, through the Performance and Innovation and Social Exclusion units in the Cabinet Office, set out to coordinate departmental policies and services.

PRESSURES & INFLUENCES

Let us imagine that your American cousin has arrived in Britain for a holiday just as you have finished reading the first six chapters of this book. Your cousin is fascinated by British politics but is also confused because of the profound differences between British and American politics at all levels—the party and electoral systems, the constitution and so on. She asks you to summarise the essential characteristics of British and Scottish politics so that she can understand what is really happening in the UK. Since you have been revising for an exam on British politics you set about the task with great enthusiasm. A number of very well-known phrases trip off your tongue: 'Parliamentary System'; 'Cabinet or maybe Prime Ministerial government'; 'Representative government'; 'Party Discipline'; 'Unitary State'; 'Devolution, not Federalism' and so on. Above all you say that Britain is a 'democracy', 'the oldest democracy in the western world'.

As you go through the list you notice that your cousin looks a bit puzzled. Each phrase you have offered captures an essential element of the British political system. You describe with great clarity reform of the House of Lords and the establishment of a Scottish Parliament. Power is to be placed even more firmly in the 'hands of the people'. Nevertheless, your cousin is not convinced. Above all, she is amazed by the fact that the Chief Executive is not directly elected by the people and by your failure to mention 'the Lobby'.

"It does not look to me as if there is much representation in the 'oldest democracy in the western world'; we elect every political official from the President down to the local sheriff. If your wonderful political parties are so centralised and disciplined, how on earth do you influence what the government does in between elections? If your executive, be it Prime Minister or Cabinet, is so much stronger than the American President, why is Labour meeting so much opposition to its proposals for reform of public services? I live in a pluralist society which is more democratic than yours because our people have more opportunities to influence what the government does. We can stop the government doing what it wants to do just as we rejected President Clinton's plans for reform of health care in 1994."

Now it is your turn to be puzzled. 'Pluralism'? 'The Lobby'? What do these terms mean? You realise that the story is not complete. You need to know more about the political process in your own country; you need to go beyond elections and parties, beyond manifestos and campaigns. What is missing from your description of Britain's 'Representative Democracy'?

96

Many groups combine 'interests' and 'cause'. In December 1997 there were rumours that Labour's review of the welfare system would result in cuts in various types of benefit and in some benefits being made conditional on going to work. Several groups receiving benefit reacted by protesting outside the gates of Downing Street, throwing paint on the gates and chaining themselves to the railings. In February 1998 one protest was organised by the Disabled People's Direct Action Network which feared that disabled people would lose benefit which in some cases paid for goods or medicine 'which they could not otherwise afford'. Other disabled groups such as Radar supported the action. These groups see the fight to safeguard the economic interests of disabled people and to safeguard their benefits as a 'cause' since the disabled need special protection.

(Royal Association for Disability and Rehabilitation)

The answers to these questions are given in this chapter in which the 'representative system' is extended to include pressure groups and interest groups, and the increasing role of public opinion. This can be expressed in protest demonstrations against such issues as benefit cuts, fox-hunting and fuel prices, and in the polls on every imaginable political issue which are published weekly in the media.

Party leaders cannot satisfy all sections of their parties all of the time. The government is not too concerned about satisfying the policy aims of the people who did not vote for it. Also, people who have little interest in party politics will sometimes be provoked into political action by an issue which affects them intimately. Consequently, many people have specific interests or political objectives which may be threatened by or are unlikely to be satisfied by the government of the day. For these reasons, individuals seeking to achieve political objectives often have to go beyond party politics to achieve their aims.

Other avenues of political participation and representation are available. One of the most famous political sayings is Aristotle's ancient dictum: "Man is by nature a social animal". Society breeds organisations. Sport, religion, work, leisure, 'good causes', 'social problems' and personal problems all stimulate the existence of organisations such as the Scottish Football Association, the Church of Scotland and the Roman Catholic Church, the Transport and General Workers Union, the Ramblers Association, the Salvation Army, the Howard League for Penal Reform and Alcoholics Anonymous. The list seems endless.

When government decisions seem likely to affect their members adversely, social organisations will enter the political process to advance or protect the interests of these members. Pressure groups are social organisations rather than political parties and seek to influence governmental decision making in favour of their members. Most social organisations are created for reasons which have nothing to do with politics. Some organisations are explicitly political and others are established to promote a view on a single issue

and may be only temporary in duration. All social organisations are potential pressure groups.

Groups become involved in politics, some on a temporary basis, others more permanently. Religion provides one source of pressure group activity. In the 1997 Election campaign one of the few adverse moments for the Labour Party in Scotland occurred when Archbishop Winning reprimanded the Party for its refusal to take a pro-life stand on the abortion issue. The General Assembly of the Church of Scotland makes known its views on a wide range of issues. Legislative proposals either by the government or by backbenchers often stimulate pressure group responses. After the 1997 Election a Private Members' Bill to introduce a ban on fox-hunting stimulated many organisations to campaign for or against the proposed legislation—the League Against Cruel Sports supported the Bill while the Countryside Alliance opposed it. The 2000 Pressure Group in Scotland to retain Section 28 of the *Local Government Act* involved a whole range of organisations and individuals. (See page 133.)

TYPES OF PRESSURE GROUP

There are two basic types of pressure groups.

- *Interest groups*—so called because they represent the economic interests of their members. Their distinguishing feature is who they represent.

- *Promotional or 'cause' groups* Promotional groups are defined by the cause they represent—by what they stand for. The Howard League for Penal Reform promotes a particular view of prison policy (what prison should be for; conditions of inmates). Membership of promotional groups is open-ended; anyone who believes in the cause can join.

Trade Unions

The best known interest groups, and the biggest, are trade unions and employers' federations. Trade unions were created and still exist primarily to defend and improve the wages and working conditions of their members. Their principal adversaries are the firms employing their members and whose main activity is to compete in the marketplace and make profits. Interest groups have closed memberships. In other words, individuals have to work in a particular industry or possess a particular skill in order to join the general or craft union which represents workers in that industry or with that particular skill.

The two sides of industry are represented by the most powerful pressure groups in Britain. Trade unions individually and collectively represent millions of workers. By the end of the 1970s there were over 13 million trade unionists, though the number had fallen to 7.3 million by 2000 (almost 30% of the British workforce). In 2001 the biggest union was UNISON which had over 900,000 women amongst its 1.27 milion members.

Collectively, unions are organised into the Trades Union Congress (TUC) which acts as an 'umbrella' organisation for the union movement. TUC leaders and the leaders of individual unions are frequently consulted by the government because their approval may make the difference between success and failure in respect of many economic and industrial policies.

The political role of British trade unions has been a central issue in recent years for two reasons. Firstly, the role of unions within the Labour Party raised questions about their political power. Many people believed that the unions possessed too much power. Secondly, trade union power and organisation was one of the major targets of 'Thatcherism' in the 1980s. There was much trade union reform which has, for the most part, been accepted by New Labour. (See page 99.)

Employers' Organisations

The links between the 'other side' of industry—companies who are the employers—and the Conservative Party are much less formal than the links between Labour and the unions. There is no equivalent of trade union affiliation to the Labour Party. The most obvious connection between business interests and the Conservative Party is financial. Many companies contribute large sums of money to the Conservatives. Industries form their own federations to make representations to the government when necessary, for instance the Engineering Employers Federation. The top business pressure group is the Confederation of British Industry (the CBI) which is the TUC's counterpart. Other umbrella associations on the business side are the British Chambers of Commerce, the Small Business Association and the Institute of Directors.

PRESSURE GROUP TARGETS

Pressure groups 'target' elements of the political system which will help them to achieve their objectives. The most obvious targets are:

1 The executive branch (Ministers and civil servants).
2 The legislature (backbench MPs).
3 Party factions (left, centre and right wings of the major parties) sympathetic to specific pressure group interests or causes.
4 Public opinion and voters.

In Britain decision making is much more narrowly concentrated than in the USA. The focus of most pressure group activity has traditionally been Whitehall. Policy making in Britain, once the general election is over, is concentrated in government departments which means government Ministers or the civil servants advising them. A government which has just been elected, especially if it has replaced a government of the rival major party, will have certain policy objectives from which it is unlikely to be diverted. The scope for influencing policy will not be great when a government transforms its manifesto proposals, for example devolution, into legislative form. On the other hand, the government will also have to cope with problems which arise unexpectedly. In these cases the government may be open to suggestions from 'interested parties'.

In contrast to American Senators and Representatives, British MPs have long been considered to be much less useful to pressure groups because voting in the legislature in Britain is determined much more by party loyalty and discipline enforced by the Whips. Most British MPs feel compelled to vote with the party majority most of the time unless they feel very strongly about an issue. For this reason, although MPs may be useful to pressure groups as far as publicity is concerned, they do not usually cross party lines to vote in accordance with these objectives when party interests clash with pressure group interests.

Conservative governments in the 1980s reformed industrial relations and weakened the political power of trade unions. Secondary picketing was made unlawful. Ballots were required both for the election of union executives and before strike action could be taken. The unions which had prevented the implementation of Edward Heath's 1972 Industrial Relations Act and frustrated Labour's efforts to enforce an incomes policy in the late 1970s (leading to the famed 'winter of discontent' which contributed to the Conservative election victory in 1979) were unable to prevent Mrs Thatcher from introducing these detested reforms.

The titanic struggle between the Conservative government and the miners in 1985 was won by the government. Unemployment strengthened the hand of the government in the battle with the unions. Conservative success encouraged Labour in opposition to speak about reforming its constitutional links with the unions which had created the Party at the beginning of the twentieth century.

In 1998 striking workers at Magnet in Darlington manned the 20-month-old picket line against the company's dismissal of 320 staff. This became Britain's longest-running industrial dispute.

PRESSURE GROUPS IN ACTION

Pressure group participation in politics takes various forms. The larger economic interest groups, which are often consulted as of right when the government is formulating policy, will try to 'persuade' the government to grant their wishes or demands. Promotional groups are more likely to resort to aggressive though non-violent protests against policy decisions which have been taken or are thought likely to be taken.

Pressure group actions vary according to the nature of the groups involved and the stages of the government decision making process. The principal decision making stages are:

1   Formulation of policy where the emphasis is on consultation and persuasion for groups who have access to the government.

2   Legislative stages where the emphasis is on the publicity generated by MPs speaking in support of group interests or causes.

3   Implementation where the emphasis may be on protest on behalf of those who lost out when decisions were taken.

Consultation

Often the government will invite groups and organisations to comment on policy proposals which have been published in the preliminary form of a White or Green Paper. At this stage the government is still open to persuasion. In the autumn of 1997 the Labour government invited the public to respond to its proposals to encourage saving which involved replacing TESSAs and PEPs with Individual Savings Allowances (ISAs).

The consultative access granted to many, but not all, pressure groups as representative institutions has long been accepted as a necessary and legitimate part of the democratic process. Politicians and civil servants spend much time and effort listening to pressure group demands. This is done in order to persuade public opinion of the validity of the government's policy and to make implementation of that policy easier once it has

entered the Statute Book. Groups, in turn, realise that they need to persuade the government to give them some of what they want. A process of consultation has therefore emerged in which representatives of groups and interests are in frequent contact with the policy makers (government Ministers and civil servants) in Whitehall.

The process of consultation between groups and government developed much earlier and is much more pronounced in the USA where it has become known as 'lobbying'. Pressure groups are known collectively in the USA as the 'Lobby' because their representatives lie in wait for important policy makers in the corridors in the Congress buildings (Capitol Hill) and in government departments. For many years 'lobbying' and 'lobbyists' were regarded with suspicion in Britain because they were associated with giving undue influence to a limited number of groups and with corruption because it seemed that votes were for sale in Congress where party discipline is much weaker than in the House of Commons. However, in recent years the business

DIFFERENCES BETWEEN POLITICAL PARTIES & PRESSURE GROUPS

	POLITICAL PARTIES	PRESSURE GROUPS
Principal Objectives	Winning elections Forming government Implementation of broad policy platforms	Protecting specific economic interests or promoting a specific cause Influencing government
Membership	Open-ended: anyone may join	Interest Groups (closed): confined to members e.g. trade unions Cause Groups (open-ended): anyone may join
Methods	Putting up candidates in elections Putting MPs into government	Persuasion Protest Campaigns to influence public opinion Sponsoring parliamentary candidates

of political consultants has developed significantly in Britain and accusations of 'sleaze' against some consultants, a few government Ministers and some MPs have hit the newspaper headlines.

Protest

Consultation may not give pressure groups what they want from the government. Sometimes groups want to influence the government before policy is formulated. In such cases pressure groups may feel the need to move from consultation and persuasion to protest. Groups may act as vehicles of protest in the hope of influencing public opinion in their favour as illustrated in the case study on pages102–103.

Opponents of fox-hunting have demonstrated vigorously against it at strategic times such as the many Boxing Day Hunts up and down the country. Sometimes these demonstrations have led to violent clashes between the two sides. The objective of the protesters is to generate publicity for their cause. Public opinion polls have suggested that opposition to fox-hunting has been growing because of such publicity. (See The Wild Mammals (Hunting with Dogs) Bill on page 59.)

PRESSURE GROUPS:
A LEVEL PLAYING FIELD?

On the positive side, pressure groups add to the representative and democratic dimensions of politics and government by widening participation in the decision making process of the state. The political participation of pressure groups has given rise to a relatively new theory of politics which is 'pluralism'.

A 'pluralist' political system is one in which power is widely distributed throughout society and not confined to the rich, the government, MPs, or powerful groups such as large companies, the 'Establishment' and trade unions. If all sections of society are able to form groups which give them some effective influence when important decisions affecting them are being made, then a strong element of pluralism is present. Society will be that much more democratic if political participation is widespread—if no significant sections of society are excluded from political decision making.

The positive side of pressure group activity may be summed up as follows: pressure groups enlarge democracy by representing the views of individuals and social organisations beyond the contribution of voting, parliamentary representation and political parties.

The negative side of pressure group politics is the claim that there is not a level playing field; that in the world of pressure groups God favours the big battalions; that some pressure groups are much more equal than others. Welfare Benefit groups such as Child Poverty Action were unable to prevent the Labour Party cutting benefits to one parent families and the disabled

MONEY AND INFLUENCE
IN BRITISH POLITICS

Groups, rather than individuals, finance British political parties. They provide parties with money to fight election campaigns and to fund other party activities such as publicising party policies in between elections. Some MPs accept payment for acting as spokespersons for particular interests or causes. Such financial links between groups and both parties and legislators have long been accepted as legitimate as long as certain safeguards are met. For example MPs have to declare their interests and there are limits on campaign spending by parliamentary candidates.

In recent years, financial links between MPs, parties, groups and individuals have become suspect and open to criticism because of alleged abuses. Groups representing economic and other interests have been accused of attempting to buy 'influence' by being overly

THE NEILL REPORT

There has been public concern about the methods used by political parties to raise funds. The 'cash for questions' scandal in 1994 and the £1 million donation to the Labour Party by Formula 1 boss Bernie Ecclestone in 1997 increased the clamour for action.

In response to the cash for questions scandal John Major had set up a Committee on Standards in Public Life. He had refused, however, to include party funding within the Committee's remit. The new Labour government extended the Committee's remit to cover party and election finance, and in 1998 the Committee, chaired by Sir Patrick Neill, made its recommendations.

1. All donations of over £5,000 national and £1,000 for a single constituency to be disclosed.
2. Foreign donations banned.
3. Anonymous donations exceeding £50 banned.
4. Blind Trusts abolished.
5. The existing system of a ban on paid election advertising on TV and radio would be continued, as would the free party election broadcasts.
6. A national spending limit of £20 million for elections to be introduced.
7. State funding to help opposing parties in Parliament to be tripled and a new £2 million fund for political research to be introduced.
8. Shareholders should approve company donations and sponsorships.

The government acted swiftly to implement many of the Committee's recommendations. The spending limit was set at £15 million. In the 1997 Election the Conservatives had spent £15 million, Labour £13 million and the Liberal Democrats about £1 million. All organisations, including pressure groups and businesses, must disclose donations to the Electoral Commission.

generous in their gifts to parties in the hope of policy being changed to meet their wishes. This issue came to a head after Labour's 1997 victory when it became known that the head of Formula 1 motor racing, Bernie Ecclestone, had given Labour £1 million before the Election. Motor racing depends

for its survival on massive sponsorship which has been provided mainly by tobacco advertising. Formula 1 racing cars are festooned with the names of cigarette manufacturers such as Rothmans and Marlborough. The new Labour government announced its intention to ban all sponsorship of

sport by tobacco interests because of the health risks inherent in smoking. However, motor sport was to be exempt from this ban temporarily. The reason given for this controversial decision was that a lot of British jobs were at stake which would go to Europe

(continued on page 104)

THE PRESSURES OF DIRECT ACTION

The Fuel Protests of September 2000

For British road haulage firms the higher price of fuel in Britain cuts down profits and puts the very survival of some of them at risk. They allege that higher fuel prices in Britain amount to unfair competition with French and German hauliers which is totally inappropriate given that fair competition is one of the principal objectives of the European Union.

The discontent of small businesses in the road haulage industry and in other industries depend-ent on using petrol and diesel, such as farmers and fishermen, was at the heart of an embar-rassing crisis for the Labour government and for the Prime Minister in particular which erupted in early September 2000. The crisis centred on the use of direct action against the government in an attempt to force it into lowering the price of fuel. The use of direct action by a small section of British society followed more traditional pressure group activities over a long period of time.

Before every Budget, Chancellors have been advised by the CBI, the Association of Road Hauliers, the NFU and many other organisations to lower or at least not to increase duties on petrol and diesel. Such advice usually fell on deaf ears.

The direct action began spontaneously, as far as we know, on the evening of 7 September 2000 when a number of pro-testers started to picket the entrance to a large oil refinery at Stanlow in Cheshire. Within four days hardly any petrol was being delivered to petrol stations through-out Britain. Most of the pickets protesting against the high cost of fuel were from the small business sector. One of the origi-nal pickets said later that they had intended to go home in the morning after making their point. However, the number of protesters increased although it did not exceed 2,500 at any point.

The government was not immediately aware of the dangers in the direct action which was more typical of French than of British politics. By Monday 11 September it was clear that the problems were escalating as petrol supplies were not getting out of the refineries either because the petrol tanker drivers could not get out due to intimidation or would not cross the picket lines out of sympathy with the protesting pickets.

What was the government to do? Its major aim was not to be seen to give in to the protests. If it did give in, it would be perceived as weak and the strategy could be used again by other groups enraged by government policies. The principal danger in letting the protests continue was that essential services such as the NHS would be deprived of vital supplies such as blood and ambulance services as vehicles ran out of fuel. Individuals who went to work by car would not be able to do so, supermarkets would run out of staple foods such as milk and vegetables, and public transport would come to a halt. There were soon reports of panic buying in supermarkets and at petrol stations. Nonetheless, to begin with the public, many of whom buy petrol, were sympathetic to the protesters. Drivers passing pickets tooted their horns in a gesture of support. The media reported the protests sympathetically, portraying the pickets as supporters of the common man against an uncaring and remote government. The pickets did allow

some tankers out to supply the essential services such as ambulances.

The pickets claimed that their actions were peaceful. Tanker drivers claimed that they were being intimidated by the pickets. The police were on hand to deal with any threat of violence. The government accused the oil companies, who own and run the refineries where petrol is produced, of not doing enough to get the tankers out safely and of not doing enough to persuade the drivers to take their tankers out on the road. There were claims that the oil companies were sympathetic to the protesters. The oil companies do not make much profit out of retailing petrol. If duties were lowered they would benefit from increased sales and would find it easier to increase prices which would increase profits. There were also claims that the picketing was not universally solid and that more tankers could have got out of some refineries. The Prime Minister summoned oil company bosses to 10 Downing Street on Wednesday 13 September and 'read them the riot act'. The oil industry leaders informed the Prime Minister that many of the tanker drivers were not oil company employees

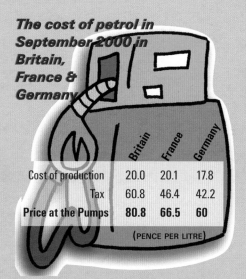

The cost of petrol in September 2000 in Britain, France & Germany

	Britain	France	Germany
Cost of production	20.0	20.1	17.8
Tax	60.8	46.4	42.2
Price at the Pumps	**80.8**	**66.5**	**60**

(PENCE PER LITRE)

but worked under contract as self-employed owners of their tankers. The oil companies felt they could not put pressure on drivers who were not their own employees.

Unlike the notorious Miners' Strike of the 1980s the trade unions this time were on the side of the government against the pickets. The General Secretary of the TUC, John Monks, urged the tanker drivers to cross the picket lines and claimed that the protests were supported by right-wing opponents of the Labour government such as the Countryside Alliance who had already been provoked into opposition by the Labour government's apparent sympathy for attempts by Labour backbenchers to ban fox-hunting. Monks did not share the original media view of the protesters as a popular and populist spontaneous direct action by sections of the small business community supported by public opinion.

By Friday morning the pickets had withdrawn and the tankers were

supplying petrol stations once more. What had happened to bring the crisis to an end? The government did not climb down by promising to reduce petrol and diesel taxes nor did it need to bring in the troops to drive the petrol tankers out of the refineries as had been suggested in some quarters. What persuaded the pickets to end their protests peacefully was a change in the public mood registered by the tabloid newspapers. *The Mirror's* headline on Thursday morning was: 'Enough is Enough'. Once it became clear that essential services could be damaged, that supermarkets could run out of staple foods, and that people could not get to work on time or at all the protesters realised that they would soon run out of sympathy.

In the Chancellor's November 2000 economic statement he announced that there would be a freeze on fuel duties until April 2002 and a package for motorists that effectively reduced the price of petrol by 4p and the price of diesel by 8p. The direct action had worked to some extent without the government climbing down abjectly. Whether direct action will develop into a routine political strategy for social groups which do not get satisfaction from consultations with the government remains to be seen. Public support or indifference is essential for such tactics to succeed.

The financial probity of MPs hit the headlines in the 1990s. The long-standing right of MPs to speak in Parliament on behalf of groups and organisations which they supported fell under a cloud when 'sleaze' became an issue. Some MPs and a few junior Ministers were accused of taking money in return for asking questions on behalf of pressure groups. Some admitted their guilt; others did not.

Party donations
2001 General Election

£12.4 million

£5.3 million

£840,000

Conservative	Labour	Liberal Democrats
• The bulk of the Conservative funds were donated by just three rich donors: Sir Paul Getty – £5 million Stewart Wheelar – £2.5 million Edward Haughey – £1 million	• The bulk of Labour's funds were donated by the trade unions giving £3.8 million in total. The Communication Workers Union gave £1 million • Eddie Izard, the comedian, gave £10,000 • Richard Wilson, the actor, gave £6,500	• Joseph Rowntree Reform Trust gave £207,000 • Lord Jacobs gave £60,000

Figure 7.1

Bernie Ecclestone, who controls F1 Motor Racing, donated £1million to the Labour Party before the 1997 election. Suspicions were voiced about the reasons for the donation and whether this gave him influence over government decisions regarding tobacco sponsorship.

or elsewhere if Britain alone banned the sponsorship by tobacco firms. Labour handed back the £1 million donation but the case for reform of party finances had received a major boost. Ironically, Labour is known to be in favour of such reform.

Party Finances

The fundamental facts about the funding of British political parties and election campaigns can be stated simply.

1   Both major parties rely heavily on one particular source of finance: Labour gets most of its money from the unions and the Conservatives get their money from 'big business'.

2   Until the Neil Report (see page 101) there were virtually no restrictions on contributions to parties either in terms of how much could be donated or of who could donate.

3   Campaigning through the broadcasting media is controlled but there are no limits on other forms of advertising such as the press and hoardings. Time on radio and television is strictly limited and is free, though parties have to pay for producing their election broadcasts.

4   The Conservatives receive more income than Labour and both receive much more income than the Liberal Democrats. In the 2001 Election Conservative income was £12.4 million, Labour's income was £5.3

million and the Liberal Democrats received £0.84 million. (See Figure 7.1.)

5 In 1996–97 approximately 60% of Labour's income came from the trade unions in the form of 'affiliation fees' which are related to the number of members in each union, and contributions to Labour's General Election Fund. Another 5% of the £12.2 million total came from the affiliation fees paid by Constituency Labour Parties.

Conservative income was dominated by donations from firms and individuals who contributed 87% of total Conservative income. Constituency contributions were 6%.

Does money buy favours?

The crucial question is: what does this money 'buy'? Does money win elections? Do contributions to parties 'buy' or influence policy decisions when one of the parties controls the government departments which make policy?

At the electoral level, Labour has won elections in spite of being financially weaker than the Conservatives. On the other hand, the Conservatives have had the stronger electoral performance overall in the period since 1945. How much money is available to the parties may be less significant than how well the money is spent. In 1987 and 1992 the Labour Party campaigns were considered to be superior to the Conservative campaigns but Labour did not win. In 1987 there was very little move-

MPs may speak on behalf of group interests and causes in Parliament as long as they declare their 'interest' before they speak. Groups may pay MPs to represent them in Parliament as long as the MPs record such payments in the Register of Members' Interests. In recent years MPs have found additional employment as consultants working for professional lobbyists. Such behaviour is legitimate as long as it is acknowledged. The twin forces of party loyalty and party discipline were considered to be sufficient to ensure that MPs behaved properly and did not allow themselves to be unduly influenced by pressure groups and individuals who paid them.

The 1990s witnessed a large increase in charges of improper behaviour against MPs who were accused of taking money and favours without proper acknowledgement. The most publicised case centred on 'cash for questions' allegations against a number of Conservative MPs including two junior ministers who resigned their posts. It was alleged that Tim Smith and Neil Hamilton asked questions in the Commons and

'CASH FOR QUESTIONS'

Neil Hamilton with his wife Christine became household names in 1997. He was found guilty of corrupt practices when found to have accepted money for asking questions in the House of Commons.

performed other services on behalf of Mohammed Al Fayed without declaring their interest or the payments they received for the services rendered. Smith admitted the charges and stood down as Conservative candidate before the 1997 Election. Hamilton denied the charges and refused to stand down. He was defeated by Martin Bell who stood against him as an anti-corruption candidate. Hamilton was found 'guilty' by both the Parliamentary Commissioner for Standards and by the Commons Select Committee on Standards

and Privileges. Ironically, the Commons could not punish Neil Hamilton because he was no longer an MP.

The 'Cash for Questions' raises two issues:

1 Who should 'police' MPs to ensure that they do not exert undue influence on behalf of groups or individuals who pay them for their services?

2 Should MPs be allowed to work for political consultancy firms and to receive money for political services even

if these services and the money are publicly acknowledged?

There remain strict limits in Britain on what MPs can do for their own constituents, for pressure groups and for individuals. Yet MPs are being allowed to act as 'political fixers'. One solution would be to pay MPs high enough salaries to justify banning all such paid work as consultants who know their way around Whitehall where many important government decisions are made.

ment in the opinion polls during the campaign which seems to have had little impact on the result.

It is difficult to assess the relationship between policy decisions and financial contributions. The unions and private companies finance the respective parties because the parties stand for their interests. This was certainly true in the heyday of the two-party system. Even now the common interests of the parties and their financial backers becomes clear in an issue such as the minimum wage legislation which was one of Labour's main campaign promises in 1997. Such legislation was designed to improve the incomes of the poorest wage earners and to prevent 'sweat shop' labour which exploits the young and the unskilled. Labour's egalitarian outlook and its long-standing union links explained the Party's long-term commitment to a statutory minimum wage. Conservative opposition to such legislation was also understandable in the light of the Party's fundamental philosophy which is favourable to business and encourages reliance on the market as a key economic decision maker. Conservative spokespersons argued that a minimum wage would mean higher costs for some manufacturers and services and could make Britain less competitive in the international marketplace. Both parties supported their 'natural allies' in their stances on the minimum wage issue. Both claimed that their policy would be 'good for the country'.

At the collective level the financial links between the two major parties and their backers are a legitimate part of the political process. There is more concern at an individual level. Do donations by individual firms and by individuals bring a reward? Mere suspicion that this might be so explains why Labour handed back the £1 million donation from Bernie Ecclestone so quickly once the story broke.

There have been some changes in the links between parties and pressure groups since 1979. It became obvious during the Thatcherite era that the CBI did not always agree with the Conservative government's economic and industrial policies. A government with radical intentions is less likely to be influenced by any views put to it, even those of groups which are usually supporters of the party of government. Mrs Thatcher was an opponent of the corporatist attitudes of the Conservative Leader she replaced, Edward Heath. It was a sign of the times in Britain that the business community became a little less favourable to the Conservatives in the 1990s. Certain well-known businessmen made substantial contributions to the (New) Labour Party and (fewer) to the Liberal Democrats before the 1997 Election. To that extent the link between pressure groups and parties has been slightly changed in British politics. It is more difficult to envisage trade unions supporting the Conservative Party politically and financially in spite of the reform of Clause IV in Labour's Constitution. However, Tony Blair and Gordon Brown devoted considerable time and effort before the 1997 Election to speaking at conferences of business organisations whose loyalty had been committed traditionally to the rival Conservative Party.

THE MEDIA AS 'PRESSURE AND INFLUENCE'

The media (plural noun meaning 'means of mass communication') consists of newspapers, television and radio, cinema, publishing, telecommunications, music and the performing arts. Media channels inform, educate, entertain, and influence those who read, watch and listen. They also convey to their readers and audiences the opinions of those who control the media and use it to advertise what they have to 'sell' which ranges from commercial goods and serv-

ices to political and other opinions and values.

Media industries have grown enormously as a result of technological advances such as satellite, cable and digital television, computers and the Internet. Increasing standards of living have brought everyone within reach of the media's offerings. The advertising industry, which uses the media intensively, has become one of the leading economic sectors; the British stock market fell significantly in June 2001 when a leading advertising company announced a fall in revenues indicating an unwelcome decline in economic activity at a time when recession in the USA was threatening to repeat itself in Europe.

Controversy surrounds the subject of the media's influence on individuals and on society. Reading books and newspapers, watching television, listening to music and going to the cinema all expose individuals to the opinions and images 'communicated' by these activities. Cultural attitudes, social values, morality and political opinions are all thought to be subject to the influence of the channels of mass communication. Does behaviour described by the media affect social behaviour? Is our view of 'foreigners' such as refugees based on media images? Does the media have a significant impact on individual voting behaviour to the extent of determining the results of general elections or referenda?

These are controversial questions which bring the media into the political spotlight not only as the means of communicating political opinion and values but also as a subject for governmental regulation to ease any undesirable aspects of the media in operation.

Newspapers and television

The media's primary role is the almost neutral-sounding one of reporting the news. However, even

The increasing intrusion of the media into politics is indicated by the emergence of recent additions to the language of politics such as 'spin doctors', 'sound bites' and 'transparency'. Governments and opposition parties attempt to influence what the media says about them and their opponents. They employ 'spin doctors' who interpret for the benefit of the media the meaning of political events in the hope that the media will accept their partisan point of view. Parties also rely heavily on the media during election campaigns to get their side of the story through to voters.

Alastair Campbell (left), Labour's 'spin doctor', was said to be more powerful than most elected Ministers.

straight reporting can have political implications because the messages or images conveyed may favour some sections of society at the expense of others. Reporting the run on the pound in September 1991 showed the Major government in a poor light but the media could hardly be expected not to report such unfavourable news.

Even more significantly, the media conveys 'opinion' as well as news, and such opinions are often clearly 'biased' in favour of particular political parties or ideologies. Many newspapers and political magazines openly proclaim their political allegiance and partisan attachments. Studies of British general elections always include a chapter on the influence of the media on the results at both constituency and national levels.

Politicians and the media

The relationship between politicians and the media is ambiguous. They need each other but are suspicious and wary of each other. Politicians often complain of media bias, alleging that the press and television have misrepresented their views or emphasised events favourable to opposing political forces. At the same time politicians rely on the media to publicise their policy proposals and political views. In turn the media relies on poli-

ticians, especially those in government, to supply it with information which allows journalists to comment accurately on political matters. It is not unknown for politicians to use the media by leaking information to journalists by means of 'unattributable' briefings.

There are some controls over what is communicated by the media and how this is done. Governments are expected to regulate the media to lessen any harmful effects it might have on society, to ensure honesty and objectivity in reporting, and so on. Yet the widespread acceptance of the need for some regulation of the media often stimulates accusations of unnecessary censorship and selfish manipulation by the government. A 'free press' has long been regarded as an essential attribute of a free, democratic society. Indeed the phrase 'the Fourth Estate' was coined many years ago, when the media was confined to the printed word, to suggest that the press should be considered along with the Monarchy, the Lords and the Commons as an essential constituent part of the democratic political system.

The role of the press, and now of the much more extensive and complex media system, is to ensure that governments do not operate in secrecy and cannot therefore act like dictators. 'Trans-

parency' has entered the political vocabulary precisely because of widespread complaints that it was not always clear what governments were doing and why. Politicians now claim to strive for transparency, meaning that everyone should be able to see exactly what they are up to and why. 'What you see is what you get' has become one of the strident claims of many politicians.

THE MEDIA AND POLITICS

The media's political significance can be conveniently analysed under two main headings:

- Ownership, Control and Political Partisanship
- The Media and Elections

Ownership and Control

The media is usually divided into two main categories: print (for example daily and Sunday newspapers) and electronic (for example terrestrial and satellite television). Both have experienced a massive growth in recent decades.

Television

Television and radio have been subjected to massive changes as a result of technological change. Until the beginning of the 1990s British television was monopolised by the terrestrial channels of the British Broadcasting Corporation (BBC) and Independent Television (ITV). The BBC is a

MORE CHANNELS – FEWER QUALITY PROGRAMMES?

Technological advances

Television has experienced profound changes due to technological advances. Until the late 1980s the 'terrestrial' channels monopolised transmission. However, the commercial exploitation of satellite, cable and digital developments has reduced the hold of the terrestrial channels on the consumers of television. There has been an explosion in the number of channels available allowing producers and advertisers to reach much more specific audiences. In 1989 there were only four TV channels, all terrestrial. By 1999 there were sixty channels available to subscribers in certain parts of the country (where satellite, cable and digital channels were in operation). More channels are not universally regarded as a 'good thing' in spite of the triumph of the 'market' as the preferred economic mechanism in contemporary British society. To many 'more' TV channels and competition among them will mean 'less' in terms of quality. The increase in channels has reduced the share of viewers enjoyed by both the BBC and ITV. By 2001, pay-TV channels—satellite and cable companies—were present in 44% of British households and commanded 20% of all TV viewing. In the summer of 2001 ITV's share of viewers watching adverts fell below 50% for the first time.

state-owned public corporation financed by a licence fee paid by listeners and viewers. The Corporation's revenue amounted to £2.4 million in 2000.

Since its origins in the 1920s, the BBC has been associated with the concept of 'public service broadcasting'. In other words the main functions of the BBC should be to educate and inform rather than to entertain. Public service broadcasting emphasises factual programmes such as documentaries rather than 'soaps'. The introduction of commercial television to Britain in the 1950s forced the BBC to compete with ITV channels which derive their revenue from selling advertising space during and between programmes. The principal defence of the BBC being financed by a licence fee is that to produce good quality

public service programmes the BBC must be protected against the 'dumbing down' in programme content which would undoubtedly follow from dropping the licence fee system and subjecting the BBC to the whims of the marketplace.

The BBC is governed under a Royal Charter by a Director General responsible to a Board of Governors. The Charter requires the BBC to be politically neutral. In recent years the appointments of both the Director General and the Chairman of the Board of Governors have aroused political controversy. In 1998 Greg Dyke was appointed as Director General by the fairly new Labour government elected in 1997. Dyke's appointment caused controversy in certain quarters because he was known to be a Labour supporter who had contributed £50,000 to

Party funds. The Conservative Leader, William Hague, declared that he could not support Dyke's appointment which went ahead regardless. A new Chairman of the BBC's Board of Governors, Gavin Davies, was appointed in 2001. Individuals on a short list of five were interviewed by a panel headed by the Permanent Secretary (senior civil servant) at the Department of Culture, Sport and Media, a relatively new government Department whose name indicates the increasing social importance of these three features of modern life. The panel's recommendation was then submitted to the Prime Minister who had the final say.

Independent television including the relatively new satellite and cable channels is subject to the authority of the Independent Tele-

*has been accused of political bias towards Labour govt.
* ie. Jack Straw + modern'veds → not reported by BBC.

Ownership and Political Allegiance of Major British Newspapers

Newspaper	Owners	Circulation	Party Preference and/or Endorsements		
			1992	1997	2001
Daily Mail	Daily Mail & General Trust Group	2,336.856	Conservative	Conservative	Conservative
Express	MAI	929,271	Conservative	Conservative	Labour
Mirror	Mirror Group	2,056,412	Labour	Labour	Labour
Sun	News International	3,288,291	Conservative	Labour	Labour
Independent	Mirror Group	197,084	No Endorsement	Labour	Labour
Times	News International	667,096	Conservative	'Eurosceptic'	Labour
Financial Times	Pearson	176,499	Did not want Conservative majority	Labour	Labour
Telegraph	Telegraph Group	989,302	Conservative	Conservative	Conservative
Guardian	Scott Trust	361,799	Labour	Labour	Labour

Table 7.1 Source: ABC (Audit Bureau of Circulation) August 2001

vision Commission (ITC) which is responsible for a code of practice ensuring quality of service and dealing with complaints. Its members are appointed by the government.

The position of the BBC and the quality of its programmes have been threatened by the triumph of the market and the arrival of new channels. During the Thatcher era the Conservative government, which had privatised much of the public sector, set up the Peacock Commission to investigate the BBC's status as a public corporation financed by a licence fee. It was widely assumed that the government wished to abolish the licence fee and make the BBC dependent on advertising revenue. Nevertheless, the Peacock Commission reported in favour of the BBC's existing status which

was guaranteed until 2006. The BBC has been able to acquire additional revenue from its publishing interests including the *Radio Times* and by selling programmes abroad. However, there appears to be a never-ending debate about the quality of service offered by the BBC at a time when competition for viewers has intensified. Television has been generating huge revenues for sports such as football which sell access to the highest bidder. The BBC has lost the televising of cricket test matches to Channel 4 and 'Match of the Day' to

ITV. Should the BBC 'waste' its public revenue by spending hugely on sport in an attempt to match the attractions of commercial television?

The Press

The British press is renowned for its massive circulation figures but its ownership is notable for being concentrated in a few hands, including multinational firms and foreign nationals. The current ownership of the major British national newspapers is shown in Table 7.1

The press is usually divided into two types—tabloid, also known as the popular press, and quality broadsheet. The tabloids include the *Sun*, the *Express*, the *Daily Mail*, the *Mirror*, and the *Daily Star*. The quality papers are *The Times, The Guardian, The Financial Times, The Independent* and *The Telegraph*. The quality press carry more in-depth articles and emphasise political reporting and opinion. The tabloids sell more copies daily than the broadsheets with the *Sun* enjoying prime position as Britain's best-selling paper. The highest selling newspaper in Britain is not one of the dailies but the *News of the World*, published on Sundays, which sold an average of 3,674,787 copies on Sundays in May 2001.The staunchly Conservative *Daily Telegraph*, which retained this political stance in 2001, is the biggest selling quality broadsheet.

Britain is one of the most media conscious societies in today's world. Circulation figures are high. About 80% of households receive a national paper. The papers listed in Table 7.1 are British papers in that they are sold throughout the United Kingdom. In addition there are significant national/regional papers in many parts of Britain such as the *Daily Record, The Herald* and *The Scotsman* in Scotland. Almost 90% of the population read a regional or local newspaper. The *Daily Record*, Scotland's largest selling paper and the sister paper of the *Mirror*, reaches 50% of Scottish adults. The *Record* sold 576,603 copies daily in May 2001. *The Scotsman*, one of Scotland's two papers claiming to be national in scope and quality in content, sold 88,110 copies daily during the same period.

News International, which owns the tabloid *Sun* and the 'quality' broadsheet *The* (London) *Times*, is run by the Australian born American citizen Rupert Murdoch. *The Financial Times* is owned by a Canadian citizen Conrad Black. The importance of ownership was clearly illustrated when the Labour supporting peer, Lord Hollick, took over the *Express* in 1999. The *Express* changed its political preference from Conservative to Labour in time for the 2001 Election.

The Media and Elections

The British press is politically much more partisan than television because of the strict rules governing television and radio. The BBC's public status requires it to be non-partisan and this requirement is extended to the other television channels. There is no equivalent of the BBC in the newspaper world which is permitted to be partisan.

Historically the British press has been predominantly Conservative in political orientation. In 1945 the circulation of pro-Conservative newspapers reached 6.7 million compared to 4.4 million for pro-Labour papers. In 1992 the Conservative advantage in press support reached its climax. There were 8.7 million readers of newspapers favouring the Conservatives compared to 3.3 million readers of pro-Labour papers. Partisanship on the part of the press was seen at its most dramatic in the Sun's 1992 election day headline:

"If Kinnock wins today will the last person to leave Britain please put out the lights".

Some former Conservative supporters did not share the *Sun's* viewpoint. *The Independent* refused to endorse any party. *The Financial Times* was not in favour of a Conservative victory but did not feel able to recommend voters to elect a Labour government.

There were several reasons for the strong Conservative allegiance of the British press for almost fifty years following World War II. Newspaper owners are in business to make money and have accordingly supported the party most favourable to a free market capitalist system. That party was the Conservative Party for most newspaper owners. They also wanted to oppose the regulatory image of 'Old' Labour before it jettisoned

much of that image along with Clause IV. Certainly at election time most of the press called on its readers to vote Conservative. Often Labour support was confined to the *Mirror* and *The Guardian.*

The 1997 election marked a significant turnaround in the party preferences of Britain's newspapers. For most of the Thatcher years Labour support was confined to *The Guardian* and the *Mirror*. In 1997 no fewer than eleven of nineteen major daily and Sunday newspapers preferred Blair and New Labour to Major and the warring Conservatives. The *Sun*, so hostile to Labour in 1992, now recommended its 3 million plus readers to vote Labour on election day. *The Independent* felt able to endorse Labour as did the *Financial Times*. The *Daily Mail,* the *Daily Express* and *The Telegraph* remained loyal to the Conservatives. *The Times,* by now tending to favour Blair and New Labour but opposed to their stance on European issues, took the independent line of recommending its readers to vote for 'Eurosceptic' candidates irrespective of their party affiliation.

By 2001 only *The Telegraph* and the *Mail* supported the Conservatives. This turnaround was due to several factors.

➡ The Conservative government's internal conflicts over European issues after the 1992 Election contributed to Labour's 1997 landslide which in turn emphasised the decline of the Conservatives' image as the natural party of government.

➡ Labour leaders, including Blair and Brown, undertook a clear campaign to convert media barons to the view that 'New Labour', having dropped Clause IV and its longstanding socialist image, was now the natural party of government.

➡ Labour maintained a comfortable lead over the Conservatives in public opinion polls between the 1997 and 2001 elections so that a Labour victory in 2001 was widely regarded as a foregone conclusion. In such circumstances clinging to a Conservative partisan preference when the party was in the doldrums no longer made sense to some newspaper owners and editors. (no sense in supporting failing Tory party)

The changes in Labour's internal politics symbolised by the popular usage of the term 'New Labour' and evident in constitutional changes (removal of Clause IV and decline in trade union influence) persuaded many people, newspaper owners as well as voters, that Labour could be trusted to govern effectively. Labour leaders like Blair and Brown contributed to the view that the press did indeed influence the formation of political opinion by undertaking a clear campaign to persuade 'media moguls' and others in the newspaper fraternity that New Labour is located ideologically in the centre ground of British politics, no longer on the socialist left. What mattered now, Labour leaders argued, was not ideological space between the parties, because there was none, but the ability of the parties to govern Britain effectively. That campaign was successful. Shortly after the 1997 Election the allegiance of the previously Conservative *Daily Express* changed to Labour because the Labour peer, Lord Hollick, took control of the former Conservative stalwart.

Most studies of the political influence of the press during election campaigns have found that the Conservatives benefited to some extent from the media bias in their favour. However, that benefit was limited and did not prevent Labour winning elections in 1945, 1950, 1964, 1966 and 1974. The main question was whether the press made the difference when Labour or the Conservatives won narrowly. Was Labour's majority reduced to uncomfortable proportions in 1950, 1964 and 1974 by press comment? Did the press ensure Conservative victories in 1951 and 1970?

Whether the changes in the partisan allegiance of sections of the press will be permanent remains to be seen. A feature of British party politics in recent decades has been an intensification of internal disputes over policy issues. This has opened the way for newspapers to be generally supportive of a political party but opposed to some of its policies. If a referendum is held on whether Britain should join the European common currency it is likely that some newspapers will oppose joining while maintaining their general support for Labour.

Others may revert back to a previous Conservative allegiance.

The influence of newspapers on voting behaviour and on election results is difficult to evaluate. There are distinct correlations between the partisan stances of particular papers and the partisan preferences of their readers. In 1997, 72% of readers of the traditionally pro-Labour *Mirror* voted Labour and 57% of the strongly Conservative *Telegraph* voted Conservative. Only readers of the *Daily Mail,* the *Daily Express, The Telegraph* and *The Times* preferred the Conservatives. Eight million voters read papers favourable to Labour compared to 4.5 million reading the pro-Conservative daily press.

Do these readers vote for their preferred party because they are influenced by the paper's clear political stance or do they buy the paper because they already support its preferred political party? Not all readers are aware of the partisan preference of the papers they read. In 1979, 68% of *Sun* readers did not know its partisan stance, so it is not clear that the press changes the way that individuals vote. It has been argued that the main political impact of the press is on committed voters. In other words, reading a paper which reflects the individual's own political views reinforces those views.

DEVOLVED POWER

What you will learn

1   *The historical and electoral background to devolution.*

2   *The Scottish party system.*

3   *The operation of the additional member electoral system.*

In May 1999 a Scottish Parliament met in Edinburgh for the first time since 1707. Its first major action was to support the establishment of the Scottish Executive. This Executive was drawn from the Labour Party and the Liberal Democrat Party who agreed to form a coalition government following the first elections to the Scottish Parliament on 6 May 1999. The creation of the Scottish Parliament and Executive, along with their Welsh counterparts, constituted a major reform of the British Constitution—known as devolution—whose political consequences will be worked out gradually in the years to come. For some, devolution threatens to cause the eventual break-up of the United Kingdom. For others, devolution was a necessary step to prevent precisely such a break-up.

DEVOLUTION

The electoral and opinion poll successes of the nationalist parties in Scotland and Wales in the late 1960s turned devolution into a critical issue in British politics in the 1970s. The SNP's capture of seven seats in February 1974 forced the new minority Labour government at Westminster to commit itself to devolved government for Scotland and Wales. The objective of this commitment was to minimise further SNP and Welsh Nationalist gains in future elections which may have been at Labour's expense. Labour was much more dependent than the Conservatives on winning Scottish and Welsh seats in order to achieve a parliamentary majority.

Between 1974 and 1979 Labour's attempt to implement its commitment to devolution ended in failure. A *Scotland Act* was passed by Parliament and secured the Royal Assent in July 1978. However, implementation of the Act was subject to the requirement that 40% of the Scottish electorate give their consent. This 40% threshold was not reached. The combination of an unexpectedly small majority for the YES camp in the devolution referendum on 1 March 1979 and the Labour government's defeat in a vote of confidence on the devolution issue in the Commons on 28 March led to a general election in which Labour was defeated.

Margaret Thatcher at the checkout of a supermarket in Stirling where she was campaigning with the then Scottish Secretary Michael Forsyth.

The victorious Conservative Party led by Margaret Thatcher was completely unsympathetic to devolution. This meant that there could be no progress on the issue until the Conservatives lost their parliamentary majority at Westminster. The eventual defeat of the Conservatives in 1997 after eighteen years in power was immediately followed by the new Labour government announcing the date of devolution referenda for both Scotland and Wales. Details of a new scheme of devolved government comprising legislative and executive institutions was also announced. The devolution referenda held on 11 September 1997 produced a massive majority in favour in Scotland and the narrowest of majorities in favour in Wales. Labour proceeded to establish 'devolved government' in both countries. The powers, composition and functions of a Scottish Parliament and Executive were laid down in the *Scotland Act* which became law in 1998.

The establishment of the Scottish Parliament and Executive following the first elections prompts a number of questions about Scottish politics and about Scotland's political and constitutional position within the United Kingdom.

? Why did devolution become a crucial issue in British politics in the second half of the twentieth century?

? Why did Labour commit itself to a Scottish Parliament in spite of claims by opponents of devolution, some from within the Labour Party itself, that devolution could lead to independence from the United Kingdom?

? What will be the long-term political and constitutional impact of devolution on the United Kingdom and on Scotland?

? To what extent will Scottish politics within the devolved framework be any different from established British norms and trends?

Answers to these questions are to be found in two distinct areas:

➡ the historical background to devolution

➡ the developments in Scottish politics in the late twentieth century.

DEVOLUTION IN HISTORICAL PERSPECTIVE

The roots of the devolution issue which emerged in the last thirty years of the twentieth century are visible in the Treaty of Union of 1707 which eliminated Scotland's independence and its Parliament but which also recognised that 'Scotland was different'. Ever since, Scotland has demonstrated both 'British' and 'Scottish' characteristics.

For over 250 years the Scots accepted the Union characterised

---

SCOTLAND'S DEVELOPING RELATIONSHIP WITHIN THE UK

There have been four principal elements in the evolution of Scotland's relationship with the United Kingdom:

1 Scotland the Nation—the cultural, social and political institutions, which 'survived' the Union of 1707 or were established after the Union. These institutions have ensured that Scotland has effectively been more than a region of Britain.

2 Scottish political behaviour, including voting behaviour, political parties and perceptions of national identity which have indicated fluctuating degrees of satisfaction or dissatisfaction with the 'Union'.

3 Administrative devolution—the administration of Scottish affairs by executive institutions such as the Scottish Office and, more recently, the Scottish Executive.

4 Legislative devolution—the legislative process for dealing with Scottish matters by Westminster institutions such as the Select and Grand Committees and, since 1999, the Scottish Parliament.

---

by parliamentary sovereignty, the Monarchy and a strong British executive (Cabinet government) without mounting any major objections. There was a certain amount of 'tinkering' (minor reforms) with the arrangements for the 'government of Scotland', usually in response to indications of Scottish dissatisfaction with existing arrangements expressed through voting behaviour and the party system. Nonetheless, the 'British' dimension in the government of Scotland prevailed over the 'Scottish' until the 1960s. Then the two important developments of (i) Scotland swinging to Labour from the 1959 Election onwards and (ii) the dramatic impact of the Scottish National Party in the 1970s set in motion political forces which could no longer be contained by 'tinkering'.

The establishment of a Scottish Parliament and Executive represents a decisive strengthening of the Scottish dimension and a profound reform of the British Constitution. The question which remains, and which will dominate

discussions about Scottish politics for years to come, is whether the Scottish Parliament and executive will permanently ensure Scotland's position within the United Kingdom or will instead lead to independence and the ending of the 'UK connection'.

DISTINCTIVE SCOTTISH INSTITUTIONS

The Scottish dimension was prominent from the outset of the British state. The social institutions which were retained at the time of the Treaty of Union almost 300 years ago are still significantly Scottish today.

Scotland's 'distinctiveness' was not insignificant. It led to Scotland being granted representation in the British Cabinet and a separate government department to look after its interests—the Scottish Office was established in 1885. Later Scotland would have legislative recognition through the establishment of a Scottish Grand Committee in the House of Commons. Scotland

The Church of Scotland

The Church of Scotland is Presbyterian in character and the product of a much stronger Reformation than occurred south of the border. It is Scotland's Established Church though by no means its only Church. The influence of the Church was particularly strong until the mid-nineteenth century in relation to education, poor relief and moral and social welfare. Today the Church functions politically as a pressure group, especially at the time of meetings of its General Assembly when the views of the Church are extensively reported by the Scottish media. Scotland has become much more heterogeneous in terms of religion. 16% of the Scottish population is Roman Catholic (30% in Glasgow). Significantly the elevation of Archbishop Winning to Cardinal was regarded as a matter of deep national pride and a recognition by the Vatican of Scotland's independence from England in terms of Church affairs.

retained a national consciousness which refused to die in spite of the loss of independence and the growth of a strong, centralised British state with its centre in Westminster and Whitehall.

The distinctive Scottish identity was maintained by several cultural and social institutions which survived the transition from independence to Union. Foremost among these are:

➤ the educational system

➤ the Church of Scotland

➤ the legal system.

Education

Education has long been thought of as a key defining feature of Scottish life. The principle of access to education based on merit was accepted in Scotland from the time of the Reformation at the end of the sixteenth century. Consequently, there was a national system of education open to all in Scotland, largely organised at parish level by the Church of Scotland, long before this developed

in England. Accordingly, Scottish education was widely believed to be 'democratic' in character and less socially exclusive than its English counterpart. Nonetheless, the Scottish upper classes opted for English public school education for their children. University attendance was more widespread in Scotland for most of the nineteenth and early twentieth centuries, though England has caught up in recent decades. Scottish education was much more centralised and 'national' or nationwide in character than its English counterpart until Thatcherism centralised English education in the 1980s.

Education remains one of the most significant functions of government in Scotland involving local authorities, the Scottish Executive Education Department and the Scottish Qualifications Authority (formerly the Scottish Exam Board). Decisions about subject curricula, teachers' salaries, and reform of examinations have long been among the most significant to be taken within the 'Scottish political system', although autonomy has

not been absolute when British governments have been adamant about comprehensive education and the publication of school league tables.

The Scottish legal system

The Scottish legal system and Scots Law constitute the third defining characteristic of Scottish distinctiveness inherited from the independent Scotland before 1707. The legal system has perhaps been the most significant politically because it has required the passage of separate Scottish legislation through the British Parliament and its implementation by devolved governmental institutions in Scotland itself.

Occasionally the distinctive features of Scots Law such as the majority verdict and the 'Not Proven' verdict hit the headlines. There have been efforts to abolish the 'Not Proven' verdict which may demand a greater burden of proof to convict on serious offences than would be the case if it did not exist. The separate Scottish legal

National consciousness in Scotland was traditionally expressed on football terracings.

system has meant that the education of lawyers and the practice of law have both remained rigorously Scottish. English lawyers are not qualified in or familiar with Scots Law (the reverse is also true) and therefore cannot practice in Scotland without acquiring the necessary training and qualifications.

National consciousness

What is significant about education, the law and the Church of Scotland is that decision making in those areas has been largely a matter for Scots living in Scotland and for Scottish institutions based in Scotland. The fact that this has happened generates the belief that this is how it should be. Also, it has maintained a degree of national consciousness which extends beyond the regionalism associated with Geordies in the North-east of England or Yorkshire Tykes or 'Essex Man'. Such national consciousness has also been kept alive by Scottish culture which supports a Scottish element in the broadcasting and news media ('Real Scots read the Record') and by Scottish sport which enjoys separate national status in some sports such as soccer (the World and European

Nations Cups), rugby (the Six Nations Championship), golf (the Dunhill Cup) and so on.

National consciousness has been evident in surveys of whether Scots perceive themselves as Scottish and/or British. One of the first modern surveys undertaken in the 1960s found that many Scots perceived themselves as Scottish rather than British while still voting for essentially British political parties in what may now be described as the last decade of the pre-devolution era.

DEVOLUTION: THE ELECTORAL BACKGROUND

Despite the Treaty of Union in 1707, Scotland was to develop politically in two areas in a way which suggested that it constituted a separate, if subordinate, political system within the United Kingdom.

Firstly, the Treaty of Union recognised the distinctiveness of Scotland's social and cultural institutions and their right to survive within the new state. This recognition eventually provided the force behind the establishment of

the Scottish Office and Scottish committees in the Commons. These Scottish political institutions, however, stopped far short of federalism and did not affect parliamentary sovereignty.

Secondly, Scottish political behaviour (political parties and the way in which people voted) recently acquired distinctive features which pushed the issue of how Scotland should be governed to the forefront of British politics. Labour's victory in the 1997 General Election was followed by the publication of a White Paper on Scotland's Parliament in July and of the Scotland Bill in December of that year.

There can be little doubt that the voting behaviour of the Scottish electorate over the last thirty years prompted Labour to reform Scotland's constitutional position within the United Kingdom.

Four-Party Politics

The Scottish electorate supports a four-party system with the Labour Party, the SNP, the Conservatives and the Liberal Democrats all enjoying significant levels of support, though the Scottish Conserv-

The Scottish Party System: Votes and Seats 1955–2001

Percentage Share of the Vote in British General Elections

	1955	1959	1964	1966	1970	1974[1]	1974[2]	1979	1983	1987	1992	1997	2001
Labour	46.7	46.7	48.7	49.9	44.5	36.6	36.2	41.5	35.1	42.4	39.0	45.6	43.9
Conservative	50.1	47.2	40.6	37.7	38.0	32.9	24.7	31.4	28.4	24.0	25.7	17.5	15.6
Liberal	1.9	4.1	7.6	6.8	5.5	7.9	8.3	8.7	24.5	19.0	13.1	13.0	16.4
SNP	0.5	0.8	2.4	5.0	11.4	21.9	30.4	17.3	11.0	14.0	21.5	22.1	20.1

Number of Westminster Seats Won

	1955	1959	1964	1966	1970	1974[1]	1974[2]	1979	1983	1987	1992	1997	2001
Labour	34	38	43	46	44	40	41	44	41	50	49	56	56[3]
Conservative	36	32	24	20	23	21	16	22	21	10	11	0	1
Liberal	1	1	4	5	3	3	3	3	8	9	9	10	10
SNP	0	0	0	0	1	7	11	2	2	3	3	6	5

Table 8.1   Note: There were two elections in 1974 in February[1] and October[2]; [3] includes the Speaker

Four significant developments in Scottish electoral politics, which explain the radical changes in the arrangements for the government of Scotland proposed by Labour in 1997, are illustrated in Table 8.1.
● Scotland has developed a four-party system which has implications for the government of Scotland under the proportional electoral system of the Scottish Parliament.
● The Scottish Conservatives have suffered a long-term decline since the late 1950s ending in the emergence of Scotland as a 'Tory-free zone' after the 1997 General Election.
● The Liberal Democrats and the SNP have been beneficiaries of the move from two-party to four-party politics in Scotland.
● Labour has maintained a dominant position in spite of the existence of four parties because the first-past-the-post electoral system employed for the Westminster Parliament works in its favour. In 2001 Labour won 78% of Scotland's seventy two seats with 43.9% of the vote.

atives won no Scottish seats in 1997 and only one in 2001. The ebb and flow of the Scottish vote is illustrated in Table 8.1. Since 1974, fluctuations in the relative strengths of the parties within the electorate have had a far-reaching impact upon the attitudes of the parties towards the issue of how Scotland should be governed.

The existence of four parties is significant because of the introduction of a measure of proportional representation in the electoral system which is used to elect the Scottish Parliament. Scotland has a Parliament much more representative of Scottish public opinion than one elected by the first-past-the-post system. (See pages 5–8.)

Conservatives

The Scottish Conservatives have suffered a sustained decline in support since 1955 when they won two more seats than Labour with just over 50% of the popular vote, the only party to do so in Scotland in the sixteen elections since 1945. The Conservatives were relegated to the status of the second party in the late 1950s and early 1960s when Scotland swung to Labour against the British trend. That status was challenged by the SNP in 1974 when the Nationalists came second in the popular vote in October, winning eight of their ten gains from the Tories.

The Conservatives recovered votes and seats in Scotland in the first of their four consecutive British victories in 1979 but they lost out to the other parties from 1987 onwards. Their Westminster representation was halved in 1987 and then eliminated in 1997. The limited Conservative recovery in 1979 and a stronger than expected electoral performance in 1992 bolstered Conservative opposition to demands for devolution temporarily. However, the 1997 result suggested strongly that the Conservatives were out of touch with Scottish opinion. The new Conservative leader, William Hague, announced shortly after his election that the Conservatives would

Conservative Seats Lost in 1997

To Labour
✗ Aberdeen South
✗ Ayr
✗ Dumfries
✗ Eastwood
✗ Edinburgh Pentlands
✗ Stirling

To the Liberal Democrats
✗ Aberdeen West & Kincardine
✗ Edinburgh West

To the SNP
✗ Galloway and Upper Nithsdale
✗ Perth
✗ Tayside North

Table 8.2

accept the result of the 1997 referendum on devolution. The Scottish Tories recovered only one seat in 2001 (Galloway & Upper Nithsdale).

Liberal Democrats and SNP

The fortunes of the formerly 'minor' parties have fluctuated since the mid-1960s when the Liberals made inroads into Tory seats between 1964 and 1966 and the SNP enjoyed their 'annus mirabilis' in 1974. The SNP have prospered in terms of votes, but the Liberals have enjoyed more success since 1983 in terms of seats won. SNP votes (20.1% in 2001) have been fairly evenly distributed throughout Scotland but the Liberal Democrats have managed to concentrate their strength sufficiently to win more seats than their nationalist rivals. Both have been winning rural and agricultural seats in the North and the South of Scotland leaving Labour dominant in urban seats. (See Figure 8.1.)

The electoral successes of the Liberal Democrats and the SNP, along with the demise of the Conservatives, strengthened the pro-devolution forces. However, that camp is itself divided into the British parties, Labour and the Liberal Democrats, who do not wish to proceed any further down 'the slippery slope to independence', and the SNP whose aim is 'independence within Europe'. This division is reflected in the Scottish Parliament with Labour and the Liberal Democrats forming a coalition in the Scottish Executive and the SNP acting as the major opposition party.

Labour

Labour has retained and even strengthened its dominant position within the four-party framework in spite of the transition from two-party to four-party politics. In 1997 Labour won fifty six seats, almost twenty more than in 1959, in spite of winning a slightly smaller share of the popular vote than it did then. Of the eleven seats lost by the Conservatives in 1997, Labour won six, the SNP won three and the Liberal Democrats won two. Labour has won the great majority of former Conservative seats in urban areas while the Liberal Democrats and the SNP have 'evicted' the Conservatives from rural and small town constituencies beyond the central belt. Labour is represented in the periphery, winning the Western Isles from the SNP in 1987 and gaining Inverness, Nairn and Lochaber from the Liberal Democrats in 1997.

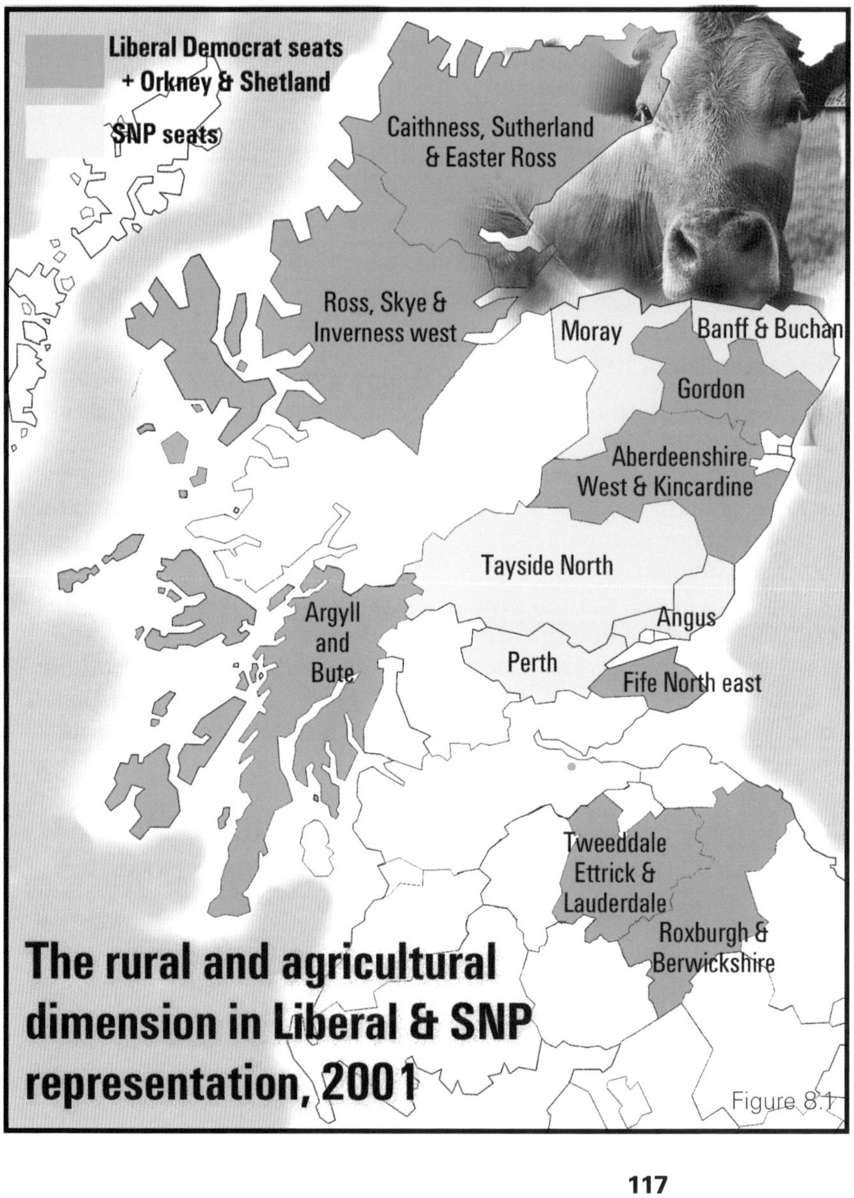

Labour's commitment to legislative devolution for Scotland was undertaken in the 1970s with British electoral considerations playing a decisive role. In 1974 the potential threat to Labour from the SNP (see Table 8.1) forced the Party's mainly English leadership to force-feed devolution to a largely unenthusiastic Labour Party in Scotland. Even though the first attempt to achieve legislative devolution suffered a humiliating failure in 1979, the issue had been established so firmly that it was unlikely to go away. With both the SNP and the Scottish Liberals committed to devolution for its own sake or as a first step towards independence, Scottish Labour became more enthusiastic. The Conservatives' immovable stance against the issue also strengthened the pro-devolution forces. By 1997 Labour was strong enough to be confident of sufficient public support to proceed with plans for a Scottish Parliament based on a proportional electoral system.

1979 Devolution Referendum

The disadvantage of using a referendum to decide a prickly issue was demonstrated in 1979 when Labour's first attempt at devolution ended in failure and sub-

Liberal Democrat seats + Orkney & Shetland

SNP seats

Caithness, Sutherland & Easter Ross

Ross, Skye & Inverness west

Moray

Banff & Buchan

Gordon

Aberdeenshire West & Kincardine

Tayside North

Argyll and Bute

Angus

Perth

Fife North east

Tweeddale Ettrick & Lauderdale

Roxburgh & Berwickshire

The rural and agricultural dimension in Liberal & SNP representation, 2001

Figure 8.1

An interesting feature of the devolution saga is that a Labour government twice gave the device of the referendum a key role in the decision making process.

A referendum has two advantages:
● A referendum is democratic in that it gives 'the people' a direct role in the decision making process which adds legitimacy to the decision taken whether the answer is Yes or No. The Conservatives, who opposed devolution strenuously, quickly moved to accept the result of the devolution referendum in 1997.

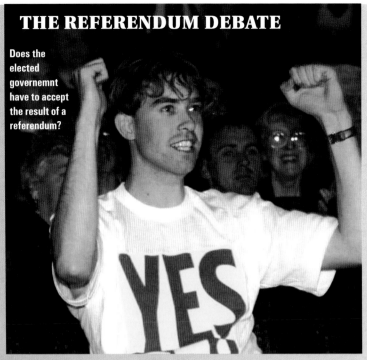

Does the elected governemnt have to accept the result of a referendum?

● A referendum allows a government not to decide. Basically, this means that difficult decisions may be put to the people and the government does not have to resign if the people reach a decision which the government does not really want. The British government resorted to referenda in 1975, 1979 and 1997 to decide on issues of constitutional reform.

On the other hand, the critics of referenda in a parliamentary system argue that a government which resorts to a referendum is renouncing its responsibility to legislate.

There is a conflict over whether a government should carry out the decision reached by the people.

sequently in electoral defeat. The Labour government which felt forced to introduce devolution for Scotland and Wales was weak in the House of Commons. It started off in October 1974 with an overall majority of four which it lost within three years, forcing it to rely on Liberal support in the division lobbies of the House of Commons—the 'Lib-Lab Pact'. The Labour Party itself was by no means unanimous in support of even the principle of devolution. The government was forced to hold a referendum and to accept the '40% rule'. This was proposed by a Labour MP, a Scotsman representing an English constituency, and required that 40% of the registered Scottish electorate, not merely 40% of those turning out to vote, must support the proposals. Worse, a significant minority in the Labour Party took part in a 'Scotland Votes No' campaign.

The result was a narrow victory for the Yes camp but the margin was much smaller than anticipated. (See Table 8.3.) The Yes vote amounted to only 32.9% of the registered electorate. The government decided it could not proceed to implement devolution.

A motion of no confidence was brought against the government. The Conservatives and the SNP voted against the Labour government which lost by 311 to 310 votes. The government resigned and the Conservatives, led by Mrs Thatcher, won the resulting election by a comfortable margin.

1997 Devolution Referendum

The 1997 devolution referendum provided a vastly different outcome. Held at the beginning of a Labour government elected by a massive majority, the referendum resulted in comfortable majorities in favour of both the Scottish Parliament and the proposed tax-varying powers. Labour was united—there was no 'Labour Votes No' campaign. The SNP and the Liberal Democrats both supported the proposals even though this was a short-term tactic on the part of the SNP whose objective remains independence. There was no 40% rule in 1997. Almost 45% of the registered electorate voted for the Parliament, but only 38.3% voted for tax varying powers. The 1997 vote emphasises the near to impossible constraint imposed in 1979 by the 40% rule.

Support for the Parliament ranged from 84.7% in West Dunbartonshire and 83.6% in the City of Glasgow to 57.3% in Orkney and 60.7% in Dumfries and Galloway. Support for the tax-varying powers ranged from 75% in Glasgow to 47.4% in Orkney and 48.8% in Dumfries where the 'Noes' won, narrowly, their only 'victories'. Some local council areas in the 'periphery', the regions farthest away from the densely populated urban and industrial central belt were least enthusiastic about the prospect of a devolved Scotland in which they might have different interests from the majority. Thus the Scottish Liberal Democrat leader, Jim Wallace, at that time MP for Orkney and Shetland and a strong devolutionist, represented an area suspicious of what devolution might bring.

ELECTION OF THE SCOTTISH PARLIAMENT

The first elections to the Scottish Parliament were held on 6 May 1999 using the two-ballot, mixed electoral system laid down in the *Scotland Act*. The 129 MSPs are selected by two distinct methods. Every voter is given two ballot

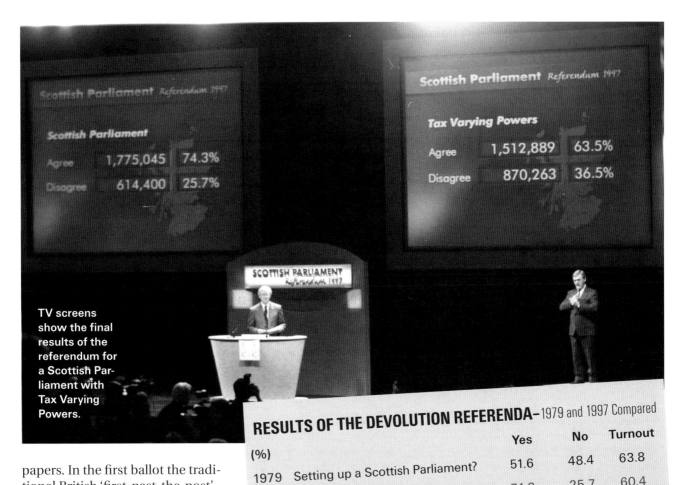

TV screens show the final results of the referendum for a Scottish Parliament with Tax Varying Powers.

RESULTS OF THE DEVOLUTION REFERENDA – 1979 and 1997 Compared

(%)		Yes	No	Turnout
1979	Setting up a Scottish Parliament?	51.6	48.4	63.8
1997	Setting up a Scottish Parliament?	74.3	25.7	60.4
1997	Tax-Varying Powers?	63.5	36.5	60.4

Table 8.3

papers. In the first ballot the traditional British 'first-past-the-post' system returns seventy three constituency representatives who represent the same constituencies as do Westminster MPs except that Orkney and Shetland each count as one constituency in the Scottish Parliament. In the second ballot another fifty six MSPs are selected from party lists in eight regional constituencies (seven MSPs per regional constituency) by the additional member system (AMS).

The government's White Paper on Devolution justified this system on the grounds that its "greater proportionality" would "build stability into the overall settlement". However, the government stopped short of the high level of proportionality associated with the single transferable vote in multi-member constituencies. (The operation of the additional member system used to allocate seats from second ballot votes is explained on page 122.)

The familiar results associated with the first-past-the-post electoral system are illustrated in Table 8.4. Labour won the most votes in the

first ballot (39%), but was well short of a majority and of the 45.6% won in the 1997 British General Election in Scotland. Nevertheless, Labour won almost three-quarters of the seventy three constituency seats available in the first ballot. The Liberal Democrats were also clear beneficiaries winning twelve seats with only 14% of the votes. In sharp contrast the SNP won only seven constituencies with double the Liberal Democrats' share of the popular vote and the Conservatives won no seats in spite of attracting 2% more of the vote than the Liberal Democrats.

The main reason for the discrepancy between percentage shares of votes and number of seats under this electoral system lies in variations between the parties in the geographical distribution of the popular vote. The Liberal Democrat vote is heavily concentrated in seats it has a chance of winning.

The considerable SNP vote in the first ballot, the second party in the popular vote, was more evenly distributed across the seventy three constituencies which placed the SNP in the familiar position of the Liberals in British elections.

Only three parties won seats in the first ballot. The seventy third seat (Falkirk) was won by the Labour dissident, Dennis Canavan, who held the same British parliamentary seat. Canavan was not selected by Labour for the Scottish Parliament elections. In a highly publicised and controversial move Canavan decided to run independently for the seat against the official Labour candidate. Canavan won by a comfortable margin because he attracted more Labour votes (18,511) than the official candidate(6,319) who came second.

The Referendum count at the Meadowbank Stadium in Edinburgh.

The 1999 Scottish Parliament Election Results

Party	FIRST BALLOT Constituency MSPs			SECOND BALLOT Regional List MSPs			Overall Result	
	Percentage of Vote	Number of Seats (73)	Percentage of Seats	Percentage of Vote	Number of Seats (56)	Percentage of Seats	Number of Seats (129)	Percentage of Seats
Labour	39	53	72.6	33	3	5.4	56	43.4
SNP	29	7	9.6	28	28	50.0	35	27.2
Conservative	16	0	0	13	18	32.0	18	13.9
Lib. Dem.	14	12	9.2	15	5	8.9	17	13.2
Green				4	1	1.8	1	
SSP				2.1	1	1.8	1	
Other		1					1	
Totals		73			56		129	

Turnout 59%

SSP *Scottish Socialist Party;* Other *Dennis Canavan*

Table 8.4

IMPACT OF THE NEW VOTING SYSTEM

The additional member system was introduced to alleviate some of the biases of the first-past-the-post system. The impact of the AMS counting system on the allocation of the second ballot list seats is clearly in evidence in Table 8.4.

Small parties rewarded

The first obvious feature of the second ballot result is the number of seats won by small or minor parties with very small shares of the popular vote. The Greens won one seat in the Lothians regional constituency with 6.9% of the vote. The

Scottish Socialist Party won one seat in the Glasgow regional constituency with 7.25% of the popular vote. These successes would not have occurred under the first-past-the-post system.

The electoral fortunes of Tommy Sheridan, the Scottish Socialist leader, have varied according to the size of the constituencies he has contested and the electoral system in use. Sheridan has represented the Pollok ward on the City of Glasgow Council since 1995. Although these elections are decided by the first-past-the-post system Sheridan has defeated the major party candidates because he has built up strong support in a small, relatively deprived

area where he is well known. In 1999, on the same day as the Scottish Parliament elections, Sheridan won his local government seat (2,972 voted) with 42.5% of the vote beating the Labour candidate into second place. In the first ballot of the Scottish Parliament elections (first-past-the-post), Sheridan stood in the Pollok parliamentary constituency (26,080 voted) winning 21.5% of the vote and coming third behind the Labour/Co-op and SNP candidates. The AMS counting system in the second ballot in the Glasgow regional constituency, with an electorate exceeding half a million, returned Sheridan and the Liberal Democrat Robert Brown to the Scottish Parliament with 7.25% and 7.21% of the vote respectively.

Greater voter choice

The second ballot gives voters the opportunity to change their allegiance. The major change in party support between the two ballots lies in the 6% fall in Labour's share of the popular vote. The beneficiaries of this behaviour were the small parties. The Greens won 4% and the SSP 2% of the Scottish popular vote in the second ballot. Both parties are to the left of the party spectrum and attracted support from Labour voters who may have been aware that their party would not win many seats in the second ballot where the counting system penalises parties which win the most seats in the first ballot.

Successful parties rewarded

The SNP, which did badly in the first ballot when seats are compared to votes, won exactly 50% of the fifty six seats from the second ballot. The Conservatives also did well in the second ballot winning eighteen seats compared to none at all first time round. In contrast the Liberal Democrats won only five seats in the second ballot compared to twelve in the first though their popular vote share was very similar in the two ballots.

A fairer result

The overall impact of AMS is also illustrated in Table 8.5. Above all the AMS system corrects many of the biases of the first-past-the-post system. The gaps between percentage shares of seats and votes are considerably reduced. There is much greater proportionality in the results achieved by the AMS electoral system. These consequences of AMS can be seen by comparing the party composition of the Scottish Westminster delegation returned in the 1997 and 2001 British General Elections (see Table 8.1) with the party composition of the Scottish Parliament. Labour's share of MSPs (43.4%) was much closer to its popular vote share (39%) in the 1999 Scot-

tish Election than was the case in Scotland in the 1997 and 2001 British General Elections. Above all, for the first time since 1955 Labour did not win a majority of seats in a Scotland-wide election.

Coalition government

The most dramatic consequence of AMS was seen in the formation of a Labour-Liberal Democrat coalition government with Donald Dewar (Labour) as First Minister and Jim Wallace (Liberal Democrat) as his Deputy. This coalition was made possible by the fact that no party, especially Labour, won enough seats to form a majority administration on its own. To enjoy a comfortable working majority in the Scottish Parliament

on its own a party would have to win at least half of the overall composition of the Parliament (129 in total) in the first ballot. Labour won fifty three seats in the first ballot which left it twelve seats short of an overall majority.

Future elections are more likely to produce coalition government than single party government in Scotland. Whether the current coalition will survive the next elections to the Scottish Parliament remains to be seen. Other coalitions are possible. Whether any will materialise after future elections will depend upon which parties can get on with one another. It is difficult to envisage a Labour-SNP coalition or a Labour-Conservative coalition.

Gender Representation in the Scottish Parliament.

One of the most striking features of the results of the first elections to the new Scottish Parliament in 1999 was that 48 of the 129 MSPs elected were women, 37% of the total. This is double the proportion of women MPs at Westminster, and is close to the 40% achieved in Sweden.

In the first ballot, 41% of the successful candidates were women and in the second ballot 32% of the successful candidates were women. Labour selected many more women candidates than any of the other major Scottish parties, choosing equal numbers of men and women as candidates in the seventy three first ballot constituency seats. Labour succeeded in electing 70% of its women candidates in the first ballot. Labour's dominance of the first ballot meant that other parties had a very low success rate in electing men and women in that part of the election. In the second ballot when the SNP was the most successful party, 46% of its successful list candidates were women. The SNP and Labour put more women in the top list positions than the other two major parties.

Women Candidates and MSPs by Party:
1999 Scottish Parliament Elections

Party	Constituency Seats		Additional Member List Seats	Total N°. of women elected
	N°. of women candidates	N°. of women elected	N°. of women elected	
Labour	37	26/53	2/3	28/56
Conservative	13	0/0	3/18	3/18
Liberal Democrat	20	2/12	0/5	2/17
SNP	19	2/7	13/28	15/35
Others	NA	0/1	0/2	0/3
Total	89/292	30/73	18/56	48/129

Table 8.5 Source: Scottish Parliament Election Results reported in *The (Glasgow) Herald*, 8 May 1999.
Notes: The 'Others' elected were Dennis Canavan (dissident Labour), Tommy Sheridan (SSP) and Robin Harper(Green).

The counting method for the additional member system is described in the White Paper on the Scottish Parliament.

1   "Each elector will be entitled to cast two votes: one for a constituency MSP and one for the party of his/her choice."

2   "Votes for constituency MSPs will be counted on a 'first-past-the-post' basis."

3   The fifty six additional members will be elected in eight 7-member constituencies (the existing European constituencies) as follows:

- "The number of votes cast for each party ... will be counted."
- "The number of votes cast for each party will then be divided by the number of constituency MSPs gained in Parliamentary constituencies ... plus one".
- "The party with the highest total after the (above) calculation is done gains the first additional member."
- "The second to seventh additional Members are allocated in the same way but additional Members gained are included in the calculations."

The operation and impact of the AMS counting system is illustrated below by working out the counting of votes from the second ballot and the subsequent allocation of the seven additional list seats for the Glasgow regional constituency.

GLASGOW VOTING RESULTS IN SCOTTISH PARLIAMENT ELECTIONS

	No. of MSPs from 1st ballot	Votes from 2nd ballot
Labour	10	112,588
SNP	0	65,360
Conservative	0	20,239
Liberal Democrat	0	18,473
SSP	0	18,581
Greens	0	10,159

Allocation of MSPs from the Second Ballot using the formula: $\dfrac{\text{Number of Second Ballot Votes}}{\text{Number of MSPs} + 1}$

	1ST COUNT	2ND COUNT	3RD COUNT	4TH COUNT	5TH COUNT	6TH COUNT	7TH COUNT
LABOUR	$\frac{112,588}{10+1}=10,235$	$\frac{112,588}{10+1}=10,235$	$\frac{112,588}{10+1}=10,235$	$\frac{112,588}{10+1}=10,235$	$\frac{112,588}{10+1}=10,235$	$\frac{112,588}{10+1}=10,235$	$\frac{112,588}{10+1}=10,235$
SNP	$\frac{65,360}{0+1}=\mathbf{65,360}$	$\frac{65,360}{1+1}=\mathbf{32,680}$	$\frac{65,360}{2+1}=\mathbf{21,786}$	$\frac{65,360}{3+1}=16,340$	$\frac{65,360}{3+1}=16,340$	$\frac{65,360}{3+1}=16,340$	$\frac{65,360}{3+1}=\mathbf{16,340}$
CONSERVATIVE	$\frac{20,239}{0+1}=20,239$	$\frac{20,239}{0+1}\;20,239$	$\frac{20,239}{0+1}=20,239$	$\frac{20,239}{0+1}=\mathbf{20,239}$	$\frac{20,239}{1+1}=10,119$	$\frac{20,239}{1+1}=10,119$	$\frac{20,239}{1+1}=10,119$
LIBERAL DEMOCRAT	$\frac{18,473}{0+1}=18,473$	$\frac{18,473}{0+1}=18,473$	$\frac{18,473}{0+1}=18,473$	$\frac{18,473}{0+1}=18,473$	$\frac{18,473}{0+1}=18,473$	$\frac{18,473}{0+1}=\mathbf{18,473}$	$\frac{18,473}{1+1}=9,236$
SSP	$\frac{18,581}{0+1}=18,581$	$\frac{18,581}{0+1}=18,581$	$\frac{18,581}{0+1}=18,581$	$\frac{18,581}{0+1}=18,581$	$\frac{18,581}{0+1}=\mathbf{18,581}$	$\frac{18,581}{1+1}=9,290$	$\frac{18,581}{1+1}=9,290$
GREENS	$\frac{10,159}{0+1}=10,159$	$\frac{10,159}{0+1}=10,159$	$\frac{10,159}{0+1}=10,159$	$\frac{10,159}{0+1}=10,159$	$\frac{10,159}{0+1}=10,159$	$\frac{10,159}{0+1}=10,159$	$\frac{10,159}{0+1}=10,159$
MSP awarded to	SNP	SNP	SNP	Conservative	SSP	Lib Dem	SNP

Table 8.6

Labour won all ten of Glasgow's constituency MSPs in the first ballot, so Labour's second ballot vote is divided by eleven in the first count; the vote totals for all other parties are divided by one because none of them won a seat in the first ballot.

Thus Labour with over 40% of the popular vote in the second ballot won no list seats because its monopoly of seats in the first ballot meant that its second ballot vote total was divided by eleven. The votes of four other parties exceeded Labour's 10,235 votes in the first count. The SNP won four Glasgow list seats because it came a strong second in the second ballot with 25.5% of the popular vote. This enabled the SNP to win the first three list seats. The Conservatives, the Liberal Democrats and the SSP each won about 7% of the vote, enough to win one list seat. The Greens would have won the ninth seat if there had been two more list seats available.

SCOTTISH GOVERNMENT

HISTORICAL BACKGROUND

The Scotland we know today existed as a unified and independent state from the eleventh century until the beginning of the eighteenth century. A determined effort by the English King Edward I to add Scotland, like Wales, to England's territorial domain was beaten off by the Scots in 1314 at the Battle of Bannockburn which confirmed Scotland's independent status. In 1603 the Crowns of Scotland and England were united by an accident of birth. Elizabeth I, the Virgin Queen, had no children and no immediate heirs. The English throne fell into the hands of her nearest relative, King James VI of Scotland, son of the executed Mary, Queen of Scots. James hurried off to London to claim his inheritance, never to return. For the next 104 years Scotland and England shared a Head of State but continued as independent countries with independent Parliaments. The 'government of Scotland' was still completely 'Scottish'. This state of affairs ended in 1707 when the Treaty of Union brought England and Scotland together as the Kingdom of Great Britain.

As we have already noted, the Treaty of Union gave legislative sovereignty exclusively to the new British Parliament. For almost 300 years Scotland did not possess a legislative assembly to provide any popular Scottish control over politics and administration north of the border. However, the Treaty of Union did make separate provision for the administration of those aspects of Scottish life which were deemed to differ significantly from their English counterparts. Although education, law and religion were clearly Scottish in character, the 'government of Scotland' was essentially carried out by British institutions located in Westminster and Whitehall.

Scotland's lack of legislative authority ended in 1999 when the new devolved Scottish Parliament and Executive were established after the passage at Westminster of the *Scotland (1998) Act*. This was introduced by the Labour government which took office following the 1997 British General Election. Devolution does not signify the return of formal constitutional independence. However, devolution does mean that individuals living in Scotland and sitting on Scottish political institutions will exercise much more political control over social, cultural and economic affairs in Scotland.

This brief historical account of the political status of Scotland suggests that there has been and remains competition and tension between three territorial dimensions: the British, the Scottish and the local. Until the Treaty of Union early in the eighteenth century such government as existed in Scotland was provided by the Monarch and the Scottish Parliament in Edinburgh and by local institutions such as the royal burghs. Scotland's relationship with England, often one of conflict, determined much of the character of Scottish politics. With the Treaty of Union the British dimension, in which England was dominant due to population size, gained the upper hand and politically ambitious Scots sought advancement through British institutions such as Parliament, the government and the Armed Services.

Until 1999 the most significant feature of the 'government of Scotland' was that it was almost exclusively administrative in character and was subject to overriding British constitutional principles of collective ministerial responsibility and the sovereignty of Parliament. (See Chapters 5 and 6). However there were distinctive Scottish institutions at both executive (for instance the Scottish Office) and legislative (for example the Scottish Grand Committee) levels which allowed commentators and politicians to talk of and to write about 'the government of Scotland'.

The Scottish Office

The Treaty of Union established one Parliament but it did not transfer all public sector functions to the British executive in Whitehall. Until the Jacobite Rebellion of 1745 there was a Scottish Secretary of State. Following the Rebellion, Scotland increasingly came to be administered from London. In the second half of the nineteenth century there was considerable feeling that the arrangements made for the government of Scotland were remote and insufficiently 'Scottish'. The post of Secretary for Scotland was re-established in 1885 though it was not elevated to the status of Secretary of State until 1926. The Scottish Office was also established in 1885. It was located mainly in Dover House in Whitehall. Until 1939 the Edinburgh wing of the Scottish Office had only around thirty civil servants. There was a major reform of the Scottish Office in 1939 when it was moved to St Andrew's House in Edinburgh and civil servants were transferred north of the border to staff it. The size and functions of the Scottish Office have been severely reduced by the introduction of the Scottish Parliament and Executive which have taken over many of its functions.

The Scottish Office was an acknowledgement of the political need to bring the business of government closer to the people it affected most. The job of the modern Scottish Office before devolution was to carry out the functions of government which were in some sense at least as much 'Scottish' as 'British'. The areas of Scottish life which required separate Scottish administration are indicated by the five major departments which were still in existence in the 1990s: Agriculture and Fisheries, Education, Economic Planning, Development, and Home and Health.

Secretary of State for Scotland

At the head of the Scottish Office is the Secretary of State for Scotland who has overall responsibility for its activities. The Scottish Secretary has a seat in the Cabinet where he or she is expected to represent Scottish interests. However, as well as being Scotland's 'representative in the British Cabinet' the Scottish Secretary was long regarded as the 'Cabinet's representative in Scotland'.

As a consequence of devolution, the 'government of Scotland' has become a complex, multi-level process. The 'British' element continues in that Scotland remains an integral part of the United Kingdom of Great Britain and Northern Ireland. Many important political decisions, for example the running of the economy and foreign policy, will continue to be taken in Westminster and Whitehall and implemented in Scotland in exactly the same way as in the rest of the United Kingdom. Scottish MPs still sit in the House of Commons and some, such as Gordon Brown, John Reid and Robin Cook, occupy leading positions in British government and in British political parties.

The 'Scottish' element in the 'government of Scotland' has been significantly extended by the establishment of Scottish-based legislative (popularly elected) and executive institutions taking political decisions which used to be taken in London. Early decisions of these Scottish institutions on issues such as teachers' pay, university tuition fees, Section 28 and care of the elderly suggest that many political decisions will be different from those which would have been taken in the absence of devolution. The 'British' and the 'Scottish' will struggle for supremacy as the 'government of Scotland' unfolds in the years to come.

SCOTLAND IN THE BRITISH CONSTITUTION

In constitutional terms the British dimension remains dominant in the post-devolution era. In spite of the significant constitutional reform of a Scottish Parliament and Welsh Assembly, Britain remains a unitary state. The constitutional relationship between the Scottish Parliament and the British Parliament is defined clearly in the following crucial paragraph in the White Paper on Scotland's Parliament:

The Scotland Office, as it is now called, was inevitably reduced in terms of both personnel and functions by the coming of the devolved institutions. There are now only two principal Ministers, the Secretary of State and a Minister of State with unspecified responsibilities. Before devolution there were five whose responsibilities paralleled the functions of the departments in the Scottish Office.

Scotland in the British Parliament

Since 1983 Scotland has sent seventy two MPs to Westminster to represent its 5.1 million inhabitants (3,946,113 voters in 1997). Scotland has thus been over-represented in the House of Commons relative to population compared to England, Wales and Northern Ireland. This apparent democratic discrepancy was justified in terms of Scotland's distinctive peripheral regions such as the Western Isles, Orkney and Shetland and the Highlands which merited separate representation in spite of low population densities. Scotland's over-representation is scheduled to be reduced in the light of devolution.

We have already seen that Scotland's special circumstances derived from history gave rise to special administrative arrangements in the establishment of the Scottish Office. Similarly, separate legislation was often required to deal with Scotland's social and cultural circumstances such as a separate educational system. Consequently, parliamentary procedures were developed to ensure that Scotland's MPs had a major say in the passage of Scottish legislation and had an opportunity to scrutinise the government's administration of Scottish affairs. These procedures included Scottish Questions, the Scottish Grand Committee, Scottish standing legislative committees and a Select Committee on Scottish Affairs.

Scottish Grand Committee

For many years the Scottish Grand Committee was a poor substitute for a separate Scottish parliament. It was one of the largest committees in the House of Commons because it included, and still includes all Scottish MPs. It was established in 1894 to meet the criticism that Scottish legislation was being discussed and decided by the English majority. Allowing all Scottish MPs to serve on the Grand Committee was intended to convey the impression of an approximation to a Scottish Parliament, though the Grand Committee remained subservient to the will of the Commons as a whole. It dealt with the committee stage of non-controversial legislation, all Scottish legislation still having to secure the consent of the House at the second and third readings however.

The politics of devolution encouraged Conservative governments after 1979 to adapt the Grand Committee to meet the demand for greater Scottish control over Scottish affairs. Michael Forsyth, Scottish Secretary of State, attempted to distract attention away from widespread demands for a Scottish Parliament and meaningful legislative devolution by holding meetings of the Grand Committee in different Scottish towns. Scottish Questions, adjournment debates and Third Reading debates were added to the Grand Committee's procedures. The Grand Committee survived the coming of devolution.

In 1999, the Scottish Secretary of State, Donald Dewar, gave up that position to take up the office of Scotland's First Minister at the head of the new Scottish Executive. Dewar was succeeded as Scottish Secretary of State by John Reid and then by Helen Liddell (above), both of whom retained the seat in the British Cabinet.

"... the UK Parliament is and will remain sovereign in all matters; but as part of the government's resolve to modernise the British constitution, Westminster will be choosing to exercise sovereignty by devolving legislative responsibilities to a Scottish Parliament without in any way diminishing its own powers."

This means that in post-devolution Britain, legislative sovereignty remains with the Westminster Parliament which could legitimately, as a last resort, overrule or veto the enactments of the elected Scottish (and Welsh) legislatures.

In choosing devolution as the vehicle of "significant constitutional reform" the founding fathers of Scotland's new institutions deliberately rejected federalism. In a federal state like the United States the sub-national territorial units, the American states, are constitutionally assigned legislative powers which in theory cannot be overruled by the national government. Disputes between the two levels of government often have to be resolved by the Supreme Court.

The provisions of the White Paper in effect point to a critical distinction between the 'constitutional' and the 'political'. What is permissible and legitimate constitutionally may not be viable politically. Relationships between the British and Scottish institutions of government are in their infancy. How they develop depends on many factors such as election results in Scotland and in Britain, variations in popular support for Scottish independence, and the impact of any conflicts of economic and other interests between Scotland and Britain. Relationships between a Labour government in London and a Labour-Liberal Democrat coalition in Scotland are unlikely to stimulate the use of the right to veto Scottish legislation. The same cannot be confidently asserted about the likely relationship between a Conservative government in London and a Labour dominated coalition in Scotland.

JUSTIFYING DEVOLUTION

In his foreword to the Labour government's White Paper on Scotland's Parliament, Donald Dewar, then Secretary of State for Scotland, and soon to become Scotland's first First Minister, justified his devolution proposals by claiming that the new system of Scottish government would "strengthen democratic control" and "make government more accountable". 'Control' and 'accountability' are two key attributes of democracy which should be achieved through elections and the parliamentary process. Elections allow voters to 'control' government by linking the selection of the people's representatives to the policies they stand for thereby effectively subjecting the executive branch to the test of re-election or rejection. The parliamentary process makes the government 'accountable' by requiring Ministers to defend their policy and administrative decisions and actions in front of the representatives of the people.

Devolution is expected to improve both 'democratic control' and 'accountability' in relation to Scottish government and politics in two ways.

☛ The number of Scottish decisions on Scottish issues have been greatly increased as the Scottish Parliament and Executive take over functions previously carried out by 'British' institutions.

The establishment in the nineteenth century of the Scottish Office signified an acceptance of the principle that certain areas of Scottish life were sufficiently distinctive to merit a separate decision making process and separate institutions. The Scottish Parliament extends that principle by vesting much of such decision making in an elected legislature, bringing 'control' much closer to the Scottish people.

☛ The electoral system chosen for the Scottish Parliament includes a strong element of proportionality compared to the tra-

DEVOLVED MATTERS
The Scottish Parliament has control over the following areas:
1. Health
2. Education and Training
3. Local Government, Social Work and Housing
4. Economic Development & Transport
5. Law and Home Affairs
6. Sport and the Arts
7. Agriculture, Fishing & Forestry
8. Environment
9. Other Matters

THE RIGHT TO LEGISLATE?

The White Paper laid down several procedures to deal with the possibility that disputes could arise over whether the Scottish Parliament or the British Parliament has the right to legislate on particular matters. Under the heading of 'Liason' the White Paper foresaw the potential for disputes between Scottish institutions and their UK counterparts being dealt with and resolved by:

1. "Good communication" between the Scottish Executive and UK Departments at civil service and political or ministerial levels.

2. The Scottish Parliament's Presiding Officer is assigned responsibility for ensuring that proposals for legislation by the Scottish Parliament are 'intra vires'—within the 'devolved matters' defined in the Scotland Act.

3. "In the event of a dispute between the Scottish Executive and the UK government about vires (powers) remaining unresolved, there will be provision for it to be referred to the Judicial Committee of the Privy Council."

4. The Scottish Secretary of State, whose job description has been severely reduced by devolution, is expected to promote "communication between the Scottish Parliament and Executive and between the UK Parliament and government on matters of mutual interest ...".

ditional British first-past-the-post system. Democracy is almost universally defined as 'rule by the people'. In most modern democracies the people's rule is 'indirect' through their elected representatives. PR usually gives more of the people an influence over the identity of their representatives and over the composition of the government which rules them.

The appearance of a Labour-Liberal Democrat coalition in the Scottish Executive in 1999 means that 53% of the Scottish electorate (first ballot) is represented by that coalition government compared to the 42% of the British electorate which voted for the Labour government which emerged from the 2001 British General Election. Scottish government could be said to look more 'democratic' than its British equivalent.

THE CONSTITUTIONAL PLAN

The structure and functions of Scotland's devolved government are to be found in the Labour government's White Paper 'Scotland's Parliament' published in July 1997 and in the *Scotland Act* passed by the British Parliament in 1998. It is made clear in the White Paper that Scotland's devolved institutions are to follow British constitutional and political practice and traditions: "The Scottish Executive will operate in a way similar to the UK government and will be held accountable to the Scottish Parliament".

The Policy Making Remit

'What the Scottish Parliament Can Do', Chapter 2 of the White Paper, lists the devolved matters which could be addressed by the Scottish Parliament. No fewer than forty seven 'devolved matters' are listed under nine headings. (See page 126.) These headings indicate a wide range of matters important to any society and provide ample tasks for the Scottish Parliament and Executive.

The scene inside the Scottish Parliament in Edinburgh as SMP's are sworn in during the opening ceremony.

The White Paper also lists the 'reserved matters' which remain the preserve of the UK government and Parliament—those matters "which can be more effectively and beneficially handled on a United Kingdom basis". Without such 'reserved matters' there would be no need for Scotland to remain within the United Kingdom.

The UK's 'reserved matters' include some of the most vital functions of the modern state. Reserved to the UK are such matters as:

- the Constitution
- foreign policy
- defence and national security
- macroeconomic, monetary and fiscal affairs other than Scotland's limited tax varying powers
- employment
- social security
- transport safety and regulation

The Scottish institutions are not confined to forty seven 'devolved matters'. The *Scotland Act* also assigns the Scottish Parliament legislative power over "all matters which are not reserved". This provision amounts to an open invitation to the Scottish Parliament to take up any issue or problem not falling into the matters reserved to the UK Parliament.

THE INSTITUTIONS OF SCOTTISH GOVERNMENT

The Scottish Parliament

Members of the Scottish Parliament, known as MSPs in order to avoid confusion with MPs (Members of the House of Commons) and MEPs (Members of the European Parliament), serve a fixed term of four years.

The fixed term provision may be cut short if two-thirds of the MSPs support a motion to this effect or if there is a stalemate when attempting to appoint the First Minister. The two-thirds provision means that the Parliament could bring down the Executive and enforce a general election. However, that strategy may be difficult to follow. Building a two-thirds majority may prove to be impossible. In the first Parliament Labour won 43% of the seats, thus denying a two-thirds majority to any other combination of parties including the Liberal Democrats if they left the governing coalition. In that situation, which could well be repeated after future elections, some Labour MSPs would have to rebel to bring down the Executive.

The social composition of the 1999 intake was notable for an acclaimed closing of the 'gender gap' compared to the House of Commons. Of the 129 MSPs, forty eight (37%) were women compared to 20% at Westminster.

Labour eliminated the gender gap altogether, twenty eight of Labour's fifty six MSPs being women. The SNP came close to doing so with fifteen women (43%) among its thirty five MSPs. The Conservatives and the Liberal Democrats lagged behind with three out of eighteen and two out of seventeen respectively.

The role of Speaker is carried out by the Presiding Officer and his or her deputies. The first Presiding Officer was David Steel, the former leader of the Liberal Party.

The Scottish Executive

The Scottish Executive is drawn from within the ranks of MSPs except for the Law Officers, the Lord Advocate and the Solicitor General, who are not members of the Parliament. Consistent with the parliamentary system, the White Paper laid down that the First Minister and his or her executive colleagues "will be accountable to the Scottish Parliament".

The most outstanding feature of the first Scottish Executive, illustrated in Table 9.1, is that it is a coalition between the Labour and Liberal Democrat Parties. This is a relatively novel departure in British politics although coalition or power-sharing executives have been seen in recent decades either as one way of bridging acute social divisions (Northern Ireland) or as more 'democratic'. Coalition is a frequent consequence of PR electoral systems so the decision to use the Additional Member System for elections to the Scottish Parliament was taken in the full knowledge of the probable consequences. The coalition feature was foreseen by the supporters of devolution in the 1980s/1990s either as desirable in its own right or as the necessary price to pay for maximising cross-party support for devolution itself.

Labour was the dominant partner in the coalition to emerge from the 1999 Election, with nine of the principal Ministers drawn from the most successful party. It had

been clear for years before this Election that Labour would be reluctant to bring either the Conservatives or the SNP into a coalition, and indeed neither would have been willing to participate. The Liberal Democrats were suitable coalition partners because they had shared Labour's enthusiasm for devolution during the years of Conservative dominance at Westminster which meant that devolution would not be implemented until the Conservatives lost a British general election. The SNP preferred and continues to prefer the independence option which makes it wary of participating in a coalition in a devolved Scotland which falls a long way short of independence.

Choosing the First Minister and the Executive

In a parliamentary system the leader of the executive branch will be the political party leader who can command majority support in the legislature. In Britain that is normally the leader of the party which wins the most seats in the general election. Problems arise only if no party wins an overall majority.

On 13 May 1999, the Scottish Parliament elected Donald Dewar as First Minister. His election was

part of the broader 'Partnership for Scotland' agreed by the Labour and Liberal Democrat parties as the method chosen to establish an Executive able to survive in the multi-party Parliament. Not all Labour and Liberal Democrat MSPs agreed with the 'partnership' strategy of their party leaders. Some Labour MSPs did not want a coaliton, preferring to go it alone with a minority single-party executive and daring the other parties to bring down the new government of Scotland, a move which would not have gone down too well in public opinion. Some Liberal Democrat MSPs did not wish to make the policy compromises which they believed the 'partnership' would make inevitable. Minority single-party government remains an option following future elections.

Once the Scottish Parliament decides on its First Minister the relationship between the Scottish and British Constitutions is again emphasised. The Monarch then appoints the First Minister "on the advice of the Presiding Officer after the Scottish Parliament has nominated a candidate ...". The appointment of other Ministers to the Scottish Executive lies in the hands of the First Minister, just as the Prime Minister appoints members of the British Cabinet, but

THE COMPOSITION OF THE SCOTTISH EXECUTIVE JANUARY 2002				
DEPARTMENT	MINISTER	PARTY	DEPUTY	PARTY
First Minister	J. McConnell	Labour		
Justice & Deputy First Minister	J. Wallace	Lib. Dem.	R. Simpson	Labour
Education and Young People	C. Jamieson	Labour	N. Stephen	Lib. Dem.
Enterprise, Transport and Lifelong Learning	W. Alexander	Labour	L. MacDonald	Labour
Environment and Rural Development	R. Finnie	Lib. Dem.	A. Wilson	Labour
Tourism, Culture and Sport	M. Watson	Labour	E. Murray	Labour
Health and Community Care	M. Chisholm	Labour	H. Henry M. Mulligan	Labour
Parliament	P. Ferguson	Labour	E. Robson	Lib. Dem.
Social Justice	I. Gray	Labour	M. Curran	Labour
Finance and Public Services	A. Kerr	Labour	P. Peacock	Labour

Table 9.1

When Donald Dewar was elected First Minister he received seventy one votes compared to thirty five for the SNP leader, Alex Salmond, eighteen votes for the Conservative leader, David McLetchie, and three votes for the Labour dissident turned Independent, Dennis Canavan. Dewar received all but two of the combined total of Labour and Liberal Democrat MSPs' votes. One Liberal Democrat MSP abstained and the Presiding Officer felt that it was inappropriate for him to vote.

Scottish Parliament is similar to that in the American Congress in that the committees parallel government Departments and deal with both legislative proposals and the administration relevant to the Department in question.

FINANCING THE GOVERNMENT OF SCOTLAND

How should the expenditure of the new Scottish government departments and their policies be financed? This is one of the most difficult questions facing politicians on both sides of the border. It threatens good relations between Scotland and the rest of the United Kingdom. It is not a new question in so far as it has long been claimed that Scotland received more than its fair share of British public expenditure in the pre-devolution era. Treasury figures released in 1997 suggested that public expenditure per capita (the most common test of 'fairness') was higher in Scotland than in any other British 'region' except Northern Ireland. The amounts disclosed in Figure 9.1 include expenditure by both British Departments in Scotland and the Scottish Office.

Such 'discrepancies' are partly based on different levels of deprivation across British regions. In respect of Scotland's apparently favoured and privileged position, part of the explanation lies in its relatively large territorial size and low population density outside the central belt which means that expenditure per person for the same level of services such as education and health care is higher.

Differences such as those shown in Figure 9.1 stimulated political debate along regional and party political lines in the pre-devolution era. For electoral and political reasons Labour was sympathetic to Scottish and Welsh claims that differences in expenditure were justifiable. The coming of devolution intensifies the inevitable controversy along national lines with English regions complaining that

the Monarch's approval of these appointments is assumed to be forthcoming. These provisions pay formal lip service to the continuing existence of a constitutional monarchy but make clear the political reality that the Monarch will have no effective political power in respect of appointments.

In 1999 the Liberal Democrats received two significant ministerial posts. Their leader, Jim Wallace, was appointed Deputy First Minister and Minister for Justice, and Ross Finnie was appointed Minister for Agriculture and Rural Development. Finnie's role became critical during the foot and mouth epidemic which struck early in 2001. There are ten Deputy Ministers, not including

Jim Wallace, of whom two are Liberal Democrats.

The major spending departments are Education, Enterprise Transport and Lifelong Learning, Health andCommunity Care, Justiceand Environment and Rural Development.

Committee structure

The Parliament's committee structure parallels the structure of the Scottish Executive, with a committee covering the work of each Department. Committee convenerships are shared among the parties with nine Labour, four SNP, two Conservative and two Liberal Democrat. (See Table 9.3.) The committee system adopted for the

they are unfairly treated and the Scots replying that the differentials are justifiable on the grounds of needs and Scotland's contribution to the British Treasury from North Sea Oil revenues. The ultimate Catch 22 for any English politicians looking for a reduction in Scottish public expenditure was that reducing Treasury-sourced Scottish expenditure might drive Scotland along the route to independence. That is a dilemma which carries on into the post-devolution age.

The Barnett formula

The main source of finance for Scottish Office spending prior to devolution was a block grant from the Treasury calculated according to the Barnett formula (named after the Treasury Minister who devised the formula in 1979). The crucial feature of the Scottish block grant was that it paid for spending programmes which reflected both Scottish social and economic realities and British government spending priorities decided by the British Cabinet. The arrival of devolution brought with it an expectation that such spending priorities in Scotland would now be more at the discretion of Scottish institutions.

In order to give the new Scottish institutions discretion in their policy making and expenditure initiatives Labour decided on two types of funding. The first would be "a continuation of the existing 'Block Grant' system of funding". Whereas the pre-devolution issue centred on claims that the Barnett formula was too generous to Scotland (though that opinion was not universally agreed), the post-devolution debate focuses on Scottish claims that Scotland is no longer receiving a fair share of increases in government spending. The reason for this is that the Barnett formula rests heavily on population trends. The Scottish population is declining whereas the English population is increasing. This will result in Scotland receiving a declining share of overall increases in future British gov-

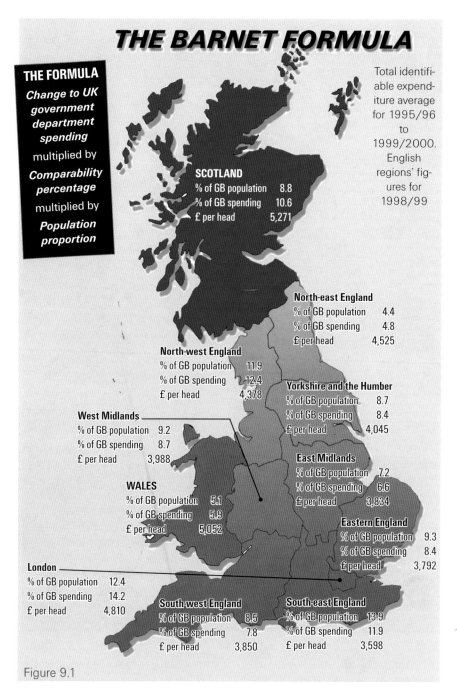

Figure 9.1

ernment spending totals decided by the Treasury. Thus discussions on the impact of the Barnett formula have been changing from the widespread belief that 'Barnett' has been generous to Scotland to talk of a 'Barnett squeeze'.

Scottish taxation powers

The second possible way of funding Scottish public expenditure lies in the power granted by the *Scotland Act* to vary income tax rates. Tax rates, which are determined by the Chancellor of the Exchequer, can be varied by up to three pence in the pound up or down. The Scottish Execu-

tive and Parliament could decide to increase the rate of income tax levied in Scotland by 3p in the pound. (If currently deployed, Scots would pay 25% rather than 22% at 2001 rates.) If it is decided to increase income tax in Scotland, the extra income will be additional to the Scottish block grant from the Treasury. If it is decided to decrease the rate of tax paid by individuals living in Scotland, which would mean that Scots would contribute less to the British Treasury from which the block grant comes, then the loss in revenue will be subtracted from the amount given to the Scottish block grant.

THE SCOTTISH PARLIAMENT IN ACTION

The result of the 1999 Scottish Parliament election produced a healthy start for the new government of Scotland in that Labour was confirmed as the strongest political force in Scotland which complemented its dominance of the Westminster Parliament. The Labour government in Britain and the Labour-Liberal Democrat coalition government in Scotland both wanted to make the new system work well because both parties had effectively been coalition partners in the struggle for devolution against the Conservatives (including the Thatcher and Major governments), who preferred the status quo, and the SNP, who preferred independence. The coalition partners occupied 56% of the seats in the Scottish Parliament, seventeen more than the other parties combined. The popularity of and respect for the first First Minister, Donald Dewar, who had fought strenuously for Scottish devolution after 1979, meant that the new Scottish political system looked as if it would succeed. At the same time it was clear that several sets of new political relationships would have to be worked out under the full glare of media attention and that there were political issues requiring immediate resolution which would test the strength of the various essential commitments to coalition government.

Testing the coalition

The relationship between executive and legislature in Scotland depends ultimately on the behaviour of the party leaders and their followers. Coalitions may break up simply because leaders can no longer agree on policy, or they may break up because backbenchers can no longer stomach the compromises which coalitions inevitably entail. Backbenchers may be tempted into rebellion by the prospect of alternative coalitions which are as acceptable to them as the existing coalition. First Ministers might be persuaded to resign by backbench revolts leading to the formation of a new executive based on the same partners but led by different individuals.

Several critical issues soon arose to give shape to these relationships, including student tuition fees, Section 28 and the teaching of sex education in schools, teachers' pay, European Union fisheries policies, the death of the First Minister, and the foot and mouth crisis. Several of the potential conflicts duly arose to test the strength of the coalition within both executive and legislature.

STUDENT TUITION FEES

This was the most serious issue because it threatened to bring several possible conflicts into play and thus to endanger the survival of the governing coalition. The two coalition partners appeared to be on opposing sides on an issue which was now within the remit of the Scottish system but which had already been decided for Britain as a whole two years earlier.

In 1997 the new Labour government decided to introduce tuition fees for all students studying at institutions of higher education throughout Britain. Until then no British students had had to pay tuition fees, a situation which always amazed American students coming to Britain to study. Labour also decided to replace any remaining grants for students' subsistence while studying with an extension of the loans system introduced by earlier Conservative governments. This policy surprised many Labour supporters who had associated the Party for many years with free state education. Support for state education was very strong in Scotland where young people were supposed to benefit from a particularly good and democratic educational system. Politically, Labour's policy was seen as being especially harmful to the poorer sections of British society. The policy was due to be applied in Scotland at a time when the new Scottish political institutions would be in their first stage of development.

The tuition fees issue duly became significant in the 1999 Scottish Election campaign. The Labour Party defended the decision of the London government; the other parties campaigned for the abolition of tuition fees in Scotland. The probability that Labour would not win a majority of seats in the new Scottish Parliament, because of PR, ensured that the fees issue could not be settled on its own by Labour as it had been in the British Parliament in 1997. Something had to be done immediately to allow the coalition between Labour and the Liberal Democrats to get off the ground and then to enable it to survive once it had been established. It was clear that Liberal Democrat MSPs would not accept the status quo—the application of Labour's tuition fees policy north of the border.

The leaders of the two potential coalition parties had to head off revolt in the ranks of the junior partner. The device chosen was the age-old one of a Committee of Inquiry to study the problem and recommend solutions. The would-be coalition partners quickly agreed to make it a condition of their partnership that Parliament be asked to set up a Committee of Inquiry. This was not only necessary from the Liberal Democrat standpoint but it also showed due deference to the newly elected members of the Scottish Parliament whose behaviour in the novel situation of no majority party was not completely predictable.

The Scottish Parliament set up the (Cubie) Committee of Inquiry on Student Fees on 2 July 1999, one day after its official opening by the Queen. The Committee, named after its chairperson, reported on 21 December, 1999. Its main recommendations were that tuition fees in Scotland should be abolished for Scottish students studying in Scotland, and that graduates should pay into a fund to finance grants for poorer stu-

Scottish student Amy Bullock, 17, from Berwickshire High School in Greenlaw (left) and English student Rosemary Hall, 18, from The High School in Alnwick, Northumberland, who took up places at university meet at Lamberton on the Scottish border with cheques to illustrate the differences in their financial circumstances as a result of the abolition of tuition fees in Scotland

dents once they had reached a certain level of income on entering employment. The Executive accepted the main thrust of the Cubie recommendations though the financial levels agreed were less favourable than the Committee had wanted. The Executive recommended to Parliament that tuition fees be abolished, that graduates start paying into the fund once they were earning £10,000 rather than the £25,000 laid down in the Cubie Report, and that means-tested grants to students be capped at £2,000 rather than at Cubie's £4,000. The abolition of fees applied to Scots and non-UK EU students studying in Scotland. It did not apply to non-Scottish UK students (English, Welsh and Northern Irish) studying in Scotland or to Scots studying outside Scotland.

The success of the committee of inquiry device and of the compromises agreed by the coalition partners became evident when Parliament voted to accept the Executive's policy by 68–53 on 27 January 2000. The coalition held within the Executive and in Parliament against Conservative and SNP opposition. Parliament sup-

ported the Executive and thus ensured its survival. Labour, reacting to public opinion influenced by events in Scotland, made changes in its policy towards students in England and Wales by introducing concessions for poorer students adversely affected by the twin attacks on fees and grants. In this case, Scottish developments influenced the course of decision making in England and Wales.

A Scottish policy at odds with the wishes of the Labour government in London was nonetheless accepted by Labour leaders as an inevitable consequence of the devolution reforms which they themselves had enthusiastically supported. Scotland and Britain (England and Wales) could diverge on policy even when the same party was in sole charge or was the dominant partner in both territories and could be accused of a lack of consistency by political opponents. However, this was a critical time for the new system of government. The Scottish Executive could not be allowed to go down to defeat because its compromise policy on tuition fees, necessitated

by the coalition factor, was unacceptable to the British political system. Acceptance was the price which had to be paid to keep the Liberal Democrats in the coalition. British Labour leaders might not always be so accommodating.

'SECTION 28'

In 1986 the Thatcher administration decided to prohibit the "promotion of homosexuality in schools". Local government was an area which, before devolution, required separate Scottish legislation, so the prohibition was included in Section 28/Clause 2A of the *Local Government (Scotland) Act* 1986. Labour in both Britain and Scotland was committed to repeal of that legislation. Devolution transferred responsibility for action on this issue to Scottish institutions.

In October 1999 the Scottish Executive publicised its intention to repeal the legislation which was offensive to several sections of the community. The issue developed into one of the most divisive issues in recent Scottish political history before and after devolution.

The battle line-up on the issues stimulated by Section 28/Clause 2A pitched most of the party political establishment against several elitist groups in society, particularly religious groups, far removed from the new devolved institutions. Three of the four main parties (the Conservatives were the exception) favoured repeal as did the Scottish Executive, so there was no doubt that the repeal legislation would go through the Parliament. At what cost to these parties though? Their problem was that opposing forces were potentially capable of whipping up public opinion against repeal which might rebound on the pro-repeal parties at the polls.

Those in favour of repeal were accused of encouraging homosexuality and of downgrading the social importance of the traditional heterosexual family. Supporters of retaining the clause were accused of discrimination against gays and against non-traditional families including one parent families, unmarried couples with children, gay and lesbian couples seeking to have children. Repeal became a 'lifestyle' issue with its supporters favouring the moral legitimacy of several family lifestyles and its opponents taking a much narrower view.

The issue was much more complex than merely whether to repeal or not. If the existing statutory prohibition on 'promoting homosexuality' in schools was to be repealed, should teachers of sex education in schools be given guidelines on how to handle issues of sexuality? Should these guidelines be included in legislation so that they would be mandatory for teachers of sex education? The supporters of repeal started off believing that a simple repeal was all that was necessary and that sex education could subsequently be left to the good sense of teachers. However, a vociferous and well-financed campaign against repeal forced the Executive to think again about the content of the necessary legislation. Supporters of repeal

FOR REPEAL	AGAINST REPEAL
● Labour Party	● Daily Record
● Liberal Democrat Party	● The religious establishment, Protestant and Catholic—especially Cardinal Winning
● SNP	● Brian Souter and Keep the Clause Campaign
● Equality Network representing Gay and Lesbian groups	● Scottish School Boards Association (SSBA)

did not wish to be in too substantial a minority position.

The campaign against repeal comprised three main elements: religious leaders, the *Daily Record* and businessman Brian Souter (owner of the Stagecoach bus company) who claimed he would spend up to £1 million to finance a 'Keep the Clause' campaign and to hold a referendum on the issue. The pro-repeal camp thereafter was divided into those who opposed statutory and mandatory guidelines and those who believed that some concessions were required as an exercise in damage limitation. The concessions brought into play the links between the Scottish and British political systems.

The passage of similar repeal legislation in the House of Commons (applicable in England and Wales) saw the Labour government grant the concession of legally enforceable guidelines explicitly favouring the traditional concept of marriage. MSPs were reporting

majority support for the anti-repeal camp in their postbags which provide one indication of the state of public opinion. This tended to reinforce the argument in favour of making some concessions along the guidelines route. The party leaders in the Executive slowly worked out some guidelines much to the discontent of many of their backbench supporters of repeal.

On 16 March 2000 the Conservatives won the Ayr constituency by-election. Did the Section 28 controversy influence the result? Historically Ayr was a relatively safe Conservative seat in British general elections, at least until the 1997 'wipe out'. Labour's majority in Ayr in the 1999 Scottish Parliament election was a mere twenty five, so the reversion of the seat to the Conservatives in 2000 was not a major surprise. Factors other than Section 28 played their part including a fair amount of adverse publicity for the Scottish Parliament such as the mounting cost of the new parliament buildings.

Brian Souter financed a private referendum to confirm public support for his campaign to retain Section 28/Clause 2A

On 28 March Brian Souter announced that a £1 million unofficial referendum would be held by the Keep the Clause campaign. On 27 April the repeal legislation, *The Ethical Standards in Public Life Bill*, began its progress through the Parliament where it would undoubtedly gain acceptance. The pro-repeal parties had not wavered on repeal although they had experienced considerable internal strife on the issue of guidelines concessions. On 30 May 2000 the results of Souter's referendum, which had been organised by a polling organisation, were announced. Almost 87% voted against repeal though only a little over one-third of those sent ballot papers bothered to reply. Many pro-repeal supporters refused to participate, claiming that the referendum should not be legitimised by a large 'turnout'.

Section 28/Clause 2A was duly repealed by the passage of the *Eth-ical Standards in Public Life Act.* It does contain statutory guidance on how to teach sex education with specific references to what should be said about family life.

The fate of Section 28 suggests the following conclusions:

➡ The Executive is able to secure the passage of controversial legislation against considerable external opposition if there is clear majority support in the legislature. The support of the SNP meant that the passage of the legislation was never in doubt.

➡ The state of public opinion on this issue was not clear. It seems likely that in the population as a whole those who opposed repeal did so more intensely than those who supported it or was that merely an impression based on a well-financed 'Keep the Clause' Campaign supported by religious leaders and favourably reported by a leading Scottish newspaper?

➡ Public support for Section 28, or opposition to its repeal, even if it was not clear how significant that would be in a general election, was sufficiently strong to persuade the coalition leaders to offer concessions without giving up on repeal.

➡ Backbench MSPs in the partnership parties, Labour and the Liberal Democrats, were unhappy about the concessions but their hands were largely tied by the fact of Conservative opposition to repeal. To carry discontent to the extent of voting against the legislation containing the repeal would have played into the hands of the Conservatives so any temptation to use the issue to assert backbench power against party leaders was resisted. The British convention of ministerial respon-

Death of Donald Dewar

On 11 October, 2000 Scotland was shocked to discover that Donald Dewar had died of a brain haemorrhage. In the spring of 2000 the 63- year-old First Minister had gone into hospital for a heart operation and Jim Wallace, his Liberal Democrat Deputy First Minister, had taken over as First Minister to enable Dewar to convalesce (thus displaying the personal trust between Dewar and Wallace and also the stability of the coalition).

The Economist magazine spoke highly of Donald Dewar and stated that Blair had had total confidence in allowing him a free hand in Scotland. It continued,
"Much of Mr Dewar's leadership skill was almost unconscious. The power of his intellect, and his love and knowledge of Scottish literature, art and music meant that he was a formidable opponent whose Scottishness could not be questioned, much though the SNP tried. His passionate commitment to reduce poverty allayed the doubts in the Scottish Labour Party and the electorate about Mr Blair's New Labour project."

Year Zero

The formal announcement on 11 October that his life had ended brought with it a sense of complete disbelief which was replicated in the reaction of each MSP colleague with whom I spoke. Donald had been such a colossus, he had been so central to the whole Scottish Parliament project that the prospect of us, the Parliament, the Labour Party, Scotland as we knew it continuing without his dominant presence was quite surreal.

Two days later, Parliament was recalled from its autumn recess for a special session to allow tributes to be paid to the First Minister …

There were speeches only from the party leaders, with Henry McLeish representing the Labour Party. It was noticeable that both John Swinney and David McLetchie referred to Donald Dewar as 'our' First Minister and their words, compassionate and heartfelt, were utterly convincing.

Sadly, though predictably, the days before the funeral were filled with media speculation as to the succession. Only after his death did anyone appreciate the require-ment—inserted in the Scotland Act by Donald himself – that the post of First Minister be filled within twenty eight days of a vacancy arising; failure to do so would result in the Parliament being dissolved and a new one being elected. The purpose of such a clause in the Act was to prevent unnecessary delay following a general election in the formation of an administration. With typical perspicacity, Donald had been determined to avoid a protracted and unseemly wrangle, inviting adverse publicity to the institution. How ironic, then, that his own pass-ing should provide the first test of its rigour.

The funeral on 18 October was an occasion worthy of the man who had done more than anyone else to deliver Scotland's parliament. The ecumenical ceremony in Glasgow Cathedral was followed by a procession through his beloved city, past fellow Glaswegians lining the route to pay their last respects, to a private family service.

Adapted from Mike Watson, Labour MSP for Glasgow Cathcar *Year Zero. An Inside View of the Scottish Parliament*

sibility (see chapter 6) was not tested. How this convention will work in the Scottish Parliament remains to be fully tested.

LEADERSHIP CHANGES

The year 2000 witnessed changes to the leadership of the SNP through the resignation of Alex Salmond and, more dramatically to the Labour Party, with the sudden death of the First Minister, Donald Dewar.

Election of Henry McLeish

While the country mourned the death of Donald Dewar, the Labour Party had to act swiftly to elect a new leader. Under the procedures for electing the First Minister, any vacancy in the post had

to be filled within twenty eight days or new elections for the Scottish Parliament would have to be declared. Dewar had devised this decree to ensure that there would be limited post-election negotiations between parties over forming a coalition.

The first step in the process was for Labour to elect a new leader who would then be chosen as First Minister by the whole Parliament. Henry McLeish, the Minister for Enterprise and Lifelong Learning, emerged as the favourite for the post as he was supported by fellow Ministers and by Gordon Brown in London. He was challenged by Jack McConnell, the Minister for Finance, who ran an effective campaign based on Labour backbench MSPs' dissatisfaction with the Scottish Executive.

The electoral college made up of Labour's fifty three MSPs and the twenty seven members of the Scottish Party's executive committee voted for Henry McLeish but only by the narrow majority of forty four to thirty six votes.

MCLEISH IN OFFICE

McLeish quickly appointed his new Cabinet and recognising Jack McConnell's popularity among backbench MPs, promoted him to the post of Education Minister. Two Cabinet members were effectively demoted. Education Minister Sam Galbraith, weakened by the SQA '2000 exam' fiasco, was given Environment, which was in turn taken from Sarah Boyack reducing her portfolio to Transport only. Wendy Alexander succeeded McLeish as Minister for

Election of John Swinney

In July 2000 Alex Salmond announced that he was resigning as leader of the Scottish National Party. Political commentators and his Party were surprised by this announcement as Salmond was only 45 and seemed prepared to lead the Party towards the 2001 General Election and the 2003 Scottish elections. Significantly, Alex Salmond had faced strong opposition from within the Party when he proposed a change to

the Party's independence strategy. His new proposal was that an election victory in Scotland would no longer be regarded as a sufficient mandate for independence. It would have to be followed by a referendum on independence and, if a successful outcome was achieved, only then would an SNP government begin negotiating to take Scotland out of Britain. The SNP's policy making national council

approved the new policy by 158 votes to 63.

There was clear division within the Party with Alex Neil, the Party's Social Security spokesperson, accusing Salmond of placing independence way down the list of priorities—a criticism he made of Salmond's 1999 Scottish election strategy. Salmond's response was that Scots would wish to be convinced that devolution works before taking a

massive leap towards independence.

Alex Neil immediately announced that he would stand against Salmond's deputy, John Swinney, who at 36 had only been an MP since 1997. John Swinney endorsed Salmond's policy of a gradualist approach to independence. The referendum strategy, he argued, gave the Party the flexibility of achieving independence even if it failed to get an overall majority in the Scottish Parliament. (The electoral PR system was deliberately chosen by Labour to ensure that the SNP would be most unlikely to achieve overall control of the Scottish Parliament.) It offered the opportunity of forming a coalition government with minority parties including the Liberal Democrats. The future battleground is the Scottish Parliament and not Westminster. The Party clearly endorsed this strategy with Swinney gaining 547 votes (67%) to 268 votes (33%) for Neil.

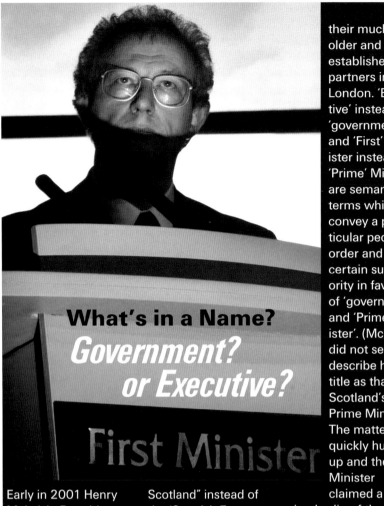

What's in a Name?

Government?
or Executive?

First Minister

Early in 2001 Henry McLeish, Donald Dewar's successor as Scotland's First Minister, caused a stir in the media by referring to the political institutions of which he was the head as the "government of Scotland" instead of the 'Scottish Executive'. Allegations were made that the leaders of the British government were upset that McLeish seemed to be claiming that Scotland's institutions are on a par with their much older and more established partners in London. 'Executive' instead of 'government' and 'First' Minister instead of 'Prime' Minister are semantic terms which convey a particular pecking order and a certain superiority in favour of 'government' and 'Prime Minister'. (McLeish did not seek to describe his title as that of Scotland's Prime Minister). The matter was quickly hushed up and the First Minister claimed a simple slip of the tongue, but the episode nonetheless hinted at an underlying tension between separate political institutions which is likely to surface from time to time.

Enterprise and Lifelong Learning. McConnell faced the difficult task of resolving pay and conditions issues with teachers, which he successfully achieved through the teachers' unions' acceptance of the McCrone Report.

Electoral Contests

Three by-elections took place in October and December 2000 which resulted in Labour retaining all the seats. The two by-elections in Anniesland (Donald Dewar's seat) for both Westminster and Scotland led to convincing victories for Labour in a low turnout. The Falkirk by-election, brought about by Dennis Canavan's resignation as a Westminster MP, was a different affair with Labour just managing to hold off the challenge of the SNP.

The Fisheries Crisis

In March 2001 Henry McLeish faced his first constitutional crisis when the Scottish Parliament rejected the Executive's proposal of a decommissioning package for Scottish fishermen. Four Liberal Democrat rebels voted to support the Opposition's motion to allocate cash to a tie-up scheme. Labour blamed its Liberal Democrat partners for this disaster but fourteen Labour MSPs missed the vote and this enabled the SNP and the Conservatives to ambush the

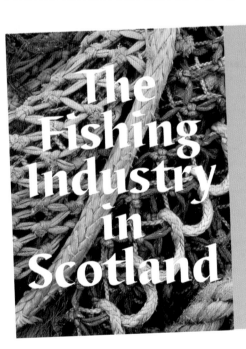

The Fishing Industry in Scotland

Around 70% of British fishing activity is based in Scotland. Peterhead, north of Aberdeen, is a key centre, accounting for 30% of Scottish fish landings, and is the largest white fish (cod and haddock) port in Europe. In February 2001 the European Union closed the cod fishing grounds in the North Sea (40,000 square miles) to fishermen for an eleven-week period. The ban was designed to enable cod stocks to recover. This threatened the livelihood of Scottish fishermen, who argued that they were now being forced to fish in waters populated by haddock too young to land, resulting in over 80% of their catches being thrown back dead.

Scottish skippers decided to tie up in harbour (to protect the fishing stock) and demanded £5 million in compensation from the Scottish Executive. On 6 March 2001 around 160 fishing boats steamed up the Firth of Forth in an impressive show of strength to demonstrate their demand for short-term compensation. Rhona Brankin, the Fisheries Minister, regarded compensation as a wasteful short-term fix. Her view was that there were too many fishermen and too few fish and she proposed a £25 million package for a voluntary decommissioning (reduction) of the Scottish fleet.

Executive. This was the Executive's first defeat in the Scottish Parliament. The crisis deepened with the resignation of Liberal Democrat Executive Minister, Tavish Scott, who represented a fishing constituency. James Anderson, a Shetland skipper, stated "In the one important vote for Shetland, Tavish Scott chose to vote against us (he had voted with the Executive) against what fishermen wanted. People here are very angry."

Mr McLeish made it clear that Labour was furious with Liberal Democrat Party managers for giving no indication of Liberal Democrat dissent. The defeat distracted media attention away from Labour's Scottish Conference in Inverness and did not endear McLeish to Labour's national leadership. The Executive ignored the will of Parliament and held another fishing debate which rubber-stamped the Executive's position.

The crisis placed great strain on the coalition arrangement and weakened McLeish's credibility given that he had earlier promised to respect the will of Parliament after MSPs had urged the Executive to provide free care for the elderly.

Long-Term Care of the Elderly

In June 2001, Henry McLeish made the long-awaited announcement that £200 million would be provided from the Executive budget to pay for free care of the elderly in nursing and residential homes. This was a significant departure from the position in the rest of the United Kingdom where Gordon Brown had ruled out such an approach.

The Labour government, in December 1997, had set up a Royal Commission on the Long-Term Care of the Elderly under the chairmanship of Sir Stewart Sutherland. In February 1999 the Sutherland Report recommended that free medical care in nursing and residential homes should be available to all elderly people who

need it. Only in Scotland has this recommendation been accepted. McLeish's decision reinforced the concept that devolution enables Scotland to find its own solutions to certain issues and to differ from the rest of the United Kingdom.

SCOTTISH PARLIAMENT COMMITTEES

One of the success stories of the new Parliament has been the workings of the Scottish Parliament Committees. (See 'Committees in Action' page 139.) Committee convenerships are shared among the parties with nine Labour, four SNP, two Conservatives and two Liberal Democrats. The committee system is similar to that in the American Congress in that the committees parallel government Departments and deal with both legislative proposals and the administration pertaining to the Departments in question.

The original committee system consisted of sixteen mandatory and subject committees with a minimum of seven MSPs and a maximum of thirteen. Two important changes were made to the committee system in January 2001.

1 An additional subject committee was created with the formation of a second Justice Committee. The Justice and Home Affairs Committee had been extremely busy dealing with complex and detailed legislation, including the Abolition of Feudal Tenure, Adults with Incapacity and the Abolition of Poindings and Warrant Sales Bills. The Committee had had little time to scrutinise the action of Departments and the Executive.

2 There was a reduction in the size of committees. Committees with thirteen members such as the Equal Opportunities Committee and the European Committee were reduced to nine members and most other committees now have seven members. (See Table 9.2.) This has reduced the number of MSPs who sit on two committees, which in turn has allowed MSPs to specialise in and concentrate on specific areas.

(continued on page 139)

THE COMMITTEES OF THE SCOTTISH PARLIAMENT OCTOBER 2001

COMMITTEE	CONVENER	PARTY	NUMBER OF MEMBERS
● Audit	A. Welsh	SNP	7
● Education Culture and Sport	K. Gillon	Labour	7
● Enterprise & Lifelong Learning	A. Neil	SNP	11
● Equal Opportunities	K. McLean	Labour	9
● European	H. Henry	Labour	9
● Finance	M. Watson	Labour	7
● Health & Community Care	M. Smith	Lib. Dem.	9
● Justice 1	C. Grahame	SNP	7
● Justice 2	P. McNeill	Labour	7
● Local government	T. Godman	Labour	7
● Procedure	M. Tosh	Conservative	7
● Public Petitions	J. McAllion	Labour	7
● Rural Development	A. Fergusson	Conservative	11
● Social Justice	J. Lamont	Labour	7
● Standards	M. Rumbles	Lib. Dem.	7
● Subordinate Legislation	K. MacAskill	SNP	7
● Transport & Environment	A. Kerr	Labour	9

Table 9.2

"TWO YEARS ON"

In June 2001 the Scottish Parliament celebrated its second birthday and Henry McLeish highlighted its achievements. (See below.) The media also gave an assessment of the Scottish Parliament. Below is a brief overview of the comments.

No argument, the Parliament has made a difference. Scottish solutions to Scottish problems are being implemented ...The Parliament or rather its Executive, scored a prodigious number of own-goals in its first two years— the Holyrood Buildings, the handling of Section 28, Henry's gaffes ... Without the Scottish Parliament and its committees the Higher Still fiasco may never have been brought to light. The only forum in which these scandals could be examined before devolution was Scottish Question Time in Westminster – a pitiful apology for democratic scrutiny.

Pride in Scotland Rises

A poll, carried out for the *Scotsman* and involving over one thousand interviews displayed a country where Scots feel more patriotic than ever before and hail Scotland as confident, modern and exciting. Below are the main findings of the survey.

● The number of people declaring they are more Scottish than British is now at its highest ever recorded level with 80% of Scots now saying they feel more Scottish than British. This represents a significant increase even on ten years ago when the figure was less than two-thirds.

● The west, east and north of Scotland feel much more Scottish than British but in the rural south the figure falls from over 80% to 65%.

● A greater confidence in the future. The words people say they most clearly identify with the Scottish nation are happy (69%), modern (67%) and exciting (60%).

Source: *The Scotsman* 29.6.01

McLeish had a hard act to follow and, not helped by being gaffe-prone ... He has been brave enough to put his neck on the line, particularly on health care for the elderly and the SQA. In its two years, the Parliament can claim some successes but it has also managed to embarrass itself on a number of occasions.

Successes

✔ Abolition of warrant sales.
✔ Commitment to free care for the elderly.
✔ Improving teachers' pay and conditions.
✔ Removing upfront tuition fees.
✔ Introducing drugs courts.
✔ Reducing quangos.
✔ The Mental Health Act blocking the loophole allowing psychopaths to be freed from the State Hospital at Carstairs.

Source: *Glasgow Evening Times* 29.6.01

Embarrassments

✘ Holyrood's soaring costs
✘ Section 28
✘ Hospital waiting lists – are they going down or not?
✘ Problems at visitscotland – appointing and then sacking a new boss before he starts the job.
✘ Compensation for fishermen debacle.
✘ SQA – no one took responsibility for botched exam results.
✘ Minister for Parliament Tom McCabe's £9,500 second home grant.
✘ Carfin – a diplomatic gaffe caused by a Westminster MP with Holyrood apparently not knowing what was happening.

Henry McLeish–First Minister

"Our new parliament is still in its infancy, yet it has passed no fewer than twenty pieces of legislation. It would have taken Westminster six, maybe seven, years to accomplish that—but you never hear that from the critics who claim devolution has not delivered.

We have a working parliament, with radical policies and careful spending. A parliament which works with Westminster to make a real difference to the people of Scotland.

So forget the Jeremiahs and their complaints. We can all be proud of our parliament's accomplishments. Just take a few examples of what has been done.

Tuition fees are gone and maintenance grants are available, meaning better opportunities for students, especially those who might otherwise have thought they could not afford to go to university.

After years of threats of industrial action in the classroom, we have delivered the pay and conditions package that our teachers deserve. The McCrone deal has been approved, the funds are in place, and it is already making a difference to teaching morale and standards.

We have established the Scottish Drugs Enforcement Agency, and it is securing arrests, prosecutions and the seizure of assets bought by dealers with their blood money.

We have started the cull of the quangos, putting two-thirds of them on notice as part of the modernisation theme underlining everything we do.

And every part of Scotland has benefited from such actions, destroying the myth that the parliament would be just for the Central Belt. This year we put together the biggest ever package to help fishermen—£26 million to given them a better future.

In health, we are building eight hospitals ... and (have) confirmed our commitment to pay for personal care for the elderly."

The Lobbygate Affair

In September 1999 newspapers published allegations that certain Ministers had provided "privileged access" to Beattie Media, a public affairs and public relations company. The fact that one of Beattie Media's employees was Kevin Reid, the son of the then Scottish Secretary, increased media speculation and public disquiet.

The reaction of the Standards Committee (responsible for the code of conduct of MSPs) was significant. It announced, to the dismay of the Executive, that it would hold its own inquiry into the affair dismissing the First Minister's internal inquiry in favour of a full and open inquiry of its own. Ministers, including Donald Dewar, had to swear an oath before they gave evidence. *The Herald's* headline 'The day parliament asserted its authority' reinforced the viewpoint that the Committee on Standards had asserted the powers of the elected Parliament over Ministers and their civil servants. The inquiry cleared all those within the Scottish Parliament accused of impropriety.

House of Commons Ministers

One of the important features of the committee system is the frequency with which Scottish Executive Ministers are called to give evidence. This contrasts with the House of Commons where Ministers seldom appear before a Select Committee and are usually represented by their Permanent Secretaries. There have been two instances where a Scottish Parliament Committee has invited a UK government Minister to give evidence and in each case he declined to attend.

Both the Finance and European Committees (undertaking a linked inquiry into European structural funds) invited the Chancellor of the Exchequer, Gordon Brown,

to attend and answer questions on the allocation of EU funds to Scotland via the Barnett formula. Brown declined and indicated that the then Scottish Executive Finance Minister, Jack McConnell, should attend in his place. The European Committee then invited John Reid, at the time Secretary of State for Scotland, to appear. John Reid stated at the Scottish Affairs Committee in the House of Commons in June 2000: "I have no intention of speaking to the European Committee … I'm accountable to this Parliament."

Donald Gorrie, Liberal Democrat
"They (Committees) have done some really good work and stuck to their guns against the Executive, unlike in the House of Commons. The Local Government Committee got good concessions from the Executive on the Ethical Standards Bill, on rights of appeal for councillors and extending the provisions to many quangos."

Brian Taylor BBC
"The Executive and civil servants are chilled at developments in the committee, especially when dealing with Bills. At the House of Commons Ministers are part of the committees considering legislation but at Holyrood they are just interested onlookers. They can seek to influence but ultimately they can't control them, nor can civil servants. They must win their case, and that's the importance of the new politics."

Margaret Smith Liberal Democrat, Convener of the Health and Community Care Committee
"The Committees have done an incredible job in terms of scrutiny, compared to Westminster. But we're seriously under-resourced; my Committee has half a researcher to assist us in scrutinising a budget of more than £3 billion."

Mike Watson, Labour
"At the outset in May 1999, I believed the Committees would become the engine room of the Parliament. With the benefit of experience, I hold that view even more strongly and I keenly anticipate the further development of their role as the driving force of Scotland's new democracy."

Kenny Gibson, SNP
"We have achieved genuine cross-party consensus. And our committee has certainly engaged with civic Scotland because we have visited fifteen local authorities in our first year."

THE RESIGNATION OF HENRY MCLEISH

After less than thirteen months as Scotland's second First Minister, Henry McLeish resigned from his post on 8 November 2001, as a result of the 'officegate scandal'. In an emotional resignation speech, the First Minister told a stunned Parliament that he had done nothing improper in sub-letting his constituency office, but he admitted that his judgment had been lacking and said that he had no option but to quit. Mr McLeish had failed to declare, in the House of Commons Register of Interests, income he had received from sub-letting his constituency office in Glenrothes, while he was a Westminster MP. Mr McLeish had claimed the full £8,700 rent allowance without declaring the sublet of his office to a succession of tenants. Mr McLeish had not benefited personally from the money which had been used to fund Labour's electoral campaigns.

After being elected as First Minister by the MSPs in Edinburgh, Jack McConnell is not officially appointed until he receives the Warrant of Appointment from the Queen.

Mr McLeish's failure to 'come clean' damaged the office of First Minister and led to a loss of confidence from the Scottish public in McLeish's leadership.

THE THIRD FIRST MINSTER

It was widely expected that Wendy Alexander would challenge the front-runner, Jack McConnell, for the post of leader of the Scottish Labour Party. She had the support of the Chancellor, Gordon Brown, but to the dismay of her supporters, she withdrew from the race citing concerns about the pressures and the personal toll of being First Minister. Malcolm Chisholm, the Deputy Health Minister, announced that he would stand but was forced to retract his statement as he embarrassingly failed to find the necessary seven MSPs to back him. This left Jack McConnell as the only candidate.

McConnell, the Scottish Education Minister, had resolved the SQA disaster and the long-running pay and conditions dispute with teachers. He had narrowly lost in the 2000 leadership battle against Henry McLeish and had not suffered from the 'Lobbygate' scandal. The former General Secretary of the Scottish Labour Party was seen as his own man and not dependent on the patronage of Gordon Brown.

In a dramatic week in Scottish politics, Jack McConnell's declaration

as sole nominee for the Labour leadership was overshadowed by his confession that seven years ago, while he was the Scottish Labour Party's General Secretary, he had an affair with a woman colleague. The *Daily Record* newspaper had declared on Saturday 10 November, "we'll pull the skeletons out of the cupboards. Each candidate's background will be examined in the most minute detail by our investigative reporters."

At a press conference, held with his wife at his side, McConnell faced the humiliation of exposing their private life to the nation. She spoke of her husband having "betrayed her trust". The McConnells hoped that, by making this bold statement, they could put an end to press speculation. On 17 November, the Labour MSPs and the members of the Party's Scottish Executive held an 'affirmative ballot' and elected McConnell leader and Labour's candidate for First Minister in Parliament. On Thursday 22 November 2001, the Scottish Parliament elected Jack McConnell as First Minister.

In a bold and controversial move, McConnell dismissed five of his former Cabinet colleagues— Wendy Alexander was the only Labour Cabinet Minister left in post. Significantly, none of those dismissed had nominated McConnell for leader and were regarded as supporters of Wendy Alexander.

THE OFFICEGATE SCANDAL

September 2000 Andrew Duncan, a pensioner researching the rateable value of Mr McLeish's office, discovers a sublet by law firm Digby Brown.

April 2001 Newspaper reports confirm that Mr McLeish had received £4,000 a year from Digby Brown since 1998. Elizabeth Filkin, the House of Commons Standards Commissioner, writes to Mr McLeish in connection with the controversy.

October 2001 Mr McLeish attempts to end the affair by stating that he has paid £9,000 to the Fees Office at the House of Commons. Mr McLeish appears on BBC TV's Question Time, stating that he does not know how much money he received from his subtenants.

6 November 2001 Mr McLeish declares his actions were a "muddle, not a fiddle". He states that he had five tenants and that the total rental income for subletting the office since 1987 was £36,000. He offers to pay back the full amount

7 November 2001 A Scottish Television phone-in survey and a poll in the *Daily Record* newspaper suggest a large majority in favour of Mr McLeish resigning. Mr McLeish discovers that *The Herald* newspaper is about to print a story which uncovers a sixth tenant with close links to the Labour Party.

8 November 2001 Prior to the Conservative-led debate of no confidence in Mr McLeish as First Minister, Mr McLeish announces his resignation.

LOCAL GOVERNMENT

Local councils impact on the daily lives of all Scottish citizens. They provide schools for our children and care for the elderly and they maintain our roads. The range of services provided by our councils is extensive (see page 143) and the money to pay for them comes mostly from general taxation and our Council Tax. We elect councillors to represent our interests and to manage budgets of millions of pounds.

The last twenty five years have witnessed dramatic changes in the role, structure and influence of local councils. Under the Conservatives (1979–1997) local authorities suffered a reduction in their income and range of services (see pages 150–152) which led to financial crisis and continual conflict with central government. The election of a Labour government determined to create a new partnership with local authorities, and the creation of a Scottish Parliament provide both opportunity and challenge for local councils to redefine their role and to restore their credibility with the Scottish people.

THE STRUCTURE OF LOCAL GOVERNMENT

The structure of local government has witnessed significant changes in recent years. Between 1975 and 1996, local government in Scotland was a two-tier system. It consisted of nine large regional councils along with fifty three district councils on the Scottish mainland, while Orkney, Western Isles and Shetland had 'all-purpose' islands councils responsible for all local government functions. Each region contained smaller districts. Grampian Region, for example, was made up of Aberdeen, Kincardine and Deeside, Banff and Buchan, Gordon, and Moray. The regions were in charge of services such as education, social work, roads and transport, and economic development which could be more efficiently and effectively delivered on a large scale. Districts were responsible for more local services such as housing and libraries.

The 1975 reorganisation also set up a third tier in the form of community councils. These councils have no formal powers, their role being to represent their local community and to put pressure on their local councillors and public bodies such as health boards.

Demands for reform of this system came from the Conservative government. While there was some criticism of the 1975 structure in Scotland, the consensus was that the benefits outweighed its deficiencies. The Conservatives' proposals to scrap the regions and districts and to replace them with twenty nine new all-purpose councils were criticised. Strathclyde Region, for example, was to be totally dismantled and replaced by twelve new authorities. Critics of the new proposals argued that the reforms were politically inspired with the Conservatives determined to destroy the political influence of Strathclyde Region which served half the population of Scotland. Strathclyde Region, with its Labour dominance, had been a thorn in the flesh of the Conservative government. The Council had opposed Conservative legislation and had mobilised the Scottish public to oppose such actions as the privatisation of water.

(continued on page 144)

THE 1996 LOCAL GOVERNMENT STRUCTURE

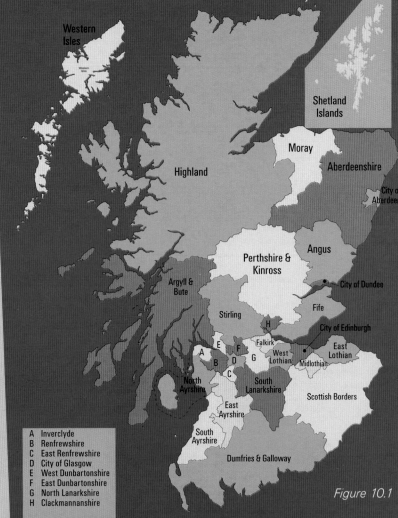

Scotland's Local Authorities

	Population	Area (hectares)
Aberdeen City	218,220	18,216
Aberdeenshire	223,630	631,736
Angus	111,020	218,396
Argyll & Bute	90,550	702,300
Clackmannanshire	48,660	15,809
Dumfries & Galloway	147,900	644,567
City of Dundee	153,710	5,500
East Ayrshire	123,820	127,527
East Dunbartonshire	110,220	17,551
East Lothian	85,640	66,558
East Renfrewshire	86,780	16,802
City of Edinburgh	441,620	26,001
Falkirk	142,610	29,300
Fife	351,200	134,045
City of Glasgow	623,850	17,472
Highland	206,900	2,611,906
Inverclyde	89,990	16,724
Midlothian	79,910	34,966
Moray	86,250	223,694
North Ayrshire	139,020	88,755
North Lanarkshire	326,750	47,648
Orkney Islands	19,760	102,498
Perthshire & Kinross	130,470	539,479
Renfrewshire	176,970	26,250
Scottish Borders	105,300	472,749
Shetland Islands	22,830	147,097
South Ayrshire	113,960	123,021
South Lanarkshire	307,100	177,789
Stirling	81,630	224,320
West Dunbartonshire	97,790	17,573
West Lothian	146,730	42,664
Western Isles	29,410	307,005

Table 10.1

A Inverclyde
B Renfrewshire
C East Renfrewshire
D City of Glasgow
E West Dunbartonshire
F East Dunbartonshire
G North Lanarkshire
H Clackmannanshire

Figure 10.1

The regions and districts were replaced by twenty nine all-purpose councils on the mainland, with three islands authorities. (See Figure 10.1 and Table 10.1.) The thirty two councils can be divided into different categories:

- ☞ the three distinctive islands councils of Orkney, Shetland and the Western Isles
- ☞ the unitary authorities based on former regions, such as Dumfries and Galloway, Fife, Highland and Scottish Borders
- ☞ the unitary authorities almost completely based on former district councils, such as Argyll and Bute, Dundee, Glasgow, Inverclyde, Moray and Stirling
- ☞ unitary authorities based on amalgamations of former councils, such as Aberdeenshire, East Ayrshire, North Lanarkshire and South Lanarkshire

The Establishment of Joint Boards

The abolition of the regions and the transfer of their powers to the small councils led to the setting up of joint arrangements between authorities in public services which involved strategic functions or in cross-authority services such as police and fire services. Critics of joint boards argue that they weaken democratic accountability as a council's involvement in a joint board is seldom subject to public scrutiny. A further criticism is that joint arrangements enable larger councils to dominate the decision making process with their larger resources thus disadvantaging smaller and weaker authorities.

Renfrewshire Council

Renfrewshire Council has a population of 178,000 and covers an area of around 270 square kilometres. Its main towns are Paisley and Renfrew and it includes rural areas such as Lochwinnoch and Kilbarchan. The Council has eight departments which provide the full range of local authority services to the people of Renfrewshire.

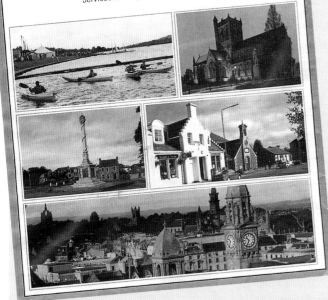

Chief Executive's Department
Key Responsibilities
- corporate strategy and planning
- community planning
- best value policy and coordination
- performance planning and management
- urban regeneration
- social policy
- Paisley partnership
- corporate communications and marketing
- press and publicity
- emergencies planning

Social Work
Key Responsibilities
- community care, including home care, day care, occupational therapy, residential and respite services, for older people and those with disabilities
- children and family services, including child protection, fostering and adoption, children with special needs and family based support
- criminal justice social work providing a range of diversionary services, probation, reports to court and support for victims of crime

Corporate Services
Key Responsibilities
- committee and member services, including servicing joint committees/boards and the children's panel advisory committee
- registration of births, deaths and marriages
- organising elections
- responding to the ombudsman on complaints of alleged maladministration
- community councils
- litigation, legal advice, contracts and conveyancing
- licensing and Renfrewshire District Court
- personnel services
- training and development
- skillseekers programme management
- health and safety

Planning and Transport
Key Responsibilities
- planning and building control
- roads and public transport
- economic development
- tourism
- European matters
- flood prevention
- conservation of the natural and built heritage of Renfrewshire
- management of the Council's internal transport operations

Education and Leisure Services
Key Responsibilities
- primary schools
- secondary schools
- early education
- community education provision for youths and adults
- libraries
- museums and the arts
- provision for those with special educational needs
- swimming pools and sports centres
- childcare and out of school care
- support services like the psychological service or educational development
- halls and community facilities

Environmental Services
Key Responsibilities
- control of pollution, noise, pets and litter
- food safety, food standards, weights and measures, counterfeit goods
- refuse collection and disposal, street cleaning, public conveniences, civic amenity sites and recycling
- building cleaning, janitorial services, catering and school crossing patrols
- research and development, information, advice and health promotion
- sustainable development and environmental issues
- maintenance of parks, cemeteries and other open spaces
- animal health and welfare

Finance and IT
Key Responsibilities
- preparation and monitoring of revenue and capital budgets
- preparation and publication of financial reports and annual accounts
- internal audit and treasury management
- administration of the billing and enforcement of Council Tax and non-domestic rates, debt recovery
- provision of information technology services

Housing and Property Services
Key Responsibilities
- housing allocations
- repairs and improvements
- rent collection and arrears recovery
- homelessness
- tenant participation
- capital investment
- private sector grants
- safer communities initiative
- management of building stock and estate
- improvement of energy consumption
- maintenance of commercial and industrial portfolios
- disposal of surplus property by way of sale or lease
- provision of project management, professional and technical services
- provision of a cost-effective construction service

Renfrewshire's Community Plan

A Pattern for Partnership

April 2001

The Conservatives were also accused of manipulating the size and diversity of some of the new authorities in an attempt to ensure a future Conservative administration. Central Region, for example, was to be divided into three small authorities—Clackmannanshire, Falkirk and Stirling; significantly, the MP for Stirling was Michael Forsyth, the Secretary of State for Scotland. A similar situation happened in Renfrewshire where Allan Stewart, the Conservative MP for Eastwood in Renfrewshire, and the Minister responsible for drawing up the Bill, ensured the creation of East Renfrewshire Council. Ironically, the Conservative strategy failed miserably; in the 1995 election for the new authorities, the Conservatives failed to win any councils.

The introduction of the new council structure was also an expensive operation. The Scottish Office had persuaded the Treasury in London that reform would reduce costs by removing a layer of councils. The reality was the opposite. The cost of redundancy payments as thousands of council workers lost their jobs, the creation of new headquarters and new structures (the cost across Scotland of new logos and signs for the new authorities ran into hundreds of thousands of pounds) ensured that the new authorities faced a financial crisis in 1996.

THE WORK OF LOCAL COUNCILS

Local councils provide a wide range of services which is illustrated in the workings of Renfrewshire Council. (See page 143.) Most of the activities performed by local authorities are mandatory (compulsory). For instance, the Scottish Executive determines overall education policy and circulates detailed regulations on educational matters which local councils must comply with.

Other services provided by local authorities are either permissive or discretionary. A swimming pool would be an example of a permissive power. Glasgow Council, in 2001, faced strong opposition from the local community when it closed down the local swimming pool in Govanhill. A sit-in by local residents took place over a period of months preventing its official closure. Discretionary services are priorities which the council decides for itself. For example, Renfrewshire Council organises an outing to Dunoon for its elderly citizens.

POLITICAL CONTROL OF LOCAL AUTHORITIES

Three clear trends have emerged in recent years in relation to political control of local authorities. These three trends are:

1 Labour's domination of local elections and political control from the 1980s onwards

2 the decline of the Conservative Party in local elections

3 the decline of Independent councillors and authorities in rural areas

Labour dominance

Labour benefits from the first-past-the-post electoral system in terms of winning seats and controlling councils, especially in the urban areas. Table 10.2 illustrates the respective performances of the four main political parties and displays Labour as being the most successful party in terms of votes and seats. Labour's performance in the 1999 Elections illustrates the crucial role of the FPTP electoral system. Labour, with 36% of the votes, received 48% of the seats; in contrast, the SNP with 29% of the votes only received 19% of seats.

The Labour Party had some setbacks in the 1999 Elections; it lost ground to the Conservatives in Stirling and South Ayrshire and to the SNP in Clackmannanshire, Dundee and East Ayrshire. Overall, Labour lost control of five councils. The SNP's 1999 performance was its best ever in terms of votes and seats (although not in terms of council control). It has consistently controlled Angus Council but its performance elsewhere has been inconsistent. The Liberal

Party performance at local elections 1978–99 (selected years)

ELECTION	LABOUR		CONSERVATIVE		SNP		LIB/LIB DEM	
	Votes (%)	Seats	Votes (%)	Seats	Votes (%)	Seats	Votes (%)	Seats
Regional 1978	39.6	177	30.3	136	20.9	18	2.3	6
Regional 1986	43.9	223	16.9	65	18.2	36	15.1	40
Regional 1994	41.8	220	13.7	31	26.8	73	12.0	60
District 1980	45.4	494	24.1	229	15.5	54	6.2	40
District 1984	45.7	545	21.4	189	11.7	59	12.8	78
District 1992	34.1	468	23.2	204	24.3	150	9.5	94
Unitary 1995	43.6	613	11.5	82	26.1	181	9.8	121
Unitary 1999	36.6	545	13.7	108	28.9	201	13.6	148

Table 10.2

Democrats displayed a consistent performance in Aberdeen, Borders, Edinburgh, East Dunbartonshire, Fife and Inverclyde where they are the main opposition party; in Aberdeenshire the Liberal Democrats are the largest party.

The decline of the Conservative Party

Table 10.2 illustrates clearly the decline of the Conservative Party. In the 1978 regional elections the Conservatives gained 30% of the votes which, in the first unitary elections in 1995, had declined to 11%. In the 1999 Elections, the Conservatives made a slight improvement gaining 13% of the votes. The Conservatives control no local authorities and remain a marginal force in Scottish local government. Formerly the Conservatives controlled Angus, Perth and Kinross and Stirling, and had periods of control in Grampian, Tayside and Edinburgh in the 1980s.

The decline of Independent councillors

Scotland has had a strong tradition of independent councillors and councils, especially in the rural areas. Table 10.3 highlights the independent tradition and its decline in Scottish local government. Local government reorganisation in 1995, with the replacement of districts by larger authorities, reduced the number of councils controlled by independents. The unitary elections of 1995 reduced independent councils to two—Argyll and Bute and Highland (independents were in coalition with the Liberal Democrats in Aberdeenshire and Borders). The 1999 elections for the Scottish Parliament further strengthened the four main political parties in the local elections which were held alongside the 'national' election. Only in Highland and Argyll and Bute did the independents gain control of a mainland authority.

The main support for independent councils is to be found in islands councils. All the islands councils are controlled by independent councillors, although the Labour Party has made some inroads in the Western Isles.

Who controls the councils?

No overall control
Independent
Labour
SNP

Orkney Islands

Shetland Islands

Western Isles

Highland

Moray

Aberdeenshire

City of Aberdeen

Angus

Perthshire & Kinross

City of Dundee

Argyll & Bute

Stirling

Fife

City of Edinburgh

Falkirk

East Lothian

West Lothian

Midlothian

North Ayrshire

South Lanarkshire

Scottish Borders

East Ayrshire

South Ayrshire

Dumfries & Galloway

A Inverclyde
B Renfrewshire
C East Renfrewshire
D City of Glasgow
E West Dunbartonshire
F East Dunbartonshire
G North Lanarkshire
H Clackmannanshire

This map shows which party controlled each council after the local elections in May 1999.

Figure 10.2

THE INDEPENDENT TRADITION IN SCOTTISH LOCAL GOVERNMENT 1974–99 (selected years)		
Election	Vote %	Seats
Regional 1974	12.4	114
Regional 1982	5.1	87
Regional 1990	4.5	73
Regional 1994	4.2	65
District 1974	14.1	345
District 1980	6.7	289
District 1988	6.4	231
District 1992	7.4	228
Unitary 1995	7.7	155
Unitary 1999	11.8	135

Table 10.3

LOCAL GOVERNMENT PERSONNEL

Councillors

Local councillors represent the interests of the people in their electoral ward and if members of the public have a problem over the local school, vandalism in the street or repairs to their council house they can approach their councillor for support and advice. Councillors often attend meetings of local organisations such as community councils, School Boards and local Gala Day Committees.

Councillors are not typical of the population. They tend to come from the older section of the population: only 9% of councillors are aged between 21 and 34, while 48% of councillors are in the age group 55–74 years. By definition, councillors have to find time to do their job and this explains why many able people are deterred from becoming councillors. The demands placed on councillors have increased significantly over the last twenty five years and councillors with special duties, such as the Provost and committee conveners, are virtually working full time for the council. The debate over whether councillors should be paid a salary is discussed on page 156.

Councillors also attend council meetings and are members of the different committees which may exist such as education or health. Councillors, unless they are independents, will belong to a political party and will attend meetings of their party's councillors where policies are discussed and decisions made. Even if they do not agree with a decision, such as closing a local school or cutting services, they are expected to follow the party line. Councillors who vote against the party can be disciplined as happened recently in West Dunbartonshire. (See page 152.) The leader of the council tends to belong to the party with the largest number of seats as does the Provost who chairs coun-

DECISION-MAKING IN LOCAL GOVERNMENT

One recommendation of the McIntosh Commission (see page 154–155) was that councils should consider moving away from the committee structure and towards a cabinet style of local government. This is not a new suggestion and was first proposed in a consultation paper on the internal management of local authorities by John Major's Conservative government in the 1990s. Below is a summary of the Conservative findings relating to the committee system.

One view is that the committee system works well, especially if the influence of 'backbench' councillors is compared with that of backbench MPs. The committee system enables councillors to have an impact on decision making and to develop an expertise on educational or housing affairs.

An alternative view is that it diminishes the role of the full council and turns it into a rubber stamp body. If councillors spent less time on committees, they would have more time to devote to the needs of their constituents and to monitor the quality of local services.

Cabinet System

This is similar to the existing central government model. An executive of elected councillors (ministers) selected from the whole council would run the council. The remaining councillors, whether from the ruling party or from the opposition parties, would scrutinise the work of the executive and concentrate on constituency matters. This is the model favoured by Tony Blair.

Directly Elected Executive

Under this model the executive (Cabinet) would be directly elected by the local electorate rather than by the leader of the majority party. This would necessitate separate elections, one for the council followed by one for the Cabinet. Such a model would be expensive and time consuming and could confuse the public.

Directly Elected Mayor

Under this arrangement, similar to that found in many cities in the USA, the 'mayor' would be elected separately from the council. In 1999, London elected its first mayor in controversial circumstances with the victory of Ken Livingstone. (See page 43.)

The McIntosh Commission, while not ruling out the election of mayors in the Scottish system, argues that there is no public demand for the creation of such a post in Scotland.

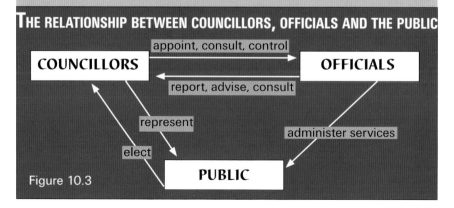

THE RELATIONSHIP BETWEEN COUNCILLORS, OFFICIALS AND THE PUBLIC

Figure 10.3

cil meetings and represents the council at official occasions like a visit from a member of the Royal Family or a delegation from abroad.

The Committee Structure

Unlike Parliament, local councils are executive bodies as well as legislative ones. While the full council is the supreme decision making body in a local authority, much of the work and powers are delegated to the committees controlled by the ruling party. The chairs or conveners of committees are elected by the full council but are usually selected from the majority party group. They chair the committee meetings and work with the full-time council officials to ensure that council policy is implemented by the various departments. Most councils have a committee known as the Policy and Resources Committee. This committee decides the overall policy of the council and the allocation of resources to departments. The chairperson of this committee is usually the council leader who works closely with the Chief Executive and the Director of Education.

Local Government Officials

All local authorities in Scotland appoint a Chief Executive who is head of the management team of directors of departments. In Renfrewshire Council the Chief Executive has his/her own department which covers the key corporate responsibilities of the Council. (See page 143.)

The traditional view of the relationship between councillors and officials is that councillors make policy which officials implement in the same way that civil servants carry out the wishes of the Prime Minister and the Cabinet. In other words, power rests with the elected councillors.

An alternative view is that senior officials are involved in policy making. Directors of Education, Social Work, Finance, etc. have technical and professional expertise which councillors lack. Given the continuity of senior officials in office and the part-time nature of the councillors' role, it is not surprising that officials can influence policy making. It is important that senior officials have a good working relationship with senior councillors. The in-fighting between Labour councillors seen in West

Dunbartonshire was triggered by the action of the Labour Group Leader in forcing the Deputy Chief Executive to resign. (See page 152.)

FINANCING LOCAL GOVERNMENT IN SCOTLAND

Labour came to power in 1997 determined to maintain tight control over public expenditure and the spending of local councils. The new government's decision to stick to Conservative spending guidelines ensured substantial financial problems for most local authorities who were still struggling to cover the cost of reorganisation. The new Labour government also carried out a review of local government finance and issued a Green Paper during the autumn of 2000. Aware of the bitter political battles raised by the poll tax, the Green Paper made it clear that Council Tax would not be reformed. (See page 149.) Outlined below are the main sources of local government income.

The main source of income is the grants given by the Scottish Executive. (See Figure 10.6.) This money is part of the Scottish Parliament's block allocation from Westminster

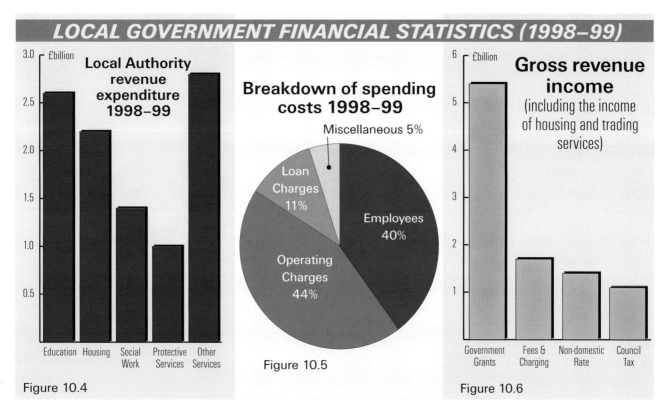

LOCAL GOVERNMENT FINANCIAL STATISTICS (1998–99)

Local Authority revenue expenditure 1998–99 (£billion)
— Education, Housing, Social Work, Protective Services, Other Services

Figure 10.4

Breakdown of spending costs 1998–99
Miscellaneous 5%
Loan Charges 11%
Employees 40%
Operating Charges 44%

Figure 10.5

Gross revenue income (including the income of housing and trading services) (£billion)
— Government Grants, Fees & Charging, Non-domestic Rate, Council Tax

Figure 10.6

and accounts for around 40% of the Parliament's expenditure. Table 10.4 highlights the range of specific government grants received by Renfrewshire Council in addition to the Revenue Support Grant which takes account of the mandatory functions which central government requires of councils.

A second source of income is through people paying their Council Tax. Every year the local authority calculates what each household will pay and sends out a Council Tax Bill. Unlike the rates system, there is a 25% reduction if there is only one adult living in a house. A third source of income for local authorities is through charges which are made for certain services. Housing is an obvious source of income. Renfrewshire Council received £40.5 million from rents in the financial year of 1999–2000.

A further important source of income is the non-domestic rate paid by owners of shops, offices and factories. Local authorities have no control over the rate set and, indeed, do not directly receive income from their own non-domestic rate.

New Financial Partnership

In November 2000, Angus Mackay, Minister for Finance and Local Government, announced improvements to the present financial system operating between central and local government. Key elements of the new system are:

❏ The Executive will give each council firm grant allocations for the next three years (2001–2004).

❏ Councils will publish their Council Tax plans for the same period.

❏ There will be a guaranteed minimum increase for the councils.

❏ The formula for distributing allocations between councils will be simpler and fairer.

❏ The Executive will scrap spending guidelines for councils. However, Ministers retain capping powers if they consider a council's spending plan to be excessive.

The new arrangements, agreed with COSLA, ensure that the annual conflict and argument over funding will no longer take place. According to the Scottish Executive, the Spending Review of

Financing Renfrewshire Council 1999–2000 (£m)

WHERE THE MONEY CAME FROM

Housing Rents	40.566
Other Income	54.432
Specific Government Grants	45.589
Income from Council Services	**140.587**
Revenue Support Grant	111.107
Non-domestic Rates	50.129
DLO/DSO Surplus	1.191
Council Tax	48.026
Contribution from Revenue Reserves	1.450
Contribution from General Services Reserves	3.820
Contribution from HRA Reserves	1.709
Gross Income	**358.019**

WHERE THE MONEY IS SPENT

Education	110.301
Housing Revenue Account	44.897
Other Housing	44.424
Social Work	47.584
Leisure Services	12.395
Environmental Services	25.618
Planning	5.377
Roads and Transport	27.734
Central Support Services	7.380
Miscellaneous Services	9.690
Joint Boards	22.068
Net Cost of Services	**357.468**

Details of Government Grants (£m)
An analysis of the figure of £45.589 million appearing above is:

Housing benefit	38.131
Education excellence funding	3.907
Social inclusion	2.399
Community services	0.481
School security	0.307
Council Tax administration	0.307
Other	0.057
Total	**45.589**

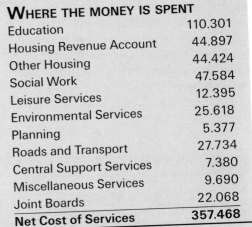

Renfrewshire Council

Source: Renfrewshire Council Annual Report and Accounts 1999–2000

Table 10.4

WHAT IS THE BEST SYSTEM OF LOCAL GOVERNMENT FINANCE?

TAX SYSTEM	FOR	AGAINST
RATES	System used in Scotland until 1988. Easy and cheap to collect. A rateable value was placed on property. A progressive tax.	*Subject to large increases during periods of inflation. An elderly person living alone paid the same rates as a family where both parents worked and who were living in an identical home.*
COMMUNITY CHARGE (poll tax)	A flat rate tax which every adult paid. On paper, a fair system with everyone contributing to the services they used. It was introduced in Scotland in 1989 and a year later in England. Students, the unemployed and other groups were given reductions.	*It was very unpopular and many people refused to pay. Proved very difficult and expensive to collect. A regressive tax whereby individuals in an area paid the same amount regardless of income. It became the focus of a huge protest movement led by such individuals as Tommy Sheridan (now a member of the Scottish Parliament). Abolished in 1993.*
COUNCIL TAX	Replaced the Poll Tax. It is easy and cheap to collect. The amount each household pays is determined by the value of the property which is placed in one of eight value bands. Rebates are available for single people and those on a low income.	*Banding can be arbitrary. May turn out to be unpopular like the rates system was during a period of inflation. People in identical homes will pay a different Council Tax depending on which local council area they live in.*
LOCAL INCOME TAX	This option was recommended by the Layfield Committee in 1976 but has been ignored by successive governments. Used in many countries and is easy to collect and to adjust. Would give local authorities greater control over their finances.	*Unpopular with the Treasury as it would be outwith the control of central government. Could be inflationary and encourage high spending by local authorities.*
UNIFORM BUSINESS RATE	Easy to collect and to understand. Linked to property values of shops, factories, etc.	*Not really a local tax, as all the revenue goes to central government and is redistributed to local authorities. Councils, such as Glasgow, are unhappy with this system.*

2001–2004 provides real growth in local council spending (within agreed priorities) and offers councils the ability to plan ahead and ensure greater financial stability and efficiency.

RELATIONS BETWEEN LOCAL & CENTRAL GOVERNMENT

The Conservative years witnessed a decline in the influence of local government. The viewpoint of the Conservative right was that local authorities, especially in urban areas, had been taken over by the extreme left who were involved in wasteful and silly politics such as setting up 'nuclear free zones'.

The Enabling Authority

The traditional view and practice of local authorities providing all the services required by their citizens was challenged. The role of councils would be restricted, and competition from the private sector would be encouraged. Councils would provide an enabling framework for the provision of services without necessarily providing all of these services themselves. Local authorities would work in partnership with private companies which would provide services such as school meals, street cleaning and rubbish collection.

149

The Convention of Scottish Local Authorities has existed since 1975 as the single representative body for local authorities in Scotland. It played a crucial role in the fight against the policies of the Conservative governments (1979–1997) and in the struggle for a Scottish Parliament. However, it now faces a financial and membership crisis.

In January 2001, Scottish councils refused to accept an increase of 11.5% in their annual levy paid to COSLA. An intense debate followed on the purpose and worth of COSLA which ended with three authorities, Glasgow, Falkirk and Clackmannanshire, leaving the Convention. This led to COSLA carrying out a review of the organisation in March 2001. COSLA argued that it carried out five key roles:

1 Representing local government interests to the Scottish Executive.
2 Influencing policy development by working in partnership with the Scottish Executive.
3 Negotiating salaries and conditions of service. It acts as the employers' organisation in, for example, deciding salaries for local government employees.
4 Promoting best local government practice.
5 Enabling councils to contribute to the work of COSLA.

The Way Forward

COSLA made the following recommendations in the summer of 2001:

☞ COSLA levy from councils to be set at 3.6% in 2001–02 in line with the overall local settlement.
☞ The three authorities, Glasgow City, Falkirk and Clackmannanshire, to be invited to join.
☞ Restructuring to take place to reduce costs.

GLASGOW'S £1.2 BILLION PRIVATE FINANCE DEAL TO REBUILD SCHOOLS

IN 1996, Glasgow had thirty nine secondary schools, many of which needed substantial refurbishment while a minority were in a desperate condition. The maintenance backlog alone was more than £100 million and many of the schools had too few pupils.

Glasgow took the painful decision to close ten secondary schools, and to involve the private sector in rebuilding and refurbishing the majority of those that remained. The Managing Director of the project 'consortium', Robin Mackie, is aware of the opposition from

trade unionists and some Glasgow councillors to private sector involvement. He argues that the project "is about lifting the quality and going for higher levels of innovation. We are getting more new schools than at any time since the Victorian age—we wouldn't have them quickly enough otherwise. They will be built on time to a very high specification and they will be looked after and maintained throughout the life of the contract and then handed back to the Council in thirty years' time."

Critics of the project argued that costs were hidden under the mantle of business confidentiality. The eleven state-of-the-art schools being built (the other ten secondary schools are being modernised) do not have swimming pools, and some classrooms, storerooms and staffrooms are too small.

There is little consultation with staff taking place. New ancillary employees do not have the same conditions of work as those under local government conditions.

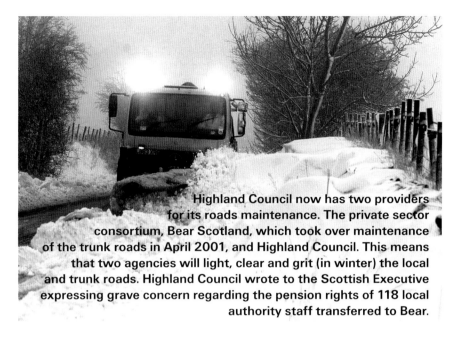
Highland Council now has two providers for its roads maintenance. The private sector consortium, Bear Scotland, which took over maintenance of the trunk roads in April 2001, and Highland Council. This means that two agencies will light, clear and grit (in winter) the local and trunk roads. Highland Council wrote to the Scottish Executive expressing grave concern regarding the pension rights of 118 local authority staff transferred to Bear.

PRIVATISATION OF LOCAL GOVERNMENT

Over the last twenty five years there has been a decline in the influence and prestige of local authorities. One important reason has been the privatisation policies of both Conservative and Labour governments. The privatisation of local authority services has taken a number of different forms.

The sale of assets

The Conservative government, through its generous discount terms, encouraged council tenants to buy their council houses. The *Housing Act* of 1980 led to over a million council houses being sold in the United Kingdom by 1990.

While some of the revenue raised from the sale of council houses (a meagre 20%) could be used to finance new house building, the remainder was tightly controlled by central government.

Deregulation

Until 1980 bus services were seen as essential social services and local authorities had a monopoly on bus provision in their area. The *Transport Act* of 1985 forced public sector operators to form private companies and to operate in competition with other private oper-

ators. Now market forces decide which bus routes will be created, how often buses will run and which companies will survive to operate them.

Compulsory competitive tendering (CCT)

Under new regulations, councils were obliged to allow private companies to bid for contracts such as refuse collection and school meals. If a private company's bid was lower than the bid from the council's direct service organisation, then the council was expected to award the contract to the private company.

CCT was fiercely opposed by the trade unions and by the Labour Party. It was claimed that CCT led to workers being paid less money and suffering a deterioration in their working conditions. Private companies are responsible to their shareholders. Their primary goal is to make a profit and that comes before providing a community service. (It is interesting to note that all the criticisms made of CCT apply to Labour's Private Finance Initiative projects.)

Removal of services from local authority control

In the early 1990s, further education colleges and polytechnics

Functions and Responsibilities of local government

- Education
- Social Work
- Police
- Fire
- Housing
- Libraries
- Archaeology
- Harbours
- Coastal Protection
- Ferries
- Urban Development
- Local Planning
- Development Control
- Strategic Planning
- Building Control
- Roads and Road Safety
- Public Transport
- Leisure and Recreation
- Administration of Housing Benefit
- General Licensing
- Listed Buildings and Ancient Monuments
- Council Tax
- Burials and Cremations
- District Courts
- Slaughterhouses
- Traffic Wardens
- Food Hygiene, Standards and Labelling
- Waste Collection and Disposal

were removed from local authority control and, in England, City Technology Colleges and grant maintained schools were encouraged to opt out of local authority control and to be directly controlled by central government. Private housing corporations were encouraged to take over the maintenance and control of designated local authority council houses.

Local authorities, under the terms of the 1993 *Community Care Act*, were forced to reduce their residential provision for the elderly and to award contracts to private and voluntary providers of the services.

(continued on page 154)

ALLEGATIONS OF CORRUPTION AND MALPRACTICE

The Scottish Executive was determined to clean up local government through legislation. It set up the McIntosh Commission to look into local government and how it can be improved. Below is a brief overview of some of the scandals which occurred in local government, centred mainly around West of Scotland councils which were totally dominated by Labour.

Glasgow

A leading councillor confessed to the *Evening Times* newspaper that Labour councillors had demanded favours, such as trips abroad, from key councillors in return for their votes. The inquiry which followed led to the suspension of Labour councillors including the Lord Provost.

West Dunbartonshire

In 2001 West Dunbartonshire Council's Labour group was in turmoil, with four councillors being suspended from the Labour group in July of that year for supporting an opposition motion of no confidence against their group leader, Andy White. This crisis in West Dunbartonshire had been ongoing for the previous two years and highlights the fragile relations which can exist between senior councillors and senior officials. Andy White had forced the resignation of Ian Leitch, the Deputy Chief Executive, and this had split the Labour Party.

Monklands

Monklands district in Lanarkshire, which was made up of the two towns of Airdrie and Coatbridge, had gained national prominence because its local MP had been the late John Smith, the former leader of the Labour Party. A long-running sense of grievance existed in Airdrie which claimed that Coatbridge was receiving far greater expenditure and was benefiting from projects such as the Time Capsule Leisure Centre and Summerlee Heritage Museum.

What gave the dispute an unsavoury taste, and attracted national publicity, was the accusation of sectarianism. Coatbridge was considered to be the 'Catholic' town with Airdrie being the 'Protestant' town. Accusations were made that the Council, dominated by Coatbridge councillors, was giving preference to Catholics applying for posts. Significantly, a number of the Council employees were related to the councillors and Airdrie councillors accused the Council of nepotism.

In 1995 the District Council agreed to an independent inquiry led by Professor Black of Edinburgh University. The outcome was that some former Monklands councillors were debarred by the Labour Party from holding office in the Party or in the new North Lanarkshire Council which came into existence in 1996.

North Lanarkshire, East Ayrshire

Both councils reported huge losses for their Direct Labour Organisations (DLOs) for the financial year 1997–98. In the case of North Lanarkshire, the loss was almost £5 million. Evidence emerged of lax management, including poor stock control and huge bonus payments leading to some workers receiving over £40,000 in wages. The Scottish Secretary threatened to abolish North Lanarkshire Council's DLO and ordered every council to examine its own DLO.

Borders Council

In June 2001, Borders Council called in fraud squad officers to investigate possible financial irregularities which had led to £3.9 million of overspending in its education budget. Clearly, financial mismanagement was a factor in this crisis and raises the issue of the ability of part-time councillors to manage complex budgets.

Dundee

In June 2001, the first woman Lord Provost of Dundee, Helen Wright, was removed from office in a vote of no confidence over an expenses row. Provost Wright had reclaimed £329 of donations that she had made to church and charity collections. Mrs Wright apologised and repaid the money which she maintained was "an honest and simple mistake".

Conclusion

The Scottish Executive, by means of the ethical framework introduced by the *Ethical Standards in Public Life etc. (Scotland) Act* 2000, has tried to improve public confidence in local councils and promote greater openness and accountability. The Scottish Executive is determined that councils, in future, will not plunge into crisis due to huge losses in their Direct Labour Organisations nor be afflicted by the allegations of 'cronyism' affecting authorities such as Glasgow. However, recent events in West Dunbartonshire suggest that political in-fighting is still part and parcel of the political culture, especially in the central belt.

DEVOLUTION AND LOCAL GOVERNMENT

The setting up of a Scottish parliament has had a considerable impact upon the roles and functions of local government. In one respect the constitutional relationship has not altered. Under the Scotland Act 1998 the Scottish Parliament is responsible for local government. Like its predecessor the Scottish Office, the Scottish Executive will control local government finance, structure, elections, etc. and also key policies such as education, housing, transport and social work.

The simple fact that a parliament totally devoted to Scottish affairs now exists means that the Executive and committees of the Parliament have more time to introduce and enact legislation affecting local government. Under Westminster rule, little time was devoted to Scottish affairs and Scottish legislation was often attached to English bills. An opportunity now exists to redefine the nature of the relationship between central and local government within Scotland.

One of the first pieces of legislation passed by the Scottish Parliament was a local government ethics bill. Wendy Alexander, Scotland's Minister for Communities, was determined to build a positive, rather than a confrontational, relationship with councils. She wanted local authorities to play their part in the modernisation of Scotland's institutions and to contribute to key government policies such as social inclusion and life-long learning.

There are two views on the impact of the Scottish Parliament on the workings of local councils.

Devolution enhances local government

1. The years of conflict between central and local government are over. The Scottish Executive wishes to involve local councils as junior partners in its policies to modernise Scotland and to tackle its health, poverty and unemployment problems.

2. There are opportunities to enhance the power and role of local councils by reducing the number of quangos and transferring their functions to local councils.

3. Local councils are already embracing policies such as PPPP (see pages 150 and 154), and are working in partnership with the Scottish Executive and private enterprise. The old ideological baggage is being jettisoned and local councils are accepting that alternative providers are not a threat to local councils. Glasgow City Council is attempting to transfer its housing stock out of Council control. (See pages 158–160.)

4. Local councils are actively involved in the modernisation process. Membership of the McIntosh Commission and Kerley Committee included a significant number of councillors (present and former). The Scottish Executive is working in partnership with local councils. Future changes to the local electoral system, payment for councillors and council structures are all aspects of this partnership model.

Devolution undermines local government

1. Devolution merely replaces domination from London with domination from Edinburgh. Moreover, the Scottish Parliament represents the economic and political interests of the central belt and is ignoring the needs of rural communities.

2. Given the limited powers of the Scottish Parliament and its inability to tackle large socioeconomic and financial issues, the Parliament is concentrating on issues such as education, housing and social work, which are key local government functions. There is a genuine fear that the Parliament will simply become a 'super' council, taking over where the previous regional councils left off and so undermining the current unitary local government system.

3. There is already evidence that the Scottish Executive is prepared to adopt a highly interventionist approach to local government. In 1997–98, the Direct Labour departments of East Ayrshire and North Lanarkshire, responsible for construction and maintenance contracts, ran up severe financial deficits. Both councils were Labour controlled and this embarrassed the Scottish Executive as it presented further evidence of the incompetence of local councils. The Secretary of State threatened to close down North Lanarkshire's Direct Labour Organisation.

The 2001 McCrone Report, which resolved the teachers' dispute in Scotland, was negotiated by the Education Minister, Jack McConnell, with COSLA playing only a minor role in the discussions.

4. Prior to devolution, COSLA and local councils played a crucial role in opposing Conservative legislation and in the fight for a Scottish Parliament. Strathclyde Regional Council, for example, carried out its own referendum on the control of water which clearly demonstrated the public's opposition to privatisation. These dizzy and exciting days are gone for ever. COSLA is divided and is criticised for being the 'poodle of the Scottish Executive', and simply carrying out its wishes.

The Best Value Approach

The new Labour government suspended CCT and introduced 'best value'. Under 'best value', local authorities must set performance targets for each service they provide which will be monitored by an external agency to ensure that 'best value' has been achieved. Services can still be delivered either by the local authority or by private contractors based on the criterion that "Best value is about effectiveness and quality, not just economy and efficiency".

In February 2001 contracts for trunk road maintenance were awarded to private companies rather than to local councils, much to the fury of local councillors. They heckled Sarah Boyack, the Transport Minister, from the public galleries of the Scottish Parliament and they were ejected after one of them, John Letford from Dundee shouted, "You are a disgrace to the Labour Party".

Removal of Educational Control

Under new regulations introduced in England and Wales, schools can now be run by private companies rather than by the local authority. This does not apply to Scotland where all state schools are under the control of the local authorities. Labour, when it came to power in 1997, passed legislation to end the opted out status of the one school in Scotland outwith local authority control.

Private Finance Initiatives

PFI was a Conservative policy which was enthusiastically embraced by New Labour. Under this initiative, private firms design, build and operate developments which require to be paid back over an agreed period of time. Labour changed the name to PPPP (Public Private Partnership Programmes) and argued that what mattered was the creation of state-of-the-art schools, where pupils could be taught in well-resourced, modern buildings, and hospitals, in which nurses could attend to patients in modern wards.

Glasgow City and Falkirk Councils, along with other councils, have embarked on ambitious PPPPs, which will transform their secondary schools, much to the fury of the trade unions. (See page 150.) Several local councils have used PFI schemes to modernise their council homes through the installation, for example, of central heating.

EURO PROTEST AS TREES GET CHOP

Furious residents are to lodge a complaint with the European Parliament after trees at a popular beauty spot got the chop to make way for a mobile phone mast.

Irate locals were fuming when a Scottish Executive Reporter overturned Renfrewshire Council's decision to refuse planning permission for the 90-foot-high mast at the Bluebell Woods on the outskirts of Elderslie.

The Reporter's intervention gave telecommunications giants One-2-One the go-ahead to cut down trees to make way for the giant pylon.

Now members of Elderslie Community Council plan to lodge a protest with their local European Parliament Member.

Tree-felling has already started at the woods which are popular with visitors just now when the bluebells are in full bloom.

Angry locals said the first they knew the trees were being chopped was when they heard the sound of chainsaws and heavy machinery.

Families setting out on walks were shocked to find a large, muddy track cut into the woodlands and trees felled to make way for the mast.

Mike Sinclair of Balmoral Road said: "I was outraged when I saw the extent of the damage. The woods are at their best at this time of year.

"The bluebells are in flower and birds, including unusual warblers, fly over from Africa to nest.

"It's a right mess where the trees were cut down. People hoping to enjoy a walk turned back in disgust when they saw the havoc.

"It's wrong the democratic process can be subverted by crass commercial interests. No one wanted this obscenity yet our elected politicians are powerless to protect chil-dren's health, let alone the unique flora and fauna of the woods."

Paisley South MSP Hugh Henry said: "I was shocked at the decision to overturn Renfrewshire Council's refusal of permission for the erection of the mast.

"It ignores local opinion and the recommendation of the Council's planning officials. I shall be tabling a question to the Scottish Parliament asking why Reporters are answerable and accountable to no one, including Scottish Ministers, for their decisions on planning appeals."

A Scottish Executive spokesperson said: "The Reporter's decision was based on written submissions by interested parties and a site inspection.

"It was reached after balancing arguments relevant to the planning merits of the case.

"Once a Reporter has made a decision on an appeal it is final."

A Community Council source said: "It's wrong that the wishes of residents and their democratically elected representatives can be by-passed by companies appealing successfully to the Scottish Executive."

They claim their human and democratic rights were infringed by the Reporter's decision and want to challenge the Reporter's right to ignore local opinion which opposed the plan.

A spokesperson for One-2-One said: "We recognise the importance of the Bluebell Woods site to local people. We shall minimise disturbance and landscape the area after work has been completed."

The Renfrewshire World 29.6.01

MCINTOSH COMMISSION

In 1998 the Scottish Executive set up a Commission dealing with local government relations with the Scottish Parliament under the Chairmanship of Professor Neil McIntosh, the former Chief Executive of the now defunct Strathclyde Regional Council. The Commission undertook an extensive consultation exercise on the best way to create a local government system more responsive and democratically accountable to local people. The Scottish public had witnessed a series of 'scandals' in several Labour controlled authorities in Monklands, Renfrewshire and West Dunbartonshire and internal Labour problems on Glasgow City Council. (See page 152.)

The Report, published in June 1999, addressed "crisis in local government" and made proposals covering inter-governmental relations, electing Scotland's councils, community councils, and political arrangements within councils. (See below.)

The reaction from the political parties was mixed. SNP leaders hailed the Report as "a breath of fresh air" and the Party's local government spokesperson said the package should be accepted as a whole and should not be "cherry-picked" by Labour to suit its own political interests. Liberal Democrats enthusiastically supported the Report and its proposals for proportional representation. In contrast, the reaction of Labour councillors was predictable, displaying open hostility to the introduction of proportional representation. (See page 157.) The Convention of Scottish local Authorities (COSLA), while welcoming the Report, argued that PR should not be introduced until at least 2005. (McIntosh recommended that it should be introduced by 2002.)

The McIntosh Commission ignored two of the main problems faced by Scottish local authorities—structure and finance. The 1996 local government structures were created before the setting up of a Scottish parliament and had a strong political agenda. (See pages141 and 144.) In terms of economic viability and strategic planning, many of the new councils are found wanting. *The Herald*, in a June 1999 editorial, stated: "No attempt has been made to deal with the question of the number of councils, and although this is a sensitive subject, given the mauling they received from the last Tory government, there are some absurdities which should be sorted out. Why Ayrshire required three councils is a mystery, especially as one of them is the utterly redundant East Ayrshire Council."

The Scottish Executive has ignored COSLA's request for an indepen-

FINDINGS OF THE McINTOSH COMMISSION

Electing Scotland's Councils

- Review of electoral arrangements to provide more open access to voting through greater use of postal and electronic voting and a more flexible and updated electoral Register.
- Local government employees below senior levels to be allowed to stand as a candidates in the authorities they work for.
- Proportional representation (PR) to be introduced as soon as possible. It did not propose any one PR system but outlined the following criteria:
  - proportionality
  - the retention of council ward links
  - fair provision for independents
  - the need to match council boundaries to natural communities
- Elections should be held every four years (three years at present) and should be timed to take place at the mid-point of the Scottish Parliament.
- Community councils should be retained and consideration should be given to extending the vote to those aged sixteen and over in community council elections. Councils were asked to review the resourcing and levels of participation in community councils.

Political Arrangements within councils

- Councils should consider adopting a Cabinet style of government ("formalising the political leadership as an executive"), but should be able to consider other options. (No significant demand for directly-elected provosts.)
- The Commission was unhappy at the present abuse of the Whip system with councillors being forced to follow the party line. Where it is applied it should be declared and minuted for public information.
- Payment for councillors should be considered by an independent review.

Inter-governmental relations

- Negotiation of a covenant between local government and the Scottish Parliament to establish a set of ground rules for inter-governmental relations.
- Based on partnership, the covenant would be modelled on the European Charter of Local Self-government.
- The Covenant would be reviewed by a joint conference of local government councillors and MSPs which would exist separately from the Parliament's Local Government Committee.
- An independent inquiry into local government finance should be set up.

PAYMENT OF COUNCILLORS

Councillors are not paid directly for the work they do. There have been several schemes introduced over the years but none has been satisfactory. When the Regions and Districts were set up in 1974, councillors were given an allowance based on attendance at meetings. This system encouraged councils to create numerous committees with some members turning up only for a short time so that they could qualify for the allowance.

The system was changed in 1996 with the government setting an upper limit of £7 million a year for basic allowances and councils were given discretion as to the number and level of special responsibility allowances. At present Charles Gordon, the leader of Glasgow City Council, receives the highest amount in Scotland—a total of £25,000 a year—which includes his basic allowance and a responsibility allowance.

Full-Time or Part-Time?

The Kerley proposals support the move towards the creation of a group of "full-time councillors, rather than the present system of a part-time job with the emphasis on voluntary 'community service'". At present, individuals who hold top posts, like provost or convener, are engaged in substantial duties. Councillors are responsible for multi-million pound budgets and deserve to be rewarded for their efforts.

Supporters of a 'salary' for councillors also argue that it will attract younger people from a wider background with the talent to serve their local communities.

---

dent commission to review the issue of local government finance, reflecting Tony Blair's reluctance to tackle such a controversial area. The McIntosh Commission proposals were widely discussed within the Scottish Parliament's Local Government Committee in 1999–2000, leading to the setting up of the Kerley Committee. The Scottish Executive also established a Leadership Advisory Panel to consider decision making within councils and a Community Leadership Forum between Scottish Executive Ministers and local government leaders.

The Scottish Executive, given the opposition from Labour rank and file, decided to procrastinate by setting up a further committee to take forward the proposals made by McIntosh.

THE KERLEY COMMITTEE

In July 1999 a ten-member committee, under the chairpersonship of Richard Kerley, and including Neil McIntosh, was set up to look into the future of local government. Significantly, the Committee had a very strong local government representation. Mr Kerley, the director of the Management School at Edinburgh University, was himself a former Labour councillor in Edinburgh.

The remit of the Committee was to examine ways in which council membership could be made more attractive to a wide cross section of society along with further examination of the introduction of proportional representation in local government elections.

The Committee issued its report in June 2000 and, as expected, it favoured both the introduction of PR and payment for senior councillors. *The Scotsman* newspaper in its headline "Up to £40,000 salary proposal for councillors to soften blow of PR", clearly regarded the findings as an incentive for councillors to accept PR.

The Report recommended that senior councillors should be paid up to £40,000 per year depending upon the size of their authority and the range of their responsibilities. To pay for the increased allowances, Kerley recommended a reduction in the number of existing councillors. Councils would be grouped into population bands with a designated number of councillors. This would result in a substantial reduction for councils like Edinburgh and Glasgow.

The Report proposed that Scottish councils should use the single transferable vote system of PR. This would create multi-member constituencies of between three and five councillors in urban councils and a minimum of two councillors in rural areas and island communities.

The Scottish Executive agreed in principle to introduce PR and announced that the next local elections would be held in 2003 on the same day as the Scottish Parliament elections. First Minister Henry McLeish favoured PR for local elections but admitted that it was an issue which "bitterly divides the Labour Party". He stated: "I acknowledge that within the Labour Party many councillors, in particular, are very opposed to PR. So let's have a debate on it."

The length of this 'debate' infuriated the Liberal Democrats who were pushing for a decision by autumn 2001 to enable the new system to be used for the 2003 elections. Labour's councillors and MSPs wish to maintain their stranglehold on Scotland's local councils. The ministerial working party on PR is aware of the bitter opposition within the Labour Party. The view of an unnamed MSP, given in July 2001, sums up Labour's dilemma: "We are not in the business of giving away power. We've compromised on a lot of things to keep the coalition going, but we could lose our local government base because of this, and, if that goes, it is going to make the election of MSPs far more difficult."

The Scottish Executive argues that it is consulting over the thirty recommendations made by the McIntosh Commission and that progress is being made which will result in a forthcoming Local Government Bill. The Scottish Executive has agreed to relax the present rules which prevent council employees standing for election to their own council (only posts designated 'politically restricted' will not be covered by the new legislation). In September 2001, Henry McLeish announced the legislative programme for session 2001–2002 and, to the dismay of the Liberal Democrats, it did not include PR for local government elections.

PR FOR LOCAL GOVERNMENT ELECTIONS?

Both the McIntosh Commission and the Kerley Committee recommended the introduction of PR for local elections. Supporters argue that the present system of FPTP ensures total dominance by Labour in the central belt. In Glasgow, for example, the Labour Party won just over half of the vote in the last council elections but took seventy four of the seventy nine council seats. Advocates of change argue that FPTP has created a Labour dictatorship in the West of Scotland which has led to corruption, public apathy at elections and public hostility towards local government.

The Liberal Democrats argue that Labour promised to "make progress" towards introducing PR for local government elections as part of the coalition deal struck shortly after the first Scottish Parliament election in 1999. However, the Labour leadership faces strong opposition from within the Party, as witnessed in the initial Labour reaction to the McIntosh Commission. The Labour leader of Glasgow City Council, Charles Gordon, condemned the proposed introduction of PR. He stated: "PR is (seen as) a cure-all for what's perceived to be a disease in local government, but the cure is potentially worse than the disease if it breaks the link between councillors and their wards; if it leads to manifestos being drawn up after polling day and not before it; and if it perpetuates the culture of the smoke-filled room and the unprincipled alliance. It creates a new generation of politicians called list people, who don't represent any community but paradoxically claim they represent the entire community."

SOUTH
LANARKSHIRE
COUNCIL

Headquarters

HOUSING

For the older generation, housing is often associated with the council. From the 1950s to the early 1970s local councils knocked down their tenements and prefabricated houses and built huge housing estates. The council built the homes and maintained them while the public paid their rent to the council. This all changed through the policies of the Conservative leader, Margaret Thatcher.

The sale of council houses through generous discounts, the ending of council house building, except for specific needs such as the elderly and the disabled, and the tight control of council spending transformed the role of local councils. The Conservatives encouraged the setting up of housing associations to take over council housing. Council tenants would then transfer from council control to housing association control, thus further weakening the power and influence of local councils.

HOUSING STOCK (%)

	SCOTLAND			UK
	1988	**1997**	**1998**	**1998**
Owner-occupied	46.7	60.3	61.3	67.3
Rented privately or with job / business	6.7	6.8	6.7	10.4
Housing association	2.8	5.1	5.3	4.9
Public sector	43.9	27.8	26.6	17.4

TABLE 10.5   Source: *Scottish Statistics 2000*, Scottish Executive

DWELLINGS COMPLETED (thousands)

	SCOTLAND			UK
	1988	**1997**	**1998**	**1998**
Private sector	14.2	17.8	18.3	154.4
Housing association	1.3	4.5	2.0	24.2
Public authorities	2.8	0.1	0.1	1.1

TABLE 10.6   Source: *Scottish Statistics 2000*, Scottish Executive

GLASGOW'S HOUSING CRISIS

- At present, Glasgow has 87,000 council houses and a housing debt of £900 million. This consumes half of every pound the city receives in rent.

- More than 80% of council houses fail to meet modern electrical standards.

- Dampness rates are 25% above the Scottish average.

- Almost 60% have no double glazing.

- Thousands of homes lie empty with prospective tenants refusing to go to 'undesirable' areas.

- Given the future costs of modernisation, Glasgow's council houses are only worth an average of £100 each.

Council house sales have removed many of the better quality houses from Council stock. One of the first improvements which the new owner-occupier often makes is to replace the front door.

THE GLASGOW SOLUTION

In 2002, the council tenants of Glasgow will vote on whether to end council control of housing by transferring it to a housing association. This action was implemented by a Labour controlled Glasgow City Council and a Scottish Executive with a Labour majority. The proposals aroused great controversy and accusations were made that Glasgow City was blackmailed into endorsing the scheme. Supporters argued that it provided an opportunity to solve Glasgow's chronic housing problems and debt.

Housing transfer

The Scottish Executive was determined to end local authority control of housing in Glasgow and 'persuaded' the Labour administration in Glasgow to accept the proposals. The Executive spent £13 million on consultancy fees alone and proposed that Glasgow Housing Association (GHA) should become the landlord of the city's council houses if tenants voted in favour of transfer. In May 2001 GHA produced a 500-page business plan which was accepted by the Council. Within 10 years GHA promised:

➤ full modernisation of all houses

➤ all houses to have new or improved heating systems and insulation by 2006

➤ rent increases will be pegged at the rate of inflation for the first five years and further guarantees for the next five years

➤ jobs for existing council staff transferring (around 2,000) and the creation of 3,000 jobs in the construction industry

➤ a concerted plan to deal with anti-social neighbours

➤ an estimated 15,000 of the city's 90,000 council homes would be demolished because they are uneconomical to repair

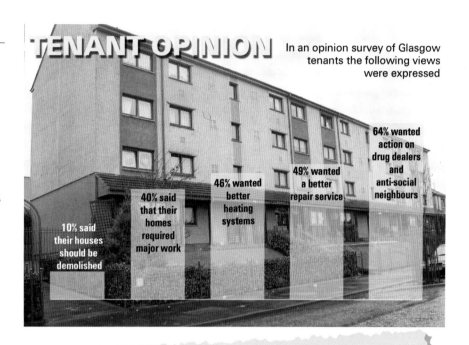

TENANT OPINION In an opinion survey of Glasgow tenants the following views were expressed

10% said their houses should be demolished

40% said that their homes required major work

46% wanted better heating systems

49% wanted a better repair service

64% wanted action on drug dealers and anti-social neighbours

"We believe that Glasgow's problems of poor housing quality and difficult neighbourhoods require a steep change in investment, better services, stronger communities, tenant control and tackling existing housing debt. The proposals for community ownership will see a £1.6 billion investment over the next ten years to provide warm, dry and modernised homes for tenants and, crucially, they will also put tenants at the heart of the process deciding how the money is spent."

Deputy Social Justice Minister, Margaret Curran, December 2000

If the tenants vote for the £4.5 billion investment and for transfer, around fifteen local housing associations would be set up enabling tenants to own their homes collectively. Tenants will be represented on the management committee of GHA. Private companies will invest in the scheme and will raise the money to carry out the modernisation programme. After the transfer, the Scottish Executive said it would take over the servicing of Glasgow's £900 million housing debt enabling rent income to be invested in improvements. However, in September 2001, the Treasury in London agreed to write off Glasgow's housing debt if the transfer to GHA went ahead.

"The transfer will fail because tenants do not trust it. It is privately financed and the markets will always put their profits ahead of social responsibility."

Sean Clerkin the Chair of the Glasgow Campaign against Stock Transfer

GLASGOW'S HOPES AND FEARS FOR IMPROVING CRUMBLING HOMES

After twelve years in Balornock waiting for her heating to fail yet again, Helen Gibson is ready for a change.

Instead of excuses about the damp in the bathroom and the slow decline of her community, she wants action.

Last Friday, the Glasgow Housing Association, the privately-financed landlord hoping to take over Helen's council house and 90,000 others like it, announced it was ready to respond.

To prove it could fix the mess at the heart of Scotland's largest city, it delivered a 500-page business plan to Glasgow City Council. It promised to turn around some of the worst slums in Europe with a £4.5 billion investment programme over the next thirty years.

New heating, new windows, new roofs, new name it.

Like every step towards wholesale stock transfer in Glasgow, it was a politically charged moment.

Tommy Sheridan railed against the privatisation of public assets, others predicted soaring rents and a return to Rachmanism.

For Helen, it was a day of belated relief.

As chairwoman of the local tenants group which has studied the transfer process for the last year, the 44-year-old housewife is an expert on the GHA's plans.

She feels comfortable with them, and tries to encourage her neighbours to become equally involved.

For her, stock transfer is the only game in town. But she is also aware that many of her fellow tenants are apathetic.

This may be the biggest shift in Scottish housing for half a century, yet thousands are still 'sleepwalking' to the crunch ballot on the GHA's offer.

"People need to wake up to what's coming," she said. "A lot of folk talk about a return to private landlords and complain. I always ask them the same thing – What else is there?

"They can never give me an answer."

On the other side of the city from Helen Gibson, in Gorbals, Maria Smith is one of the ambivalent voters waiting to be convinced.

As a member of the Norfolk Court tenants association, she knows more about the transfer than most in her 23-storey block.

Like Helen, she is no fan of Glasgow City Council's housing department, having been one of its victims for two decades.

Her bath is slowly sinking into the floor, and she has been waiting over 10 years for her windows to be fixed.

Damp blooms in both bedrooms.

She is angry, well informed and sick of the status quo.

Just the sort of person who should rush to embrace the GHA.

But like the city itself, she is hovering between the devil she knows and the devil she doesn't.

In November, Maria and Glasgow's 86,000 other tenants will be forced to stop dithering and choose.

They will be offered new jobs, better homes, more say in how their housing is run, and their city's £900 million debt taken over by the Scottish Executive.

Or they can have more of the same old misery.

That many are undecided says volumes about Glasgow's painful experience of previous 'big bang' solutions.

It also shows how propaganda has boiled the merits and demerits of Europe's biggest housing project down to a crude choice between hope and fear.

"I don't believe half of what each side is saying," Maria said.

"People aren't sure whether this is being done for the council tenants or the Council itself, so they get their debt cleared up."

Power is to be devolved down to socially excluded communities.

Neighbours will gorge on civic pride and regeneration. Fewer social ills, and further investment will all follow.

To the politicians, it must sound too good to be true.

To Paisley University's Professor Mike Danson, the author of two Unison reports on the transfer, it is just that.

He predicts the neighbourhoods with half-decent stock will prosper, while the traditional basket-case areas will either be razed or left to rot because private capital won't touch them.

"The history of Glasgow housing is that you go for these big bangs, like the high rises and the peripheral estates," said Mr Danson. "they start off great and then they run out of money."

Charities ask who will take the homeless in when the Council has no property; unions want to know about the jobs in the housing DLO when repair work goes out to tender.

But consensus hasn't broken out yet.

Elaine Smith was the first Labour MSP to break ranks on the transfer, awkwardly pointing out that it was a Tory idea Labour has never formally adopted as policy.

"If the choice is transfer and get your house patched up or no transfer and you get nothing, then that's not a real choice at all," she said.

"Tenants aren't being told about alternatives, like councils being allowed to spend more money."

Elaine Smith, Sean Clerkin and Tommy Sheridan would all prefer well-funded local authorities borrowing to pay for repairs, but the Executive are having none of it. Councils had their chance, and they blew it.

Adapted from *The Scotsman* 16.5.01